THE
NEW TESTAMENT IN THE APOSTOLIC FATHERS

BY

A COMMITTEE OF THE OXFORD SOCIETY
OF HISTORICAL THEOLOGY

WIPF & STOCK · Eugene, Oregon

Wipf and Stock Publishers
199 W 8th Ave, Suite 3
Eugene, OR 97401

The New Testament in the Apostolic Fathers
By a Committee of the Oxford Society of Historical Theology
By Lake, Kirsopp
Softcover ISBN-13: 978-1-6667-3383-9
Hardcover ISBN-13: 978-1-6667-2918-4
eBook ISBN-13: 978-1-6667-2919-1
Publication date 8/11/2021
Previously published by Oxford University Press, 1905

This edition is a scanned facsimile of the original edition published in 1905.

PREFACE

THIS work had its origin in a resolution passed by the Society of Historical Theology, in Oxford, appointing a small Committee to prepare a volume exhibiting those passages of early Christian writers which indicate, or have been thought to indicate, acquaintance with any of the books of the New Testament. Beyond the appointment of the Committee, the Society has no responsibility whatever for the work, and the judgements which are expressed belong to the Committee alone. The present volume deals with the writings of the Apostolic Fathers, in which information is scanty, and traces of dependence on the Scriptures of the New Testament are most open to doubt. The editors are quite aware that their judgements may not command universal assent ; but they may claim at least that these judgements have been carefully formed, sometimes after considerable hesitation, by men who are not without practice in this kind of investigation. It is hoped that the book will not only provide the student with useful material, but afford him some helpful direction in reaching his own conclusions.

The first duty of the Committee was to agree upon a plan. It was decided to arrange the books of the New Testament in four classes, distinguished by the letters A, B, C, and D, according to the degree of probability of their use by the several authors. Class A includes those books about which there can be no reasonable doubt, either because they are expressly mentioned, or because there are other certain indications of their use. Class B comprises those books the use of which, in the judgement of the editors, reaches a high degree of probability. With class C we come to a lower degree of probability ; and in class D are placed those books which may possibly be referred to, but in regard to which the evidence appeared too uncertain to allow any reliance to be placed upon it. Under each author the books of the New Testament are arranged in accordance with these four classes, except that the Gospels are reserved for a section by themselves after the other writings. In dealing with the Gospels the following division has been observed :—First are presented references to the Synoptical Gospels severally; secondly, references to Synoptical material, where the individual Gospel cannot be distinguished —cases to which the above classification seems inapplicable; thirdly, references to the Fourth Gospel ; and lastly, references to apocryphal Gospels. Under each class (A, B, C, D) the books follow one another in the present canonical order; and the passages cited under each head are arranged in the order of probability, according to the editors' judgement, and marked a, b, c, d—symbols to which an explanation will apply similar to that which has been given in connexion with the capital letters.

The quotations are printed in parallel columns. The first presents the quotation containing the supposed reference. The second exhibits the corresponding passage, or passages, in the New Testament, quoted from the text approved by our English Revisers, with references, when necessary, to various readings. A third column, when required, contains illustrative passages from the LXX (the text of Dr. Swete's edition being used) or from other writings. Underneath the several quotations are comments, calling attention to special points, or indicating briefly the grounds of the editors' judgement. In class D references are given without the text in several instances, because, though they have been cited in evidence, they did not appear to deserve serious recognition. In addition to these a great many passages were examined by the Committee, but are not mentioned because the Committee came to the conclusion that there was no serious ground for arguing that they showed the influence of the New Testament.

In the execution of the foregoing plan, books were in the first instance allotted to the several members of the Committee, in order that each might make a preliminary list of passages, with his own judgements and comments. These were carefully revised, passage by passage, at meetings of the Committee. They were then arranged in what was intended to be their permanent form. Finally, they were once more revised by the Committee; and in many cases previous judgements were again brought under consideration. It is obvious that the distinction of classes, especially between b and c, must often have involved delicate and doubtful deliberation; for it is extremely difficult, where several are collaborating, to retain at all times the same standard of judgement. But even if in many cases other scholars may arrive at different conclusions, the Committee hope that their labours will not be wholly without fruit in this important field of Biblical study.

The task of final redaction and the furnishing of special introductions were in each case left to the member of Committee to whom the preliminary work had fallen; so that the full consensus of the Committee must be taken to apply only to the degrees of probability assigned to the apparent traces of given New Testament books in the authors examined.

A list of the Committee is appended, in which is indicated the particular work for which each member is specially responsible—

Barnabas: J. V. Bartlet, M.A., D.D., Senior Tutor of Mansfield College.

Didache: K. Lake, M.A., Professor of New Testament Exegesis in the University of Leyden.

I Clement. A. J. Carlyle, M.A., Lecturer in Theology of University College.

Ignatius: W. R. Inge, M.A., Fellow and Tutor of Hertford College.

Polycarp: P. V. M. Benecke, M.A., Fellow and Tutor of Magdalen College.

Hermas: J. Drummond, M.A., LL.D.. Principal of Manchester College.

II Clement: (Gospels) J. V. Bartlet; (St. Paul's Epistles) A. J. Carlyle; (Catholic Epistles) P. V. M. Benecke

CONTENTS

THE EPISTLE OF BARNABAS

INTRODUCTION.

Standard of Accuracy in quotation. Our author shares the Alexandrinism so widely diffused in the first century A.D. throughout the eastern Mediterranean. This has its effect on his methods in dealing with the O. T., which he uses through the LXX, known to him in a text which approximates to our *Codex Alexandrinus* (but reads also at times as if revised from the Hebrew)[1]. In general 'the O. T. is quoted even more profusely than in the Epistle of Clement, but with less precision. The writer is fairly exact in well-known contexts belonging to the Psalter or the Book of Isaiah ; but elsewhere he appears to trust to memory, and not to concern himself greatly about the words of his author. Even when preceded by a *formula citandi* his citations often wander far from the LXX, although they are clearly based upon it (e. g. Exod. 33¹⁻³ = Barn. vi. 8 [2]). Similar liberties are taken even where the writer mentions the book which he is quoting,' e. g. πέρας γέ τοι λέγει αὐτοῖς ἐν τῷ Δευτερονομίῳ, Καὶ διαθήσομαι πρὸς τὸν λαὸν τοῦτον τὰ δικαιώματά μου—'a sentence which, though it has all the notes of a strict quotation, proves to be a mere summary of Deut. 4¹⁻²³.' The following comparison of Exod. 33¹⁻³ and Barn. vi. 8 may give some measure of the freedom [3] for which we must allow in considering possible N. T. citations or echoes.

Exodus.	Barnabas.
καὶ εἶπεν Κύριος πρὸς Μωυσῆν, Πορεύου ἀνάβηθι ἐντεῦθεν σὺ καὶ ὁ λαός σου . . . εἰς τὴν γῆν ἣν ὤμοσα τῷ Ἀβραὰμ καὶ Ἰσαὰκ καὶ Ἰακώβ, λέγων . . . καὶ εἰσάξω σε εἰς γῆν ῥέουσαν γάλα καὶ μέλι.	ἰδού, τάδε λέγει Κύριος ὁ Θεός· Εἰσέλθατε εἰς τὴν γῆν τὴν ἀγαθήν, ἣν ὤμοσεν Κύριος τῷ Ἀβραὰμ καὶ Ἰσαὰκ καὶ Ἰακώβ, καὶ κατακληρονομήσατε αὐτήν, γῆν ῥέουσαν γάλα καὶ μέλι.

(See also Nos. (1) (40) below.)

---

[1] Swete, *Introd. to the O. T. in Greek*, 411–413, for this and what follows.

[2] Comp. vi. 1, where he substitutes the correct gloss τῷ παιδὶ Κυρίου in the phrase ἐγγισάτω μοι, in Isa. 50⁸ ; and xii. 9, where he boldly adds ὁ υἱὸς τοῦ Θεοῦ ἐπ' ἐσχάτων τῶν ἡμερῶν to Exod. 17¹⁴.

[3] Sanday, *Gospels in the Second Century*, 31 ff, reckons 16 exact, 23 slightly variant, and 47 variant citations of the O.T.

Further we must remember that he freely blends passages from different quarters: e.g. ii. 7 f. = Jer. 7²² f· + Zech. 7¹⁰, 8¹⁷; iv. 7 = Deut. 34²⁸ + 31¹⁸; iv. 8 = Exod. 32⁷ + Deut. 9¹²; cf. ix. 8, xv. 1. The same applies to his quotations from apocryphal books like Enoch and 4 Ezra, which he also cites with the same phrases as introduce Scriptural allusions generally.

The formulae of citation are: λέγει, with ὁ Θεός or ὁ Κύριος, ἡ γραφή, ὁ προφήτης, expressed or understood; or again with the name of the prophet in question, Moses, David, Isaiah, Daniel, and even Enoch; or most fully λέγει Κύριος (ὁ Θεὸς) ἐν τῷ προφήτῃ, ὁρίζει (Κύριος) ἐν ἄλλῳ προφήτῃ λέγοντι. Synonymous for λέγει are εἶπε, ἐλάλησε, ἐνετείλατο. Similarly γέγραπται, used even in citing Enoch (iv. 3, xvi. 6), and γεγραμμένης ἐντολῆς (vii. 3). The general result is an absolute doctrine of inspiration, which equates the Divine and the human speaker or writer, and which neglects distinctions between canonical and apocryphal sources. In this connexion reference may be made to vi. 13 λέγει δὲ Κύριος, Ἰδού, ποιῶ τὰ ἔσχατα ὡς τὰ πρῶτα (see *Didascalia Apost.* ed. Hauler, 75 'Ecce facio prima sicut novissima et novissima sicut prima': cf. Apoc. 21⁵ Ἰδού, καινὰ ποιῶ πάντα, Hipp. in Dan. 4³⁷ ἔσονται γὰρ τὰ ἔσχατα ὡς τὰ πρῶτα): also to vii. 4, where τί οὖν λέγει ἐν τῷ προφήτῃ is followed by words not found in any other extant writing, though our author has Lev. 16⁷ ff· in mind in the context. Here the citation seems too definite (ἐν τῷ προφήτῃ coming in between γεγραμμένης ἐντολῆς and πῶς οὖν ἐνετείλατο) to be other than due to some written source, whether apocryphal or a passage that has crept from the margin into the text of a canonical book. The former view is supported by the analogous case in xi. 9 f., see below (40). So in ii. 10 θυσία τῷ Κυρίῳ καρδία συντετριμμένη, ὀσμὴ εὐωδίας τῷ Κυρίῳ καρδία δοξάζουσα τὸν πεπλακότα αὐτήν, Barnabas has been quoting certain O. T. prophets, and continues in a way which suggests that he has his mind on them still, ἡμῖν οὖν οὕτως λέγει. But while the opening words are substantially those of Ps. 51¹⁷ (θυσία τῷ Θεῷ πνεῦμα συντετριμμένον, καρδίαν συντετριμμένην, κτλ.), the whole quotation actually comes from the Apocalypse of Adam (cf. Iren. iv. 17. 2). Thus confusion of memory may explain the case in which γέγραπται introduces words found also in our Matthew (see below).

On the whole, then, we have reason to expect that, if Barnabas alludes to any N. T. writings, it will be in a free and glossing way, and that sympathy with its methods and style will be needful to appraise the likelihood attaching to alleged cases of dependence [1]. The phenomena in the section on the 'Two ways' are dealt with under the *Didache*.

<hr />

EPISTLES AND APOCALYPSE

B

Romans	**b**
(1) Barn. xiii. 7.	Rom. 4³· ¹⁰ f. (¹⁷ f·).

τί οὖν λέγει τῷ Ἀβραάμ, ὅτε μόνος πιστεύσας ἐτέθη εἰς δικαιοσύνην; Ἰδοὺ τέθεικά σε, Ἀβραάμ, πατέρα ἐθνῶν τῶν πιστευόντων δι᾽ ἀκροβυστίας τῷ Κυρίῳ (GL, Θεῷ אC).

τί γὰρ ἡ γραφὴ λέγει; Ἐπίστευσε δὲ Ἀβραὰμ τῷ Θεῷ, καὶ ἐλογίσθη αὐτῷ εἰς δικαιοσύνην . . . πῶς οὖν ἐλογίσθη; . . . οὐκ ἐν περιτομῇ ἀλλ᾽ ἐν ἀκροβυστίᾳ· . . . εἰς τὸ εἶναι αὐτὸν πατέρα πάντων τῶν πιστευόντων δι᾽ ἀκροβυστίας.

LXX. Gen. 15⁶ καὶ ἐπίστευσεν Ἀβρὰμ τῷ Θεῷ, καὶ ἐλογίσθη αὐτῷ εἰς δικαιοσύνην.

17⁴ f· καὶ ἐγώ, ἰδοὺ ἡ διαθήκη μου μετὰ σοῦ· καὶ ἔσῃ πατὴρ πλήθους ἐθνῶν· καὶ οὐ κληθήσεται ἔτι τὸ ὄνομά σου Ἀβράμ, ἀλλ᾽ ἔσται Ἀβραὰμ τὸ ὄνομά σου· ὅτι πατέρα πολλῶν ἐθνῶν τέθεικά σε.

In our author's memory the O. T. passages have become

---

[1] The final estimate of the literary dependence of our epistle cannot be separated from one's theory of its date, and this again involves that of its religious standpoint. In the view of the member of committee specially responsible for its work on Barnabas, it is most probable that the epistle was written under Vespasian (iv. 4 f), within a very few years of the destruction of the Jewish Temple, the spiritual substitute for which, the Christian Church, is alluded to as in process of being built up (xvi. 10; cf. vii. 11). The standpoint is essentially that of the Epistle to the Hebrews, as distinct from other known types of primitive Christianity. For though they differ in their attitude to O T. ritual, both interpret the 'new Law' and its people under the categories of the old, in such wise that the literal observances of Judaism are regarded as at once fulfilled in essence and superseded by the purely spiritual worship realized in and through Christ. To both, O.T. worthies like Abraham, Isaac, Jacob, Moses, and David were in the line of heirship of the Promise, but not Israel at large (cf. Heb. 3-4, 11).—J. V. B.

conflated with the comments in Rom. 4; for the phrase τῶν πιστευόντων δι' ἀκροβυστίας (by no means an obvious one), especially as qualifying ἐθνῶν in Barnabas, can hardly be explained otherwise.

d

(2)   Barn. xiii. 2–3.   Rom. 9⁷⁻¹³.

ἀκούσατε οὖν περὶ τοῦ λαοῦ τί λέγει ἡ γραφή· ... Δύο ἔθνη ἐν τῇ γαστρί σου ... καὶ ὁ μείζων δουλεύσει τῷ ἐλάσσονι· αἰσθάνεσθαι ὀφείλετε ... ἐπὶ τίνων δέδειχεν ὅτι μείζων ὁ λαὸς οὗτος ἢ ἐκεῖνος.

οὐδ' ὅτι εἰσὶ σπέρμα 'Αβραάμ, πάντες τέκνα, ἀλλ' 'Εν 'Ισαὰκ κληθήσεταί σοι σπέρμα ... ἐρρήθη αὐτῇ ὅτι ὁ μείζων δουλεύσει τῷ ἐλάσσονι· καθὼς γέγραπται, Τὸν 'Ιακὼβ ἠγάπησα, τὸν δὲ 'Ησαῦ ἐμίσησα.

Though the passages both turn on the phrase common to them, they use it differently, Barnabas seeing in it a prophecy of the Christian people, Paul citing it simply for the principle of sovereign election. Yet Barnabas often twists what he borrows, and his knowledge of Romans is otherwise probable.

C

Ephesians   c

(3) Barn. vi. 11 ff.   Eph. 2¹⁰, ²¹ f·, 3¹⁷,   2 Cor. 5¹⁷, 1 Cor.
                              4²² ff·   3¹⁶ f·

11 ἐπεὶ οὖν ἀνα-καινίσας ἡμᾶς ἐν τῇ ἀφέσει τῶν ἁμαρτιῶν ἐποίησεν ἡμᾶς ἄλλον τύπον, ὡς παιδίων ἔχειν τὴν ψυχήν, ὡς ἂν δὴ ἀνα-πλάσσοντος αὐτοῦ ἡμᾶς. ... δευτέραν πλάσιν ἐπ' ἐσχάτων ἐποίησεν· λέγει δὲ Κύριος· Ἰδού, ποιῶ τὰ ἔσχατα ὡς τὰ πρῶτα.
Comp. xvi. 8 λα-βόντες τὴν ἄφεσιν τῶν ἁμαρτιῶν καὶ ἐλπίσαν-τες εἰς τὸ ὄνομα Κυρίου ἐγενόμεθα καινοί, πάλιν ἐξ ἀρχῆς κτιζόμενοι (continued below).
14 ἴδε οὖν, ἡμεῖς ἀναπεπλάσμεθα, καθὼς

2¹⁰ αὐτοῦ γάρ ἐσμεν ποίημα, κτισθέντες ἐν Χριστῷ 'Ιησοῦ.
4²² ff· ἀποθέσθαι ὑμᾶς ... τὸν παλαιὸν ἄν-θρωπον ... , ἀνανεοῦ-σθαι δὲ τῷ πνεύματι τοῦ νοὸς ὑμῶν καὶ ἐνδύσασθαι τὸν καινὸν ἄνθρωπον τὸν κατὰ Θεὸν κτισθέντα (cf. 2¹⁵).
Cf. Col. 3⁹ f· ἀπεκ-δυσάμενοι τὸν παλαιὸν ἄνθρωπον ... , καὶ ἐνδυσάμενοι τὸν νέον τὸν ἀνακαινούμενον εἰς ἐπίγνωσιν κατ' εἰκόνα τοῦ κτίσαντος αὐτόν.

2 Cor. 5¹⁷ ὥστε εἴ τις ἐν Χριστῷ, καινὴ κτίσις· τὰ ἀρχαῖα παρῆλθεν· ἰδού, γέγονε καινά (cf. Gal. 6¹⁵).

3¹⁷   κατοικῆσαι   τὸν

... λέγει· Ἰδού, λέγει Κύριος, ἐξελῶ τούτων ... τὰς λιθίνας καρδίας καὶ ἐμβαλῶ σαρκίνας· ὅτι αὐτὸς ἐν σαρκὶ ἔμελλεν φανεροῦσθαι καὶ ἐν ἡμῖν κατοικεῖν. 15 ναὸς γὰρ ἅγιος, ἀδελφοί μου, τῷ Κυρίῳ τὸ κατοικητήριον ἡμῶν τῆς καρδίας. Comp. xvi. 8(continued)—10 διὸ ἐν τῷ κατοικητηρίῳ ἡμῶν ἀληθῶς ὁ Θεὸς κατοικεῖ ἐν ἡμῖν· πῶς; ὁ λόγος αὐτοῦ τῆς πίστεως, ... αὐτὸς ἐν ἡμῖν προφητεύων, αὐτὸς ἐν ἡμῖν κατοικῶν ... τοῦτό ἐστιν πνευματικὸς ναὸς οἰκοδομούμενος τῷ Κυρίῳ (see also iv. 11).

Χριστὸν διὰ τῆς πίστεως ἐν ταῖς καρδίαις ὑμῶν.

2²¹ f. (Χρ. Ἰησ.) ἐν ᾧ πᾶσα οἰκοδομὴ συναρμολογουμένη αὔξει εἰς ναὸν ἅγιον ἐν Κυρίῳ, ἐν ᾧ καὶ ὑμεῖς συνοικοδομεῖσθε εἰς κατοικητήριον τοῦ Θεοῦ ἐν Πνεύματι.

1 Cor 3¹⁶ f. οὐκ οἴδατε ὅτι ναὸς Θεοῦ ἐστέ, καὶ τὸ πνεῦμα τοῦ Θεοῦ οἰκεῖ ἐν ὑμῖν; ὁ γὰρ ναὸς τοῦ Θεοῦ ἅγιός ἐστιν, οἵτινές ἐστε ὑμεῖς.

Here the phenomena are most complex, but Ephesians has the advantage over 1 and 2 Corinthians in several ways. (1) The idea of re-creation in Ephesians is really the nearer. The context of 2 Cor. 5¹⁷ (and of Gal. 6¹⁵) gives the phrases a rather specific reference ; while dependence on Ephesians explains *both* Barnabas's passages. (2) Ephesians has κατοικητήριον in close conjunction with ναὸν ἅγιον, as well as κατοικῆσαι τὸν Χριστὸν .... ἐν ταῖς καρδίαις ὑμῶν (not God, as in 2 Cor. 5¹⁶) —the idea from which Barnabas starts (ἔμελλεν ... ἐν ἡμῖν κατοικεῖν)—and the notion of the spiritual temple as in process of building (cf. Barn. xvi. 10). (3) The mystical idea of Christ indwelling the Saints, or the Church, which Barnabas expands in an emphatic way in §§ 14–16, is most marked in Ephesians (and Colossians), in close connexion with the idea of the Church as the body or πλήρωμα of Christ (Eph. 1²³). This latter thought may even determine the strange turn Barnabas gives to the words of Ps. 41³, viz. ἐν τίνι ὀφθήσομαι τῷ κυρίῳ τῷ Θεῷ μου καὶ δοξασθήσομαι (LXX, πότε ἥξω καὶ ὀφθήσομαι τῷ προσώπῳ τοῦ Θεοῦ), as if the Son were *bodied* forth in the Church and so *fulfilled* as to His glory (cf. Eph. 1¹⁸ τίς ὁ πλοῦτος τῆς δόξης τῆς κληρονομίας αὐτοῦ ἐν τοῖς ἁγίοις), even if αὐτοῦ refers strictly to God.

That the ideas underlying these sections of Barnabas are so subtle and inward, points to a source beyond common Christian tradition, and to a knowledge of the Pauline writings themselves.

d

(4) Barn. ii. 1.	Eph. 5¹⁶, 2².
ἡμερῶν οὖν οὐσῶν πονηρῶν καὶ αὐτοῦ τοῦ ἐνεργοῦντος ἔχοντος τὴν ἐξουσίαν.	ὅτι αἱ ἡμέραι πονηραί εἰσιν. κατὰ τὸν ἄρχοντα τῆς ἐξουσίας τοῦ ἀέρος, τοῦ πνεύματος τοῦ νῦν ἐνεργοῦντος ἐν τοῖς υἱοῖς τῆς ἀπειθείας.

The first of these parallels is a commonplace of early Christian thought ; the latter has parallels in Jewish Apocalyptic, e.g. *Test. Benj.* iii τοῦ ἀερίου πνεύματος τοῦ Βελίαρ, cf. *Secrets of Enoch*, xxix. 5. Moreover in Ephesians it is the aerial power or spirit (collectively), not its ruler, to which ἐνεργεῖν belongs.

(5) Barn. iii. 6.	Eph. 1⁴⁻⁶.
ὁ μακρόθυμος προβλέψας ὡς ἐν ἀκεραιοσύνῃ πιστεύσει ὁ λαὸς ὃν ἡτοίμασεν ἐν τῷ ἠγαπημένῳ αὐτοῦ, προεφανέρωσεν ἡμῖν περὶ πάντων.	καθὼς ἐξελέξατο ἡμᾶς ἐν αὐτῷ πρὸ καταβολῆς κόσμου . . ., προορίσας ἡμᾶς εἰς υἱοθεσίαν διὰ Ἰησοῦ Χριστοῦ εἰς αὐτόν . . ., εἰς ἔπαινον δόξης τῆς χάριτος αὐτοῦ, ἧς ἐχαρίτωσεν ἡμᾶς ἐν τῷ ἠγαπημένῳ.

Here the resemblances, turning on προβλέψας and ἡτοίμασεν ἐν τῷ ἠγαπημένῳ, seem really striking. They can only partly be paralleled from Jewish Apocalyptic[1], which taught that God made the world with a view to His Beloved (People), i.e. faithful Israel. Yet probably 'the Beloved' was sometimes applied to Messiah in particular, even in pre-Christian usage (see Charles's note on *Asc. Isaiae*, i. 4) : and so Barnabas uses it himself again in iv. 3, 8.

Hebrews   **c**

(6) Barn. v. 5 ff. (xiv. 4, xvi. 9).   Heb. 1² ff., 2⁹ ff. (12², 13¹²).

5 εἰ ὁ Κύριος ὑπέμεινεν παθεῖν   12² ὑπέμεινε σταυρόν.
περὶ τῆς ψυχῆς ἡμῶν, ὧν παντὸς τοῦ   13¹² ἔξω τῆς πύλης ἔπαθε.

---

[1] E g 4 Ezra 6⁵⁸ 'But we thy people, whom thou has called thy First-born, thy Only-begotten, and thy fervent Lover [? Beloved], are given into their hands.' Comp. Apoc. of Baruch xiv. 18, with Charles's note.

κόσμου Κύριος, ᾧ εἶπεν ὁ Θεὸς ἀπὸ
καταβολῆς κόσμου, Ποιήσωμεν κτλ.
... πῶς οὖν ὑπέμεινεν ὑπὸ χειρὸς
ἀνθρώπων παθεῖν;
6 αὐτὸς δέ, ἵνα καταργήσῃ τὸν
θάνατον καὶ τὴν ἐκ νεκρῶν ἀνάστασιν
δείξῃ (ὅτι ἐν σαρκὶ ἔδει αὐτὸν φανερωθῆναι), ὑπέμεινεν, ἵνα τοῖς πατράσιν
τὴν ἐπαγγελίαν ἀποδῷ, κτλ.
xiv. 4 δι᾽ ἡμᾶς ὑπομείνας.
xvi. 9 αὐτὸς ἐν ἡμῖν κατοικῶν,
τοῖς τῷ θανάτῳ δεδουλωμένοις, κτλ.

1²⁻¹³, e. g. σὺ κατ᾽ ἀρχάς, Κύριε,
τὴν γῆν ἐθεμελίωσας, κτλ.
2⁹ τὸν δὲ βραχύ τι παρ᾽ ἀγγέλους
ἠλαττωμένον βλέπομεν, Ἰησοῦν, διὰ τὸ
πάθημα τοῦ θανάτου .. ὅπως ...
ὑπὲρ παντὸς γεύσηται θανάτου.
¹⁴ ἐπεὶ οὖν τὰ παιδία κεκοινώνηκεν
αἵματος καὶ σαρκός, καὶ αὐτὸς παρα-
πλησίως μετέσχε τῶν αὐτῶν, ἵνα διὰ
τοῦ θανάτου καταργήσῃ τὸν τὸ κράτος
ἔχοντα τοῦ θανάτου ...
¹⁶ οὐ γὰρ δήπου ἀγγέλων ἐπιλαμ-
βάνεται ...
¹⁷ ὅθεν ὤφειλε κατὰ πάντα τοῖς
ἀδελφοῖς ὁμοιωθῆναι.
¹⁵ (ἵνα) καὶ ἀπαλλάξῃ τούτους,
ὅσοι φόβῳ θανάτου διὰ παντὸς τοῦ
ζῆν ἔνοχοι ἦσαν δουλείας.

Apart from the actual phrasing of ἵνα καταργήσῃ .... δείξῃ,
which recalls also 2 Tim. 1¹⁰ (see (19), below), the points of
contact between Barnabas and Heb. 2 in particular seem
too important to be accidental. The probability of literary
dependence on the side of Barnabas becomes enhanced when
we consider the relation of Barn. vi. 17–19 also to Heb. 2⁵⁻⁹ (see
below), as well as the similar use of the same O. T. quotation,
Ps. 21²³, in Barn. vi. 16 and Heb. 2¹² (though the wording
differs). Further, Heb. 9⁹, ¹³, ³⁹ may well suggest Barnabas's
ἵνα τοῖς πατράσιν τὴν ἐπαγγελίαν ἀποδῷ.

(7) Barn. vi. 17–19 (xiv. 5).

ζήσομεν κατακυριεύοντες τῆς γῆς ...
εἰ οὖν οὐ γίνεται τοῦτο νῦν, ἄρα ἡμῖν
εἴρηκεν ποτέ· ὅταν καὶ αὐτοὶ τελειωθῶμεν κληρονόμοι τῆς διαθήκης κυρίου
γενέσθαι.
Cf. xiv. 5 ἐφανερώθη δὲ (sc. ὁ
Κύριος) ἵνα κἀκεῖνοι (the Jews)
τελειωθῶσιν τοῖς ἁμαρτήμασιν καὶ
ἡμεῖς διὰ τοῦ κληρονομοῦντος διαθήκην
Κυρίου Ἰησοῦ λάβωμεν.

Heb. 2⁵⁻⁹.

... πάντα ὑπέταξας ὑποκάτω τῶν
ποδῶν αὐτοῦ (sc. ἀνθρώπου) ... νῦν
δὲ οὔπω ὁρῶμεν αὐτῷ τὰ πάντα ὑπο-
τεταγμένα· τὸν δὲ ... Ἰησοῦν ...

Here note the ideas of (1) lordship over things earthly as
the destiny of man, (2) its delayed but certain realization, (3)
when union with the archetypal Heritor (ὃν ἔθηκε κληρονόμον
πάντων, Heb. 1², cf. Barn. xiv) shall reach its consummation (the

τέλος of the type, x. 11 fin.); and elsewhere the idea that all this was the *rationale* of the Divine Heritor's own 'manifestation' and especially His sufferings : see (6). Nothing short of literary dependence seems to explain the appearance in Barnabas, alone in its age, of so much distinctive of Hebrews, especially as this state of lordship is also conceived as the true Sabbatic Rest in a new world (ch. xv, cf. x. 11 ; Heb. $3^{11,\ 18}$, $4^{1,\ 9-11}$), on which Jesus has already entered (xv. 9). This idea of ἄλλος κόσμος (xv. 8) was a current Jewish one[1], but seems to come to Barnabas through Hebrews with its οἰκουμένη μέλλουσα (ii. 5) and αἰὼν μέλλων (vi. 5). Further the prominence of the ideas in κληρονόμοι τῆς διαθήκης Κυρίου and διὰ τοῦ κληρονομοῦντος διαθήκην Κυρίου Ἰησοῦ seems to point to Hebrews, which contains more on these lines than all the rest of the N. T.: e.g. Heb. 1^2 ὃν ἔθηκεν κληρονόμον πάντων (cf. 1^4), Barn. iv. 3 ἵνα ταχύνῃ ὁ ἠγαπημένος αὐτοῦ καὶ ἐπὶ τὴν κληρονομίαν ἥξῃ ; Heb. 7^{22} κρείττονος διαθήκης γέγονεν ἔγγυος Ἰησοῦς (μεσίτης, 8^6, 9^{15}, 12^{24}), Barn. iv. 8 ἵνα ᾖ τοῦ ἠγαπημένου Ἰησοῦ (διαθήκη) ἐνκατασφραγισθῇ εἰς τὴν καρδίαν ἡμῶν (cf. xiii. 1), xiv. 5 ὃς εἰς τοῦτο ἡτοιμάσθη, ἵνα αὐτὸς φανείς ... διάθηται ἐν ἡμῖν διαθήκην λόγῳ ; Heb. 6^{17} τοῖς κληρονόμοις τῆς ἐπαγγελίας (1^{14}), 9^{15} ὅπως ... τὴν ἐπαγγελίαν[2] λάβωσιν οἱ κεκλημένοι τῆς αἰωνίου κληρονομίας, Barn. xiii. 6 τὸν λαὸν τοῦτον ... τῆς διαθήκης κληρονόμον, xiv. 4 αὐτὸς δὲ Κύριος ἡμῖν ἔδωκεν (τὴν διαθήκην) εἰς λαὸν κληρονομίας. Indeed Heb. 9^{11-15} seems to underlie Barnabas's whole soteriology : cf. (11).

d

(8) Barn. iv. 9–10, 13.

διὸ προσέχωμεν ἐν ταῖς ἐσχάταις ἡμέραις· οὐδὲν γὰρ ὠφελήσει ἡμᾶς ὁ πᾶς χρόνος τῆς ζωῆς ἡμῶν, ἐὰν μὴ νῦν ..., ὡς πρέπει υἱοῖς Θεοῦ, ἀντιστῶμεν ... Μὴ καθ᾽ ἑαυτοὺς ἐνδύνοντες μονάζετε ὡς ἤδη δεδικαιωμένοι, ἀλλ᾽ ἐπὶ τὸ αὐτὸ συνερχόμενοι συνζητεῖτε περὶ τοῦ κοινῇ συμφέροντος ...

Heb. 4^1, 10^{24} f.

φοβηθῶμεν οὖν μή ποτε, καταλειπομένης ἐπαγγελίας εἰσελθεῖν εἰς τὴν κατάπαυσιν αὐτοῦ, δοκῇ τις ἐξ ὑμῶν ὑστερηκέναι. 10^{24} f. κατανοῶμεν ἀλλήλους εἰς παροξυσμὸν ἀγάπης καὶ καλῶν ἔργων, μὴ ἐγκαταλείποντες τὴν ἐπισυναγωγὴν ἑαυτῶν, καθὼς ἔθος τισίν, ἀλλὰ παρα-

---

[1] Dalman, *The Words of Jesus*, 177 f.

[2] Ἐπαγγελία very frequent in Hebrews, also in Barn. v. 6, vi. 17, xv. 7, xvi 9 (conjoined with κλῆσις, cf. iv. 14) Observe too the similar use of τέλειος (iv 3, 11, v 11, viii. 1, xiii. 7), τελειοῦν (vi. 19, xiv. 5), to express the final or absolute stage of a thing.

13 ἵνα μήποτε ἐπαναπαυόμενοι ὡς κλητοὶ ἐπικαθυπνώσωμεν ταῖς ἁμαρτίαις ἡμῶν.

καλοῦντες, καὶ τοσούτῳ μᾶλλον ὅσῳ βλέπετε ἐγγίζουσαν τὴν ἡμέραν.

Note the points in common : (1) the danger of a false sense of security amid temptations against which strenuous vigilance alone can prevail, (2) the value of frequent fellowship and stimulus to good works.

(9)   Barn. v. 1.

εἰς τοῦτο γὰρ ὑπέμεινεν ὁ Κύριος παραδοῦναι τὴν σάρκα εἰς καταφθοράν, ἵνα τῇ ἀφέσει τῶν ἁμαρτιῶν ἁγνισθῶ-μεν, ὅ ἐστιν ἐν τῷ αἵματι τοῦ ῥαντί-σματος αὐτοῦ[1]. γέγραπται γὰρ περὶ αὐτοῦ (Isa. 53⁵·⁷) . . .

Heb. 12²⁴, 13¹² (1 Pet. 1²).

καὶ αἵματι ῥαντισμοῦ κρεῖττον λαλοῦντι παρὰ τὸν ᾽Αβελ.
13¹² διὸ καὶ ᾽Ιησοῦς, ἵνα ἁγιάσῃ διὰ τοῦ ἰδίου αἵματος τὸν λαόν, ἔξω τῆς πύλης ἔπαθε.
Cf. 1³ καθαρισμὸν τῶν ἁμαρτιῶν ποιησάμενος, also 9¹⁵.
1 Pet. 1² ἐκλεκτοῖς παρεπιδή-μοις . . . ἐν ἁγιασμῷ Πνεύματος, εἰς ὑπακοὴν καὶ ῥαντισμὸν αἵματος ᾽Ιησοῦ Χριστοῦ.

Here as regards 1 Pet. 1² all depends on the reading adopted; and as ℵ is quite as likely to be right as C and a version, we must leave the phrase in question out of account. On the other hand the idea of 'sanctification' τῇ ἀφέσει τῶν ἁμαρτιῶν (see also viii. 1 ῥαντίζειν . . . . τὸν λαόν, ἵνα ἁγνίζωνται ἀπὸ τῶν ἁμαρτιῶν; cf. Heb. 1³, 2¹¹, 9²², 10¹⁸), achieved by blood of sprinkling (13¹¹ f·, cf. 9¹³, ¹⁹, ²¹, 10²²), is far more characteristic of Hebrews than of 1 Peter. Hence this passage also must be added to those suggesting the influence of Hebrews (cf. Barn. v. 5 f., 10 f., viii. 1, 3).

(10)   Barn. vi. 19.

ὅταν καὶ αὐτοὶ τελειωθῶμεν κληρο-νόμοι τῆς διαθήκης κυρίου γενέσθαι.

Heb. 6¹.

ἐπὶ τὴν τελειότητα φερώμεθα.
Cf. 12²³ πνεύμασι δικαίων τετε-λειωμένων.

The idea of τελειότης underlying these passages is similar, and is one highly characteristic of Hebrews; see 2¹⁰ διὰ παθη-μάτων τελειῶσαι, 5⁹, 7²⁸ υἱὸν εἰς τὸν αἰῶνα τετελειωμένον, 9⁹, 10¹·¹⁴, 11⁴⁰. It corresponds to δικαιωθῆναι in Barn. iv. 10, xv. 7.

[1] v. l. ἐν τῷ ῥαντίσματι αὐτοῦ τοῦ αἵματος, C, cf. Lat. 'sparsione sanguinis illius.'

(11) Barn. viii. 1 ff, xiv. 4–6.

τίνα δὲ δοκεῖτε τύπον εἶναι, ὅτι ἐντέταλται τῷ Ἰσραὴλ προσφέρειν δάμαλιν ... καὶ οὕτως ὁαντίζειν τὰ παιδία καθ᾽ ἕνα τὸν λαόν, ἵνα ἁγνίζωνται ἀπὸ τῶν ἁμαρτιῶν ... ὁ μόσχος ὁ Ἰησοῦς ἐστίν ... οἱ ῥαντίζοντες παῖδες οἱ εὐαγγελισάμενοι ἡμῖν τὴν ἄφεσιν τῶν ἁμαρτιῶν καὶ τὸν ἁγνισμὸν τῆς καρδίας.

xiv. 5–6 ἐφανερώθη δέ, ἵνα ... ἡμεῖς διὰ τοῦ κληρονομοῦντος διαθήκην Κυρίου Ἰησοῦ λάβωμεν, ὃς εἰς τοῦτο ἡτοιμάσθη ἵνα αὐτὸς φανείς ... διάθηται ἐν ἡμῖν διαθήκην λόγῳ.

xiv. 4. Μωυσῆς θεράπων ὢν ἔλαβεν, αὐτὸς δὲ ὁ Κύριος ἡμῖν ἔδωκεν εἰς λαὸν κληρονομίας, δι᾽ ἡμᾶς ὑπομείνας.

Heb. 9[13 ff.], 3[5 f.]

εἰ γὰρ τὸ αἷμα τράγων καὶ ταύρων καὶ σποδὸς δαμάλεως ... ῥαντίζουσα ... ἁγιάζει ... πόσῳ μᾶλλον τὸ αἷμα τοῦ Χριστοῦ ... καθαριεῖ τὴν συνείδησιν ὑμῶν ἀπὸ νεκρῶν ἔργων ...

[15] καὶ διὰ τοῦτο διαθήκης καινῆς μεσίτης ἐστίν, ὅπως, θανάτου γενομένου εἰς ἀπολύτρωσιν τῶν ἐπὶ τῇ πρώτῃ διαθήκῃ παραβάσεων, τὴν ἐπαγγελίαν λάβωσιν οἱ κεκλημένοι τῆς αἰωνίου κληρονομίας.

Cf. 12[24] διαθήκης νέας μεσίτῃ Ἰησοῦ.

3[5 f.] καὶ Μωσῆς μὲν πιστὸς ἐν ὅλῳ τῷ οἴκῳ αὐτοῦ (sc. τοῦ Θεοῦ) ὡς θεράπων ... Χριστὸς δὲ ὡς υἱὸς ἐπὶ τὸν οἶκον αὐτοῦ· οὗ οἶκός ἐσμεν ἡμεῖς.

Here, no doubt, there are elements peculiar to Barnabas, especially certain ritual details in viii. 1. Still he lays emphasis on the very points of contact between the Old and New Covenants which Hebrews also sets in relief, i.e. the ritual of the Heifer and the Covenant bequeathed by Jesus as the Son and Heir, as distinct from Moses who was only God's θεράπων in all his action (quite another turn being given to the idea 'servant of God' than that in Exod. 14[31], Num. 12[8], Joshua 1[2]). The probability of dependence on Hebrews is moreover increased by a like emphasis on the Rest of God (see below).

(12)   Barn. xv.   Heb. 4[1–11].

Barnabas is concerned primarily with the *hallowing* of the Sabbath, as something to find fulfilment in Christianity, as distinct from Judaism, in the Messianic Age soon to dawn. But he may have got his idea of its rest, e. g. τότε καλῶς καταπαυόμενοι ἁγιάσομεν αὐτήν ... αὐτοὶ δικαιωθέντες καὶ ἀπολαβόντες τὴν ἐπαγγελίαν ... αὐτοὶ ἁγιασθέντες πρῶτον, from the treatment of σαββατισμὸς τῷ λαῷ τοῦ Θεοῦ in Heb. 4, e.g. [10 f.] See further (7).

[Barn. i. 8, iv. 9a, xxi. 2, 7 and Heb. 12[22], 18[f.], present some similarities in the writer's attitude to his readers.]

On the whole, then, the passages severally marked as d seem to amount cumulatively to c, as suggesting that Hebrews influenced Barnabas's thinking and language in various ways. Even Barnabas's ἐν σαρκὶ φανεροῦσθαι and its relation to Christ's Passion has its parallel in Heb. 9^{26} εἰς ἀθέτησιν ἁμαρτίας διὰ τῆς θυσίας αὐτοῦ πεφανέρωται, read in the light of 2^{14}, 5^7 ἐν ταῖς ἡμέραις τῆς σαρκὸς αὐτοῦ, and 10^{20}.

D

1 Corinthians   d

(13)   Barn. iv. 11.

λέγει γὰρ ἡ γραφή· Οὐαὶ οἱ συνετοὶ ἑαυτοῖς καὶ ἐνώπιον ἑαυτῶν ἐπιστήμονες. γενώμεθα πνευματικοί, γενώμεθα ναὸς τέλειος τῷ θεῷ.

1 Cor. $3^{1,\ 16,\ 18\ ff.}$

οὐκ ἠδυνήθην λαλῆσαι ὑμῖν ὡς πνευματικοῖς· . . . οὐκ οἴδατε ὅτι ναὸς Θεοῦ ἐστε . . . εἴ τις δοκεῖ σοφὸς εἶναι ἐν ὑμῖν . . . μωρὸς γενέσθω, ἵνα γένηται σοφός . . . γέγραπται γάρ (Job 5^{13}; Ps. 94^{11}).

Here the conjunction of ideas at first seems striking, because self-sufficiency, unspirituality, and God's true temple, do not obviously suggest each other; and the citation of very similar passages from the O. T. perhaps adds to the appearance of dependence. Yet on closer examination it appears that Barnabas means by πνευματικός that obedience to God's ἐντολαί as a whole which he goes on to demand, the opposite of drowsing in sins; so that in fact it is the same as ἀγαθός in § 12.

2 Corinthians   d

(14)   Barn. iv. 11 f.

μελετῶμεν τὸν φόβον τοῦ Θεοῦ . . . Ὁ Κύριος ἀπροσωπολήμπτως κρινεῖ τὸν κόσμον· ἕκαστος καθὼς ἐποίησεν κομιεῖται· ἐὰν ᾖ ἀγαθός, ἡ δικαιοσύνη αὐτοῦ προηγήσεται αὐτοῦ· ἐὰν ᾖ πονηρός, ὁ μισθὸς τῆς πονηρίας ἔμπροσθεν αὐτοῦ.

2 Cor. 5^{10} (1 Pet. 1^{17}).

τοὺς γὰρ πάντας ἡμᾶς φανερωθῆναι δεῖ ἔμπροσθεν τοῦ βήματος τοῦ Χριστοῦ, ἵνα κομίσηται ἕκαστος τὰ διὰ τοῦ σώματος, πρὸς ἃ ἔπραξεν, εἴτε ἀγαθόν, εἴτε φαῦλον. εἰδότες οὖν τὸν φόβον τοῦ Κυρίου ἀνθρώπους πείθομεν. 1 Pet. 1^{17} καὶ εἰ πατέρα ἐπικαλεῖσθε τὸν ἀπροσωπολήμπτως κρίνοντα κατὰ τὸ ἑκάστου ἔργον, ἐν φόβῳ . . . ἀναστράφητε.

Against the obvious resemblance in word and idea to 2 Corinthians must be set the reference to a man's recompense becoming patent before his eyes (cf. Isa. 58^8, cited in iii. 4), which rather suggests some other source, possibly known to both. This view gains some support from 1 Pet. 1[17], which affords a close parallel to Barnabas's ὁ Κύριος ἀπροσωπολήμπτως κρινεῖ, a sentiment echoed in Rom. 2[11] οὐ γάρ ἐστι προσωποληψία παρὰ τῷ Θεῷ. It is to be noted, too, that in the context of all these writers 'fear' of God is present (as in a similar passage in Hipp. περὶ τῆς συντελείας, 39).

Colossians   d

(15)   Barn. vi. 12 f.   Col. 3[9 f.]

ὡς λέγει τῷ υἱῷ· Ποιήσωμεν κατ' εἰκόνα καὶ καθ' ὁμοίωσιν ἡμῶν τὸν ἄνθρωπον ... Δευτέραν πλάσιν ἐπ' ἐσχάτων ἐποίησεν· λέγει δὲ Κύριος· Ἰδού, ποιῶ τὰ ἔσχατα ὡς τὰ πρῶτα.

ἀπεκδυσάμενοι τὸν παλαιὸν ἄνθρωπον σὺν ταῖς πράξεσιν αὐτοῦ, καὶ ἐνδυσάμενοι τὸν νέον τὸν ἀνακαινούμενον εἰς ἐπίγνωσιν κατ' εἰκόνα τοῦ κτίσαντος αὐτόν.

The common reference to renewal κατ' εἰκόνα can count for little in view of the different contextual ideas : see also (3).

(16)   Barn. xii. 7.   Col. 1[16 f.]

ἔχεις πάλιν καὶ ἐν τούτοις (sc. the Brazen Serpent) τὴν δόξαν τοῦ Ἰησοῦ, ὅτι ἐν αὐτῷ πάντα καὶ εἰς αὐτόν.

τὰ πάντα δι' αὐτοῦ καὶ εἰς αὐτὸν ἔκτισται· καὶ αὐτός ἐστι πρὸ πάντων καὶ τὰ πάντα ἐν αὐτῷ συνέστηκε.

It is to be observed that the scope of the words common to the two is in Barnabas much narrower, viz. typological, ὅτι πάντα ὁ πατὴρ φανεροῖ περὶ τοῦ υἱοῦ Ἰησοῦ, as he says just below. Yet he may be echoing a striking phrase, for all that.

1 Timothy   d

(17)   Barn. v. 9.   1 Tim. 1[15 f.]

τοὺς ἰδίους ἀποστόλους ... ὄντας ὑπὲρ πᾶσαν ἁμαρτίαν ἀνομωτέρους, ἵνα δείξῃ ὅτι οὐκ ἦλθεν καλέσαι δικαίους ἀλλὰ ἁμαρτωλούς.

πιστὸς ὁ λόγος ..., ὅτι Χριστὸς Ἰησοῦς ἦλθεν εἰς τὸν κόσμον ἁμαρτωλοὺς σῶσαι—ὧν πρῶτός εἰμι ἐγώ· ἀλλὰ διὰ τοῦτο ἠλεήθην, ἵνα ἐν ἐμοὶ πρώτῳ ἐνδείξηται Ἰησοῦς Χριστὸς τὴν ἅπασαν μακροθυμίαν ...

The relation of Barnabas's οὐκ ἦλθον, κτλ., to our Synoptics is discussed under (31). But the application of this principle to Apostles in particular, as palmary proof (ἔνδειξις) of the Saviour's grace—a bold idea—is so parallel to 1 Tim. 1[15 f.] as to suggest that the latter prompted Barnabas's thought.

(18)   Barn. v. 6.   1 Tim. 3¹⁶.
—ὅτι ἐν σαρκὶ ἔδει αὐτὸν φανερω-   ὁμολογουμένως μέγα ἐστὶ τὸ τῆς
θῆναι—   εὐσεβείας μυστήριον—ὃς ἐφανερώθη
                                                          ἐν σαρκί . . .

1 Tim. 3¹⁶ certainly affords the most striking N. T. parallel
to the recurring phrase in Barnabas. But as it is itself probably quoting a current liturgical form, literary dependence
cannot be pressed either way : see also (19).

2 *Timothy*   d

(19)   Barn. v. 6.   2 Tim. 1¹⁰.
αὐτὸς δέ, ἵνα καταργήσῃ τὸν θάνα-   (χάριν τὴν . . .) φανερωθεῖσαν δὲ
τον καὶ τὴν ἐκ νεκρῶν ἀνάστασιν δείξῃ   νῦν διὰ τῆς ἐπιφανείας τοῦ σωτῆρος
—ὅτι ἐν σαρκὶ ἔδει αὐτὸν φανερωθῆναι   ἡμῶν Χριστοῦ Ἰησοῦ, καταργήσαντος
—ὑπέμεινεν.   μὲν τὸν θάνατον φωτίσαντος δὲ ζωὴν
                                                          καὶ ἀφθαρσίαν διὰ τοῦ εὐαγγελίου.

                                                     Comp. 1 Tim. 3¹⁶ ὃς ἐφανερώθη
                                                     ἐν σαρκί.

                                                          1 Pet. 1²⁰.
                                                     φανερωθέντος δὲ ἐπ᾽ ἐσχάτου τῶν
                                                     χρόνων δι᾽ ἡμᾶς τοὺς δι᾽ αὐτοῦ πιστοὺς
                                                     εἰς Θεὸν τὸν ἐγείραντα αὐτὸν ἐκ νεκρῶν.

In both 2 Timothy and 1 Peter we have the conjunction of
two ideas prominent in Barn. v. 6. The degree of likeness, however, to 2 Timothy is greater, and is supported by 1 Timothy,
though there is some additional evidence that Barnabas used
1 Peter; see (23), (24). As regards the phrase ἐν σαρκὶ φανεροῦσθαι in Barnabas, its frequency (see vi. 7, 9, 14, xii. 10, cf.
xiv. 5) calls for special notice. Its occurrence in 1 Tim. 3¹⁶,
in what looks like a rhythmical hymn (Eph. 5¹⁹ ᶠ·; Col. 3¹⁶ ᶠ·)
or liturgical form, implies that the idea of the incarnation as
a 'manifestation' (ἐπιφάνεια) of a Divine Saviour was fairly
general (see Heb. 5⁷, 9²⁶, cf. 1 Pet. 1²⁰; 2 Tim. 1¹⁰; Titus 2¹¹)
in the later apostolic age, long before the Fourth Gospel
appeared. Such a usage in Barnabas's region may explain
the hold the idea has on him. But the conjunction in
Barnabas of the two ideas blended in the latter half of 2 Tim.
1¹⁰ is striking, and suggests literary connexion, unless here
also the same holds as is probable in ἐν σαρκὶ φανερωθῆναι.

(20)   Barn. vii. 2.

εἰ οὖν ὁ υἱὸς τοῦ Θεοῦ, ὢν Κύριος
καὶ μέλλων κρίνειν ζῶντας καὶ νεκρούς,
ἔπαθεν, κτλ.

2 Tim. 4¹.

διαμαρτύρομαι ἐνώπιον τοῦ Θεοῦ
καὶ Χριστοῦ Ἰησοῦ τοῦ μέλλοντος κρίνειν ζῶντας καὶ νεκρούς.

Here in both cases a common formula of Christain faith seems to be cited; cf. 1 Pet. 4⁵; Acts 10⁴²; Polyc. ad Phil. ii. 1; 2 Clem. i. 1.

Titus   d

(21)   Barn. i. 3, 4, 6.

ἀληθῶς βλέπω ἐν ὑμῖν ἐκκεχυμένον
ἀπὸ τοῦ πλουσίου τῆς πηγῆς Κυρίου
πνεῦμα ἐφ' ὑμᾶς . . . ἐλπίδι ζωῆς αὐτοῦ
(C ἐπ' ἐλπίδι) . . . ζωῆς ἐλπίς, ἀρχὴ
καὶ τέλος πίστεως ἡμῶν.

Titus 3⁵ ff., 1².

ἔσωσεν ἡμᾶς διὰ λουτροῦ παλιγ-
γενεσίας καὶ ἀνακαινώσεως Πνεύματος
ἁγίου, οὗ ἐξέχεεν ἐφ' ἡμᾶς πλουσίως
διὰ Ἰησοῦ Χριστοῦ τοῦ σωτῆρος ἡμῶν,
ἵνα δικαιωθέντες τῇ ἐκείνου χάριτι
κληρονόμοι γενηθῶμεν κατ' ἐλπίδα
ζωῆς αἰωνίου.

1² ἐπ' ἐλπίδι ζωῆς αἰωνίου.

The parallelism of language is considerable, as also of thought. To Barnabas the presence of salvation as evidenced by the effusion of the Spirit; while, just below, he refers to 'hope of life' eternal, in the phrase ἐλπίδι ζωῆς αὐτοῦ—a phrase characteristic of Titus (here, and in 1² ἐπ' ἐλπίδι ζωῆς αἰωνίου, to which C seems assimilated in Barn. i. 4). Yet this may well be part of his own way of thinking, in view of i. 6, cf. iv. 8 ἐπ' ἐλπίδι τῆς πίστεως αὐτοῦ.

(22)   Barn. xiv. 5 f.

ὃς εἰς τοῦτο ἡτοιμάσθη, ἵνα αὐτὸς
φανεὶς τὰς ἤδη δεδαπανημένας ἡμῶν
καρδίας τῷ θανάτῳ καὶ παραδεδομένας
τῇ τῆς πλάνης ἀνομίᾳ λυτρωσάμενος
. . . λυτρωσάμενον ἡμᾶς ἐκ τοῦ σκότους ἑτοιμάσαι ἑαυτῷ λαὸν ἅγιον.
Cf. v. 7 αὐτὸς ἑαυτῷ τὸν λαὸν τὸν
καινὸν ἑτοιμάζων.

Titus 2¹⁴.

ὃς ἔδωκεν ἑαυτὸν ὑπὲρ ἡμῶν, ἵνα
λυτρώσηται ἡμᾶς ἀπὸ πάσης ἀνομίας
καὶ καθαρίσῃ ἑαυτῷ λαὸν περιούσιον,
ζηλωτὴν καλῶν ἔργων.

Here the idea of Christ preparing *for Himself* a special people, by redeeming it from ἀνομία, is present in both writings in rather similar language, and so far strengthens the presumption created by (21).

1 *Peter*   d

(23)   Barn. v. 5, 6, vi. 7.

πῶς οὖν ὑπέμεινεν ὑπὸ χειρὸς
ἀνθρώπων παθεῖν, μάθετε. οἱ προ-

1 Pet. 1¹⁰ f.

περὶ ἧς σωτηρίας ἐξεζήτησαν καὶ
ἐξηρεύνησαν προφῆται οἱ περὶ τῆς εἰς

φῆται, ἀπ' αὐτοῦ ἔχοντες τὴν χάριν, εἰς αὐτὸν ἐπροφήτευσαν. αὐτὸς δὲ ἵνα καταργήσῃ τὸν θάνατον καὶ τὴν ἐκ νεκρῶν ἀνάστασιν δείξῃ, ὅτι ἐν σαρκὶ ἔδει αὐτὸν φανερωθῆναι, ὑπέμεινεν, ἵνα καὶ τοῖς πατράσιν τὴν ἐπαγγελίαν ἀποδῷ, κτλ.

Cf. vi. 7 ἐν σαρκὶ οὖν αὐτοῦ μέλλοντος φανεροῦσθαι καὶ πάσχειν, προεφανερώθη τὸ πάθος. Cf. vii. 7, xii. 8, 10.

ὑμᾶς χάριτος προφητεύσαντες, ἐρευνῶντες εἰς τίνα ἢ ποῖον καιρὸν ἐδήλου τὸ ἐν αὐτοῖς Πνεῦμα Χριστοῦ, προμαρτυρόμενον τὰ εἰς Χριστὸν παθήματα καὶ τὰς μετὰ ταῦτα δόξας.

In Barn. v. 5, 6 the parallelism with 1 Peter is twofold; (1) prophecy foreshadows Christ's passion and its sequel, and (2) this is due to grace proceeding from Christ Himself. (1) is an idea native to Barnabas's own thought (see the parallels); but (2) is noteworthy.

(24)   Barn. vi. 2–4.   1 Pet. 2⁶⁻⁸.

καὶ πάλιν λέγει ὁ προφήτης [Isa. 50⁸ f. has been quoted], ἐπεὶ ὡς λίθος ἰσχυρὸς ἐτέθη εἰς συντριβήν· Ἰδού, ἐμβαλῶ κτλ. (Isa. 28¹⁶).

διότι περιέχει ἐν γραφῇ, Ἰδού, τίθημι ἐν Σιὼν λίθον ἀκρογωνιαῖον κτλ. (Isa. 28¹⁶).

Though Barnabas and 1 Peter cite the same passage from Isaiah (with textual variation) and Psalm 118²², they use them rather differently, as is shown by Barnabas's εἰς συντριβήν, probably suggested by Isa. 8¹⁵ καὶ συντριβήσονται. Comp. Rom. 9³³ for the idea of Jesus as ὁ λίθος τοῦ προσκόμματος of Isa. 28¹⁶.

Other seeming parallels have been treated in other connexions: 1 Pet. 1² under (9), 1¹⁷ under (14), 1²⁰ under (19).

Considered, but set aside.

1 Cor. 3¹⁶ f., cf. 6¹⁹, see (3).

Gal. 4²¹ ff.; Barn. xiii (where Isaac's sons, not Abraham's, are the types).

1 Tim. 5²⁴ f.; Barn. iv. 12.

2 Pet. 3⁸ cannot be cited as affecting Barn. xv. 4 αὐτὸς δέ μοι μαρτυρεῖ· Ἰδού, ἡμέρα Κυρίου (v. l. σήμερον ἡμέρα) ἔσται ὡς χίλια ἔτη; for such exegesis of Ps. 90⁴ seems to have become a commonplace of Judaism (cf. Charles's note on *The Book of the Secrets of Enoch*, xxxiii. 1, 2).

1 John 4², cf. 2 John 7, cannot be treated as influencing

Barn. v. 10 f. ἦλθεν ἐν σαρκί, especially in view of what is said under (19): see also (41).

The greeting in Barn. xxi. 9 recalls several N. T. epistles. Ὁ Κύριος τῆς δόξης (see 1 Cor. 2[8]; James 2[1], also Acts 7[2] ὁ Θεὸς τῆς δόξης, cf. Ps. 28[8]) καὶ πάσης χάριτος finds its most striking parallel in 1 Pet. 5[10] ὁ δὲ Θεὸς πάσης χάριτος, ὁ καλέσας ὑμᾶς εἰς τὴν αἰώνιον αὐτοῦ δόξαν ἐν Χριστῷ. But the similar thought in 2 Cor. 1[3] suggests that here too it is a common fund that is being drawn on by all; while the μετὰ τοῦ πνεύματος ὑμῶν, found also in Gal. 6[18]; Phil. 4[23]; Philem. [25], may be a recognized epistolary phrase.

UNCLASSED

Apocalypse

(25)   Barn. vi. 13.   Apoc. 21[5].

λέγει δὲ Κύριος· Ἰδού, ποιῶ τὰ   καὶ εἶπεν ὁ καθήμενος ἐπὶ τῷ
ἔσχατα ὡς τὰ πρῶτα.   θρόνῳ, Ἰδού, καινὰ ποιῶ πάντα.

Isa. 43[19] ἰδοὺ ἐγὼ ποιῶ καινὰ ἃ νῦν ἀνατελεῖ.

That Barnabas, at least, cites an apocryphal source is made highly probable by the *Didascalia* (ed. Hauler, p. 75), 'Nam id dictum est, Ecce facio prima sicut novissima et novissima sicut prima.'

(26)   Barn. vii. 9.   Apoc. 1[7, 13].

ἐπειδὴ ὄψονται αὐτὸν τότε τῇ ἡμέρᾳ   ἰδού, ἔρχεται μετὰ τῶν νεφελῶν,
τὸν ποδήρη ἔχοντα τὸν κόκκινον περὶ   καὶ ὄψεται αὐτὸν πᾶς ὀφθαλμός, καὶ
τὴν σάρκα καὶ ἐροῦσιν· Οὐχ οὗτός   οἵτινες αὐτὸν ἐξεκέντησαν . . .
ἐστιν ὃν ποτε ἡμεῖς ἐσταυρώσαμεν . . .   καὶ ἐπιστρέψας εἶδον . . . ὅμοιον
κατακεντήσαντες . . . ;   υἱῷ ἀνθρώπου, ἐνδεδυμένον ποδήρη . . .

The main reference in Barnabas is certainly to the situation described in our Gospels; see (37). Moreover common knowledge of Zech. 12[10] (Heb. and LXX cod. Γ) and the reference seen in it by early Christians (cf. John 19[37] καὶ πάλιν ἑτέρα γραφὴ λέγει, Ὄψονται εἰς ὃν ἐξεκέντησαν) will serve to explain other features common to our two passages. But the substantival use of ποδήρη, found in the N. T. only in Apoc. 1[13], might suggest that Barnabas's language was unconsciously influenced by this passage also. Yet see Ecclus. 27[8] καὶ ἐνδύσῃ αὐτὸ (τὸ δίκαιον) ὡς ποδήρη δόξης, a passage which also implies that ποδήρης was a word of dignified associations, fitting it for Barnabas's purpose.

(27)   Barn. xxi. 3.   Apoc. 22¹⁰, ¹².
ἐγγὺς ὁ Κύριος καὶ ὁ μισθὸς αὐτο.   ὁ καιρὸς γὰρ ἐγγύς ἐστιν . . . ἰδοὺ
                                               ἔρχομαι ταχὺ καὶ ὁ μισθός μου μετ' ἐμοῦ.

LXX Isa. 40¹⁰ ἰδοὺ Κύριος, Κύριος (om. κς 2° א*ΑΓΓ) μετὰ ἰσχύος ἔρχεται . . . ἰδοὺ ὁ μισθὸς αὐτοῦ μετ' αὐτοῦ. Here Barnabas, while not intending an exact quotation, seems to have Isa. 40 in mind. Perhaps his use of ἐγγύς is due to its presence in the line before, ἐγγὺς γὰρ ἡ ἡμέρα κτλ. Comp. 1 Clem. xxxiv. 3 προλέγει γὰρ ἡμῖν· Ἰδοὺ ὁ Κύριος, καὶ ὁ μισθὸς αὐτοῦ πρὸ προσώπου αὐτοῦ, κτλ., and see 1 Clem. (54).

GOSPELS.

(I) The Synoptic Gospels.

Against Barnabas's knowledge of our Synoptic Gospels (and Acts) there is one piece of negative evidence which deserves attention. In xv. 9 he argues, against the observance of the Jewish Sabbath, that the Christian day of glad festival is 'the eighth day,' ἐν ᾗ καὶ ὁ Ἰησοῦς ἀνέστη ἐκ νεκρῶν καὶ φανερωθεὶς ἀνέβη εἰς οὐρανούς. Here, quite apart from all disputes as to whether Barnabas's words must needs imply that the Ascension of Jesus, after an act of self-manifestation (φανερωθείς), was on the self-same Sunday as the Resurrection, we have to consider whether Barnabas would even have used language so ambiguous (to say the least), if he had known any of our Synoptics—unless it were Luke, before Acts (see 1³) had come into his hands. This difficulty must be borne in mind in estimating the final effect of the positive evidence adduced below: see also (31), (33) for other negative indications[1]. It tells specially against the view that any Gospel whose authority counted for so little, would be cited with ὡς γέγραπται (29).

Matthew   D

(28)   Barn. vii. 3.   Matt. 27¹⁴.
ἀλλὰ καὶ σταυρωθεὶς ἐποτίζετο ὄξει   ἔδωκαν αὐτῷ πιεῖν οἶνον μετὰ χολῆς
καὶ χολῇ.   μεμιγμένον.

Ps. 68²² καὶ ἔδωκαν εἰς τὸ βρῶμά μου χολήν, καὶ εἰς τὴν δίψαν μου ἐπότισάν με ὄξος.

[1] Cunningham, *Epistle of Barnabas*, xciii, cites also the discussion of the Sabbath in ch. xv, where 'we find not the most distant allusion to the narratives of Matt. 12, or the emphatic declarations of vv. 8, ¹², of that chapter.'

Matthew alone of the Gospels refers to χολή: but it and Barnabas seem to represent independent traditions influenced by Ps. 68, Barnabas being nearest to its wording (ποτίζειν, ὄξος). Further Barnabas must have in view the Synoptic incident in Matt. 27⁴⁸; Mark 15³⁶; (John 19²⁹ ᶠ·), not that of Matt. 27³⁴, which preceded the Crucifixion. And in general, Barnabas's handling of the Passion in terms of O. T. types, especially from the Psalms, seems parallel to, rather than dependent on, Matthew's narrative (cf. Luke 23¹¹; Barn. vii. 9 ἐξουθενεῖν): see further under John ¹.

(29) Barn. iv. 14.	Matt. 22¹⁴.
προσέχωμεν μήποτε, ὡς γέγραπται, πολλοὶ κλητοί, ὀλίγοι δὲ ἐκλεκτοὶ εὑρέθωμεν.	πολλοὶ γάρ εἰσι κλητοί, ὀλίγοι δὲ ἐκλεκτοί.

Here we may set aside the idea of direct dependence on 4 Ezra 8³ πολλοὶ μὲν ἐκτίσθησαν, ὀλίγοι δὲ σωθήσονται (or Greek to that effect). But taken along with 10⁵⁷ σὺ γὰρ μακάριος εἶ ὑπὲρ πολλούς, καὶ κατ᾽ ὄνομα ἐκλήθης παρὰ τῷ Ὑψίστῳ καθὼς καὶ ὀλίγοι, this passage points to a familiar maxim, akin to Barnabas's quotation, as lying behind both 8³ and 10⁵⁷. In 8³ it would naturally be adapted to its context, which speaks of God's creative action, cf. 8¹ 'The Most High hath made this world for many, but the world to come for few'—where the same antithesis is implied. In this light, Barnabas and Matthew probably draw on a common source for the saying, whose proverbial character seems proved by its addition to Matt. 20¹⁶ in some copies (CDN Latt. Syrr. Arm. Aeth. Orig.). There, too, Syr. Sin. and Pesh. omit the γάρ found in Matt. 22¹⁴, as if it were no part of the familiar maxim. Where it was 'written' we cannot now say. But ὡς γέγραπται in Barnabas by no means excludes an apocryphal work; witness λέγει γὰρ ἡ γραφή, of *Enoch* in xvi. 5 (cf. vi. 13). So in xii. 1 an apocryphal dictum, somewhat akin to 4 Ezra 5⁵, is cited with ὁρίζει ἐν ἄλλῳ προφήτῃ. Of course the improbability of ὡς γέγραπται being used to cite one of our Gospels (a narrative,

---

¹ Compare Sanday, *Gospels in the Second Century*, 272 · 'We know that types and prophecies were eagerly sought out by the early Christians, and were soon collected in a kind of common stock from which every one drew at his pleasure.'

not a 'prophetic,' writing), varies in degree as we put Barnabas early or late. On the other hand, Barnabas may have known the maxim in connexion with the parable of the Wedding Feast, and thence derive its exact wording, while yet thinking of it as occurring in a prophetic 'scripture.'

UNCLASSED

Luke

(30)   Barn. v. 9.   Luke 5⁸.

ὅτε δὲ τοὺς ἰδίους ἀποστόλους   ἔξελθε ἀπ᾽ ἐμοῦ, ὅτι ἀνὴρ ἁμαρ-
τοὺς μέλλοντας κηρύσσειν τὸ εὐαγ-   τωλός εἰμι, Κύριε.
γέλιον αὐτοῦ ἐξελέξατο, ὄντας ὑπὲρ
πᾶσαν ἁμαρτίαν ἀνομωτέρους . . .

Peter's exclamation might possibly contribute, like 1 Tim. 1¹⁵ f., to suggest Barnabas's turn of thought; see (17), (31).

(II) The Synoptic Tradition.

(31)   Barn. v. 9.   Matt. 9¹¹, ¹³ ; Mark 2¹⁶ f.
                                                   (Luke 5³²).

ὅτε δὲ τοὺς ἰδίους ἀποστόλους τοὺς   ἔλεγον τοῖς μαθηταῖς αὐτοῦ, Διατί
μέλλοντας κηρύσσειν τὸ εὐαγγέλιον   (ὅτι) μετὰ τῶν τελωνῶν καὶ ἁμαρ-
αὐτοῦ ἐξελέξατο, ὄντας ὑπὲρ πᾶσαν   τωλῶν ἐσθίει . . . , ὁ δὲ ἀκούσας εἶπεν
ἁμαρτίαν ἀνομωτέρους, ἵνα δείξῃ ὅτι   . . . οὐ (γὰρ) ἦλθον καλέσαι δικαίους
οὐκ ἦλθεν καλέσαι δικαίους ἀλλὰ   ἀλλὰ ἁμαρτωλούς.
ἁμαρτωλούς, τότε ἐφανέρωσεν ἑαυτὸν
εἶναι υἱὸν Θεοῦ.

This points to knowledge of a Logian tradition only partly parallel to the tradition common to our Synoptics ; for the inference as to the sinful character of *the Apostles* is excluded by the context of all three Synoptists (including Luke, who adds εἰς μετάνοιαν), as well as by the general impression which they convey. That the saying, in a more or less detached form, was a familiar λόγος among Christians, is both likely and is implied by 1 Tim. 1¹⁵ πιστὸς ὁ λόγος καὶ πάσης ἀποδοχῆς ἄξιος, ὅτι Χριστὸς Ἰησοῦς ἦλθεν εἰς τὸν κόσμον ἁμαρτωλοὺς σῶσαι (see further under (17)): compare the way Barnabas continues, εἰ γὰρ μὴ ἦλθεν ἐν σαρκί, πῶς ἂν ἐσώθησαν οἱ ἄνθρωποι βλέποντες αὐτόν. That there was no basis for Barnabas's idea in any apocryphal writing is so far proved by Origen, *Contra Celsum*, i. 63, where he traces a similar suggestion to the passage in Barnabas.

C 2

(32)   Barn. v. 11.

οὐκοῦν ὁ υἱὸς τοῦ Θεοῦ εἰς τοῦτο ἐν
σαρκὶ ἦλθεν, ἵνα τὸ τέλειον τῶν ἁμαρτιῶν ἀνακεφαλαιώσῃ τοῖς διώξασιν ἐν
θανάτῳ τοὺς προφήτας αὐτοῦ. οὐκοῦν
εἰς τοῦτο ὑπέμεινεν.

Matt. 23³⁴ f· (Luke 11⁴⁹ f·).

διὰ τοῦτο, ἰδού, ἐγὼ ἀποστέλλω
πρὸς ὑμᾶς προφήτας . . . ὅπως ἔλθῃ
ἐφ' ὑμᾶς πᾶν αἷμα δίκαιον ἐκχυνόμενον
ἐπὶ τῆς γῆς . . .

The general idea is the same, though not its exact application.

(33)   Barn. v. 12.

λέγει γὰρ ὁ Θεὸς τὴν πληγὴν τῆς
σαρκὸς αὐτοῦ ὅτι ἐξ αὐτῶν· ὅταν
πατάξωσιν τὸν ποιμένα ἑαυτῶν, τότε
ἀπολεῖται τὰ πρόβατα τῆς ποίμνης.

Matt. 26³¹; Mark 14²⁷.

γέγραπται γάρ, Πατάξω τὸν ποιμένα
καὶ διασκορπισθήσεται τὰ πρόβατα τῆς
ποίμνης.

Cod. A of LXX has all the textual agreements here presented. As the application in Barnabas (ὅτι ἐξ αὐτῶν, sc. the Jews) is quite foreign to Matthew and Mark, it looks as if he were unaware of any setting such as theirs.

(34)   Barn. vi. 6.

Matt. 27³⁵; Mark 15²⁴;
Luke 23³⁴.

The casting of lots on Christ's garments is common to all our Gospels (including John 19²⁴). Barnabas quotes Ps. 21 for it and further Messianic touches.

(35)   Barn. vi. 11.

ἐπεὶ οὖν ἀνακαινίσας ἡμᾶς ἐν τῇ ἀφέσει τῶν ἁμαρτιῶν ἐποίησεν ἡμᾶς ἄλλον
τύπον, ὡς παιδίων ἔχειν τὴν ψυχήν, ὡς ἂν δὴ ἀναπλάσσοντος αὐτοῦ ἡμᾶς . . . .

Is the clause ὡς παιδίων ἔχειν τὴν ψυχήν due merely to the 'parable' which Barnabas sees in the promise as to entrance into 'a land of milk and honey'; or is it only in the light of the idea of Christians as childlike in heart (cf. viii. 1, 3) that he perceives the parable as latent in this phrase? If the latter, then one of Christ's *logia* seems presupposed, e. g. ἄφετε τὰ παιδία . . . τῶν γὰρ τοιούτων ἐστὶν ἡ βασιλεία τοῦ Θεοῦ (Mark 10¹⁴; Luke 18¹⁶, cf. Matt. 19¹⁴), which gains special emphasis in Mark and Luke by the added words, Ἀμὴν λέγω ὑμῖν, ὃς ἐὰν μὴ δέξηται τὴν βασιλείαν τοῦ Θεοῦ ὡς παιδίον, οὐ μὴ εἰσέλθῃ εἰς αὐτήν (cf. also Matt. 18³).

(36)   Barn. vii. 3: see (37).

(37) Barn. vii. 9.

... ἐπειδὴ ὄψονται αὐτὸν τότε
τῇ ἡμέρᾳ τὸν ποδήρη ἔχοντα τὸν
κόκκινον περὶ τὴν σάρκα, καὶ ἐροῦσιν,
Οὐχ οὗτός ἐστιν ὅν ποτε ἡμεῖς ἐσταυρώσαμεν ἐξουθενήσαντες καὶ κατακεντήσαντες καὶ ἐμπτύσαντες; ἀληθῶς οὗτος
ἦν ὁ τότε λέγων ἑαυτὸν υἱὸν Θεοῦ
εἶναι.

Matt. 27²⁸ ; Mark 15¹⁷.

Matt. 26⁶³ f.; Mark 14⁶¹ f.;
Luke 22⁶⁹ f.

As to the incident of the 'red robe,' it forms part of the
Synoptic tradition (see also John 19²): the agreement between Barnabas and Matthew in the use of κόκκινος (Mark
πορφύραν, John ἱμάτιον πορφυροῦν) is due to Barnabas's reference
to τὸ ἔριον τὸ κόκκινον just above. As to the assertion of Divine
Sonship, the reference to the Synoptic incident at the hearing
before the Sanhedrin is manifest; note the τότε and the
implicit reference to the prophecy of a regal Return (Matt.
26⁶⁴, ‖). The descriptive participles ἐξουθενήσαντες (=ἐμπαί-
ξαντες: see Matt. 27²⁹, ³¹, ⁴¹; Mark 15²⁰, ³¹; Luke 22⁶³, 23³⁶, in
the light of Luke 23¹¹), κατακεντήσαντες, ἐμπτύσαντες, refer simply
to the type of occurrence seen in Matt. 27²⁸⁻³⁰; Mark 15¹⁷⁻²⁰,
prior to the crucifixion and so without reference to John
19³⁴⁻³⁷ : see also (41).

(38) Barn. vii. 11.

οὕτω, φησίν (sc. ὁ Ἰησοῦς), οἱ θέλοντές με ἰδεῖν καὶ ἅψασθαί μου
τῆς βασιλείας, ὀφείλουσιν θλίβοντες καὶ παθόντες λαβεῖν με.

These words simply state in a dramatic form (cf. vii. 5) the
moral of what goes before, viz. the allegory of the Red Wool
amid the Thorns. They are no traditional *logion* of Jesus,
falling outside our Synoptic tradition: cf. Matt. 16²⁴, ‖. For
φησίν='He means,' see x. 3 ff., 7 f., xi. 11, cf. vi. 9, xi. 8.

(39) Barn. xii. 10.

ἐπεὶ οὖν μέλλουσιν λέγειν ὅτι ὁ
Χριστὸς υἱός ἐστιν Δαυίδ, αὐτὸς προ-
φητεύει Δ., φοβούμενος καὶ συνίων
τὴν πλάνην τῶν ἁμαρτωλῶν· Εἶπεν ὁ
Κύριος . . . Καὶ πάλιν λέγει οὕτως
Ἡσαΐας (45¹) . . . Ἴδε πῶς Δ. λέγει
αὐτὸν κύριον καὶ υἱὸν οὐ λέγει.

Matt. 22⁴¹⁻⁴⁵ ; Mark 12³⁵⁻³⁷ ;
Luke 20⁴¹⁻⁴⁴.

τίνος υἱός ἐστι; λέγουσιν αὐτῷ,
Τοῦ Δαβίδ. λέγει αὐτοῖς, Πῶς οὖν
Δαβὶδ ἐν Πνεύματι κύριον αὐτὸν καλεῖ,
λέγων, Εἶπεν ὁ Κύριος . . . ὑπο-
κάτω¹ τῶν ποδῶν σου; εἰ οὖν Δ. καλεῖ
αὐτὸν κύριον, πῶς υἱὸς αὐτοῦ ἐστι;

¹ ὑποπόδιον Luke (Mark אAL)

Here the use of Ps. 110[1] is quite parallel, down to the application which concludes the argument. Textually Barnabas agrees with the LXX (Alexandrine: B *deest*) in ὑποπόδιον, where Matthew and Mark (BD) have ὑποκάτω.

(III) The Fourth Gospel.

UNCLASSED

(40)   Barn. vi. 3.   John 6[51], cf. [58].

εἶτα τί λέγει, Καὶ ὃς ἐλπίσει ἐπ᾽   ἐάν τις φάγῃ ἐκ τούτου τοῦ ἄρτου,
αὐτὸν ζήσεται εἰς τὸν αἰῶνα.   ζήσεται εἰς τὸν αἰῶνα.
v. l. ὁ πιστεύων εἰς, cf. LXX.
Isa. 28[16] καὶ ὁ πιστεύων (ἐπ᾽ αὐτῷ,
ℵAQ) οὐ μὴ καταισχυνθῇ.

Barn. viii. 5 ὅτι δὲ τὸ ἔριον ἐπὶ τὸ ξύλον; ὅτι ἡ βασιλεία Ἰησοῦ ἐπὶ ξύλῳ, καὶ ὅτι οἱ ἐλπίζοντες ἐπ᾽ αὐτὸν ζήσονται εἰς τὸν αἰῶνα.

ix. 2 τίς ἐστιν ὁ θέλων ζῆσαι εἰς τὸν αἰῶνα; Ps. 33[13] ὁ θέλων ζωήν.

xi. 10 καὶ ὃς ἂν φάγῃ ἐξ αὐτῶν (sc. δένδρων), ζήσεται εἰς τὸν αἰῶνα (as from a 'prophet' influenced by Ezek. 47[1-12]), interpreted in § 11 as meaning ὃς ἂν ἀκούσῃ τούτων λαλουμένων [the words connected with Baptism] καὶ πιστεύσῃ, ζήσεται εἰς τὸν αἰῶνα.

Compare Gen. 3[22] καὶ νῦν μή ποτε . . . λάβῃ τοῦ ξύλου τῆς ζωῆς καὶ φάγῃ, καὶ ζήσεται εἰς τὸν αἰῶνα.

Apoc. 2[7] τῷ νικῶντι δώσω αὐτῷ φαγεῖν ἐκ τοῦ ξύλου τῆς ζωῆς . . . 22[2] ξύλον ζωῆς ποιοῦν καρποὺς δώδεκα, also [14, 19].

Barnabas is clearly haunted by the phrase ζήσεται εἰς τὸν αἰῶνα, which he uses to gloss other phrases of the LXX in vi. 3, ix. 2, (xi. 10). But whether he got it from Gen. 3[22], the *Psalms of Solomon*, xiv. 2, or rather from the apocryphal 'prophet' seemingly cited in xi. 9–11 (as his use of it in connexion with ξύλον, especially in xi. 6 f. and 10, rather suggests: cf. Apoc. 2[7], &c.), or again from current Christian usage (see Ecclus. 37[26], cf. Wisd. 5[15]), is obscure. In any case he seems independent of John; for he makes no allusion to Jesus as ὁ ἄρτος τῆς ζωῆς.

(41)   Barn xi. 1 ff., 8.   John 19³⁴.

ζητήσωμεν δὲ εἰ ἐμέλησεν τῷ Κυρίῳ   καὶ ἐξῆλθεν αἷμα καὶ ὕδωρ.
προφανερῶσαι περὶ τοῦ ὕδατος καὶ
περὶ τοῦ σταυροῦ (then quotations, especially Ps. 1³⁻⁶) . . . αἰ-
σθάνεσθε πῶς τὸ ὕδωρ καὶ τὸν σταυρὸν
ἐπὶ τὸ αὐτὸ ὥρισεν· τοῦτο γὰρ λέγει,
μακάριοι οἱ ἐπὶ τὸν σταυρὸν ἐλπί-
σαντες κατέβησαν εἰς τὸ ὕδωρ, ὅτι τὸν
μὲν μισθὸν λέγει ' ἐν καιρῷ αὐτοῦ' . . .

Barnabas's treatment of the Water and the Cross (not Blood, as in John) is quite independent, being connected in his own mind with the ξύλον and ὕδατα in Ps. 1. Indeed the treatment of the Blood and the Water in John 19³⁴, 1 John 5⁶⁻⁸ ὁ ἐλθὼν δι' ὕδατος καὶ αἵματος, is so different that, had Barnabas known the Johannine writings, he could hardly have written as he does.

(42)   Barn. xii. 7.   John 3¹⁴ f.

The handling of the type of the Brazen Serpent is so different that, taken by itself, it 'makes against rather than for the theory of acquaintance with the Fourth Gospel' (Rendall, ad loc.).

On the whole, in spite of their affinities in 'the deeper order of conceptions,' to which Keim in particular has called attention (cf. Sanday, *Gospels in the Second Century*, 270 ff.), we must regard Barnabas as unacquainted with the Fourth Gospel. Its Logos conception is one upon which he would be almost sure to seize, with much else to his anti-Judaic purpose. Rather it looks as if Barnabas and this Gospel shared to some degree in a common mode of thought touching Eternal Life and feeding upon words of Life—a mode of thought visible also in the Eucharistic prayers of the *Didache*.

THE DIDACHE

INTRODUCTION.

THE treatment of apparent quotations from Scripture in the *Didache* is rendered difficult by the composite character of the document. It is impossible to treat it as an homogeneous whole, but it is hard to decide what strata are to be recognized in its composition.

It has been thought best to adopt the following arrangement, while admitting that the classification is uncertain in several respects.

1. The *Two Ways*, i–vi. In this section no attempt has been made to reconstruct the primitive text from a comparison of the Greek MS. found by Bryennios, the Latin version and the text used in Barnabas—except in the omission of the section εὐλογεῖτε . . . τῆς διδαχῆς (i. 3–ii. 1). This is treated separately, as manifestly secondary.

2. The ecclesiastical section, vii. 1–xv. 3.

3. The eschatological section in xvi.

4. The interpolation in the 'Two Ways,' i. 3–ii. 1.

The *formulae* which appear to introduce quotations are as follows :—

1. In the *Two Ways*.

Except in the interpolated section (see below) no formulae are used.

2. In the *Ecclesiastical section*.

(1) Did. viii. 2 ὡς ἐκέλευσεν ὁ Κύριος ἐν τῷ εὐαγγελίῳ αὐτοῦ . . . cf. xv. 3, 4.

(2) Did. ix. 5 εἴρηκεν ὁ Κύριος . . .

3. In the *Eschatological section*.

(1) Did. xvi. 7 ὡς ἐρρέθη . . .

4. In the *Interpolation* in the *Two Ways* (i. 3–ii. 1).

(1) Did. i. 6 εἴρηται . . . [introducing the saying Ἱδρωσάτω ἡ ἐλεημοσύνη σου εἰς τὰς χεῖράς σου, μέχρις ἂν γνῷς τίνι δῷς, which cannot be traced to any known source].

1. THE TWO WAYS, I-VI.

There are no certain quotations from or allusions to the Old Testament or to any other documents which can serve as a standard of accuracy in quotation.

ACTS AND EPISTLES.

D

Acts   **d**

(1)   Did. iv. 8.   Acts 4³².

συγκοινωνήσεις δὲ πάντα τῷ ἀδελφῷ   οὐδὲ εἷς τι τῶν ὑπαρχόντων αὐτῷ
σου καὶ οὐκ ἐρεῖς ἴδια εἶναι.   ἔλεγεν ἴδιον εἶναι, ἀλλ' ἦν αὐτοῖς
                                         ἅπαντα κοινά.

The resemblance is such as might be due to similarity of circle or of conditions of life, and is not sufficiently close to prove literary dependence, on one side or the other.

Romans   **d**

(2)   Did. v 2.   Rom. 12⁹.

οὐ κολλώμενοι ἀγαθῷ.   ἀποστυγοῦντες τὸ πονηρόν, κολλώ-
                                         μενοι τῷ ἀγαθῷ.

The verbal coincidence is close, but the phrase is not remarkable (cf. iii. 9), and seems like an ethical commonplace. In the absence of other signs of any use of the epistle, it cannot prove literary dependence on either side.

UNCLASSED

Hebrews

(3)   Did. iv. 1.   Heb. 13⁷.

τοῦ λαλοῦντός σοι τὸν λόγον τοῦ   μνημονεύετε τῶν ἡγουμένων ὑμῶν, οἵ-
Θεοῦ μνησθήσῃ νυκτὸς καὶ ἡμέρας.   τινες ἐλάλησαν ὑμῖν τὸν λόγον τοῦ Θεοῦ.

There is some similarity of thought, but the distinctive ἡγουμένων is not in *Didache*, and the phrase λαλεῖν τὸν λόγον τοῦ Θεοῦ is a natural one.

Jude

(4)   Did. ii. 7.   Jude ²² f.

οὐ μισήσεις πάντα ἄνθρωπον [ἀλλὰ   Text very uncertain.
οὓς μὲν ἐλέγξεις, περὶ δὲ ὧν προσ-
εύξῃ, om. Lat.], οὓς δὲ ἀγαπήσεις ὑπὲρ
τὴν ψυχήν σου.
See Lev. 19¹⁷ f. for wording of Did.

GOSPELS.

(I) The Synoptic Gospels.

UNCLASSED

(5)   Did. iii. 7, cf. Matt. 5⁵ (due to Ps. 36¹¹).

(II) The Synoptic Tradition.

(6)   Did. i. 2.   Matt. 22³⁷⁻³⁹.

πρῶτον ἀγαπήσεις τὸν Θεὸν τὸν   ἀγαπήσεις Κύριον τὸν Θεόν σου ἐν ὅλῃ
ποιήσαντά σε, δεύτερον τὸν πλησίον   τῇ καρδίᾳ σου . . . αὕτη ἐστὶν ἡ μεγάλη
σου ὡς σεαυτόν.   καὶ πρώτη ἐντολή. δευτέρα δὲ ὁμοία
                                        αὕτη, ἀγαπήσεις τὸν πλησίον σου ὡς
                                        σεαυτόν : cf. Mark 12²⁹ f.

Here there is juxtaposition of the two principles associated in the Gospels and with like emphasis on their order; but the addition τὸν ποιήσαντά σε suggests direct Jewish influence. See Ecclus. 7³⁰, and cf. (5).

(7)   Did. i. 2.   Matt. 7¹².

πάντα δὲ ὅσα ἐὰν θελήσῃς μὴ γίνε-   πάντα οὖν ὅσα ἐὰν θέλητε ἵνα ποιῶ-
σθαί σοι, καὶ σὺ ἄλλῳ μὴ ποίει.   σιν ὑμῖν οἱ ἄνθρωποι, οὕτως καὶ ὑμεῖς
                                       ποιεῖτε αὐτοῖς (cf. Luke 6³¹).

                                       Tobit 4¹⁵.

                                       ὃ μισεῖς, μηδενὶ ποιήσῃς.

                                       Acts 15²⁰, ²⁹.

                                       καὶ ὅσα μὴ θέλετε ἑαυτοῖς γίνεσθαι
                                       ἑτέροις (-ῳ) μὴ ποιεῖτε. c D min.
                                       pauc syr^hl c.* sah. aeth. Iren.^lat
                                       Cyprian.

The evidence seems to show that the form preserved in Tobit re-emerges in the Jewish saying ascribed to Hillel, 'What is hateful to thyself, do not to thy fellow'; and the negative form in the *Didache* may be due to such influence. On the other hand the wording ὅσα ἐὰν θελήσῃς μὴ κτλ., instead of ὃ μισεῖς (found also in Greek, attributed e.g. to Cleobulus), seems due to the influence of the evangelical form of the saying (cf. Lampridius, in *Vita Alex. Severi*, 51, 7 quod a quibusdam sive Iudaeis sive Christianis audierat... 'Quod tibi fieri non vis, alteri ne feceris'; so *Didascalia*, i. 1, adding 'ab alio'). If the saying be part of the true text of the Acts, it would here most naturally be attributed to the use of the Acts. If it be regarded as a gloss in Acts, the *Didache* may have originated such a gloss.

2. THE ECCLESIASTICAL SECTION, VII-XV.

There are no certain quotations or allusions to the Old Testament or to any other documents which can serve as a standard of accuracy in quotation, save the free quotation from Mal. 1$^{11\,ff\cdot}$ in xiv. 3, where καὶ χρόνῳ (added to ἐν παντὶ τόπῳ) finds a parallel in the Targum ad loc.

EPISTLES.
D

1 *Corinthians*   **d**

(8)   Did. x. 6.   1 Cor. 16^{22}.

μαρὰν ἀθά.   μαρὰν ἀθά.

The Aramaic words would seem, from the sudden way in which they are introduced in 1 Corinthians, to have been in common use. But it may be noted that in each case they are used to enforce a warning. In the *Didache*, εἴ τις οὔκ ἐστιν [ἅγιος], μετανοείτω. In 1 Corinthians, εἴ τις οὐ φιλεῖ τὸν Κύριον, ἤτω ἀνάθεμα.

GOSPELS.
(I) The Synoptic Gospels.
C

Matthew   **c**

(9)   Did. vii. 1.   Matt. 28^{19}.

βαπτίσατε εἰς τὸ ὄνομα τοῦ πατρὸς   βαπτίζοντες αὐτοὺς εἰς τὸ ὄνομα τοῦ
καὶ τοῦ υἱοῦ καὶ τοῦ ἁγίου πνεύματος.   πατρὸς καὶ τοῦ υἱοῦ καὶ τοῦ ἁγίου
                                    πνεύματος.

The Trinitarian baptismal formula is not found in the Canonical New Testament except in Matthew ; but on account of its liturgical use, its presence here cannot prove literary dependence on the Gospel. Further, it cannot be held certain that these words stood originally either in this section of the *Didache* or in the original text of Matthew (*om.* codd. ap. Euseb.).

d

(10)   Did. ix. 5.   Matt. 7^6.

καὶ γὰρ περὶ τούτου εἴρηκεν ὁ Κύριος,   μὴ δῶτε τὸ ἅγιον τοῖς κυσί.
μὴ δῶτε τὸ ἅγιον τοῖς κυσί.

The verbal resemblance is exact, but the passage in Matthew contains no reference to the Eucharist, and the proverbial character of the saying reduces the weight which must be attached to verbal similarity, cf. (13). It is cited as a *saying* of the Lord.

(11)   Did. viii. 1 f.

αἱ δὲ νηστεῖαι ὑμῶν μὴ ἔστωσαν μετὰ
τῶν ὑποκριτῶν· νηστεύουσι γὰρ δευ-
τέρᾳ σαββάτων καὶ πέμπτῃ· ὑμεῖς δὲ
νηστεύσατε τετράδα καὶ παρασκευήν.
2 μηδὲ προσεύχεσθε ὡς οἱ ὑποκριταί,
ἀλλ᾽ ὡς ἐκέλευσεν ὁ Κύριος ἐν τῷ
εὐαγγελίῳ αὐτοῦ, οὕτω προσεύχεσθε.
πάτερ ἡμῶν ὁ ἐν τῷ οὐρανῷ, ἁγιασθήτω τὸ ὄνομά σου, ἐλθέτω ἡ
βασιλεία σου, γενηθήτω τὸ θέλημά σου
ὡς ἐν οὐρανῷ καὶ ἐπὶ γῆς· τὸν ἄρτον
ἡμῶν τὸν ἐπιούσιον δὸς ἡμῖν σήμερον,
καὶ ἄφες ἡμῖν τὴν ὀφειλὴν ἡμῶν, ὡς
καὶ ἡμεῖς ἀφίεμεν τοῖς ὀφειλέταις
ἡμῶν, καὶ μὴ εἰσενέγκῃς ἡμᾶς εἰς
πειρασμὸν ἀλλὰ ῥῦσαι ἡμᾶς ἀπὸ τοῦ
πονηροῦ· ὅτι σοῦ ἐστιν ἡ δύναμις καὶ
ἡ δόξα εἰς τοὺς αἰῶνας.

Matt. 6¹⁶.

ὅταν δὲ νηστεύητε μὴ γίνεσθε, ὡς οἱ
ὑποκριταί, σκυθρωποί· ἀφανίζουσι γὰρ
τὰ πρόσωπα αὐτῶν, ὅπως φανῶσι τοῖς
ἀνθρώποις νηστεύοντες. ἀμὴν λέγω ὑμῖν
ὅτι ἀπέχουσι τὸν μισθὸν αὐτῶν· σὺ δὲ
νηστεύων ἄλειψαί σου τὴν κεφαλὴν καὶ
τὸ πρόσωπόν σου νίψαι.

Matt. 6⁵, ⁹⁻¹³.

καὶ ὅταν προσεύχησθε οὐκ ἔσεσθε
ὡς οἱ ὑποκριταί ... οὕτως οὖν προσεύχεσθε ὑμεῖς· πάτερ ἡμῶν ὁ ἐν τοῖς οὐρανοῖς, ἁγιασθήτω τὸ ὄνομά σου, ἐλθέτω ἡ
βασιλεία σου, γενηθήτω τὸ θέλημά σου
ὡς ἐν οὐρανῷ καὶ ἐπὶ γῆς· τὸν ἄρτον ἡμῶν
τὸν ἐπιούσιον δὸς ἡμῖν σήμερον, καὶ ἄφες
ἡμῖν τὰ ὀφειλήματα ἡμῶν, ὡς καὶ ἡμεῖς
ἀφήκαμεν τοῖς ὀφειλέταις ἡμῶν, καὶ μὴ
εἰσενέγκῃς ἡμᾶς εἰς πειρασμὸν ἀλλὰ
ῥῦσαι ἡμᾶς ἀπὸ τοῦ πονηροῦ.

Matt. v. 5 om. syrˢⁱⁿ.   ἀφήκαμεν] ἀφίομεν DELΔΠ² al., ἀφίεμεν ℵ°GKMSUΠ*
codd. recent.   πονηροῦ] add ὅτι σοῦ ἐστιν ἡ βασιλεία καὶ ἡ δύναμις καὶ ἡ δόξα εἰς
τοὺς αἰῶνας· ἀμήν. codd. recent. ; add. ὅτι σοῦ ἐστιν ἡ βασιλεία καὶ ἡ δόξα εἰς τοὺς
αἰῶνας· ἀμήν. syrᶜᵘʳ (syrˢⁱⁿ deest); add. quoniam tuum est robur et potentia
in aevum aevi amen. sah.; add. quoniam est tibi virtus in saecula saecu-
lorum. k.

In the section about fasting the only point in common is
the connexion of fasting with hypocrisy; there is also in
the *Didache* a complete perversion of the spirit of Christ's
teaching about fasting, and the specific reference to Pharisees
is wanting.

In the sections touching prayer the writer seems clearly
familiar with a definite statement of Christ's teaching, though
hardly a written one, cf. αὐτοῦ after ἐν τῷ εὐαγγελίῳ. There
is also a superficial point of connexion with Matt. 6⁵, inas-
much as both there and in the *Didache* the true method of
prayer is contrasted with a false one.   But Matthew dis-
tinguishes (cf. v. 7) between the false methods of the ὑποκριταί
(a class of Jews) and the ἐθνικοί, while the *Didache* makes no
mention of ἐθνικοί.   It must however be remembered that the
text of Matthew is doubtful on this point, as B syrᶜᵘʳ read
ὑποκριταί instead of ἐθνικοί.   It would also appear probable
from what precedes and follows that the *Didache* makes the

falsity of method on the part of the ὑποκριταί lie not so much in the spirit as in the form of their prayers.

The Lord's Prayer in the *Didache* agrees with the Matthaean version as against the Lucan, in the number of clauses which it contains, in the introduction by the words οὕτω προσεύχεσθε, and in its verbal similarity. There are no divergences from Matt. 6⁹ ᶠᶠ except in four points :—

(1) τῷ οὐρανῷ *for* τοῖς οὐρανοῖς.

(2) ὀφειλήν *for* ὀφειλήματα.

(3) ἀφίεμεν *for* ἀφήκαμεν.

(4) The doxology.

(3) may be dismissed on the ground of possible assimilation in the text of our MS. of the *Didache* to the later text of the Lord's Prayer. As to (1) and (2) the differences would be insignificant, were it not that they come in a liturgical passage, where the text is apt to be strictly fixed by use, and that the whole quotation seems to come directly from a local liturgical usage. (4) The peculiar form of the doxology does not agree exactly with any of the forms known to occur in the authorities for the text of Matthew.

These three sections, on fasting, on prayer, on the Lord's Prayer, cannot be separated from each other. They point at least to similar local conditions; but the two former rather weaken the probability that the Lord's Prayer is a direct quotation from our Matthew.

(12) Did. xi. 7.	Matt. 12³¹.
πᾶσα γὰρ ἁμαρτία ἀφεθήσεται, αὕτη δὲ ἡ ἁμαρτία οὐκ ἀφεθήσεται.	πᾶσα ἁμαρτία καὶ βλασφημία ἀφε-θήσεται τοῖς ἀνθρώποις, ἡ δὲ τοῦ Πνεύματος βλασφημία οὐκ ἀφεθήσεται.

Mark 3²⁸.

πάντα ἀφεθήσεται τοῖς υἱοῖς τῶν ἀνθρώπων τὰ ἁμαρτήματα, καὶ αἱ βλασ-φημίαι ὅσα ἂν βλασφημήσωσιν· ὃς δ' ἂν βλασφημήσῃ εἰς τὸ Πνεῦμα τὸ Ἅγιον, οὐκ ἔχει ἄφεσιν εἰς τὸν αἰῶνα, ἀλλ' ἔνοχός ἐστιν αἰωνίου ἁμαρτήματος, cf. Luke 12¹⁰.

The form of the quotation is closer to Matthew than to Mark or Luke, and a similar context for the saying is obviously implied. Yet what is true of (10) applies here also.

(13)   Did. xiii. 1.

πᾶς δὲ προφήτης ἀληθινός, θέλων
καθῆσθαι πρὸς ὑμᾶς, ἄξιός ἐστι τῆς
τροφῆς αὐτοῦ, ὡσαύτως διδάσκαλος
ἀληθινός ἐστιν ἄξιος καὶ αὐτὸς ὥσπερ
ὁ ἐργάτης τῆς τροφῆς αὐτοῦ.

Matt. 10¹⁰.

ἄξιος γὰρ ὁ ἐργάτης τῆς τροφῆς αὐτοῦ.

Luke 10⁷.

ἄξιος γὰρ ὁ ἐργάτης τοῦ μισθοῦ αὐτοῦ.

1 Tim. 5¹⁸.

ἄξιος ὁ ἐργάτης τοῦ μισθοῦ αὐτοῦ.

The verbal coincidence is exact, and is made the more noticeable by the fact that in Luke and 1 Timothy τροφῆς is replaced by μισθοῦ. But 1 Timothy seems to show that the saying was one in common Christian use, while the *Didache* does not refer it to 'the Lord,' as in clear Gospel citations.

D

Luke   d

(14)   Did. ix. 2.   Luke 22¹⁷⁻¹⁹.

πρῶτον περὶ τοῦ ποτηρίου.   καὶ δεξάμενος ποτήριον εὐχαριστήσας
                                 εἶπε, λάβετε τοῦτο καὶ διαμερίσατε εἰς
                                 ἑαυτοὺς . . . καὶ λαβὼν ἄρτον κτλ.

The R. V. goes on to give an account of another ποτήριον. But D omits, and so does the Syriac, though it inverts the order. If, then, we regard this as a 'Western non-interpolation,' the order in the *Didache* is the same as that found in what would be the earliest text of Luke. But the specific associations of the Last Supper in Luke are ignored; therefore it does not seem that the resemblance is to be explained by any literary dependence, but rather by a common traditional usage.

(II) The Synoptic Tradition.

(15) This, as implied in the *Didache*, corresponds closely to what is found in our Synoptics, particularly Matthew, and is alluded to under the phrase τὸ εὐαγγέλιον, which apparently means the Message itself rather than any special record.

Thus we have in xi. 3 the phrase κατὰ τὸ δόγμα τοῦ εὐαγγελίου. Here the closest point of connexion in the context is to be found in xi. 4 πᾶς δὲ ἀπόστολος ἐρχόμενος πρὸς ὑμᾶς δεχθήτω ὡς Κύριος, which suggests Matt. 10⁴⁰, but can scarcely be regarded as a quotation; see also (12) for xi. 7. So in viii. 2, the tense ἐκέλευσεν supports the view that the εὐαγγέλιον is thought of as uttered by the Lord, and not as written down. In view of these passages, it is not certain that the phrase ὡς ἔχετε ἐν τῷ εὐαγγελίῳ (τοῦ Κυρίου ἡμῶν), in xv. 3, 4, has any other sense.

(III) The Fourth Gospel.

UNCLASSED

Under this heading it will be proper to mention the passages in ix–x which seem reminiscent of Johannine ideas and terminology. Three are especially noticeable:—

(16) Did. ix. 2 ὑπὲρ τῆς ἁγίας ἀμπέλου Δαβὶδ τοῦ παιδός σου.

This must refer primarily at least to the Church regarded as the Messianic kingdom, and not to Christ personally (which is excluded by ἐγνώρισας διὰ 'Ιησοῦ). It may also refer secondarily to the Davidic Messianic king, who in Jewish thought is almost interchangeable with the nation in its ideal aspect. Cf. the Targum on Ps. 80¹⁴, ¹⁵, *The vine-shoot which thy right hand hath planted and the king Messiah whom thou hast established for thyself,* and Apoc. Baruch 39 '*Tunc revelabitur Messiae mei principatus qui similis est fonti et viti.*' It is relative to this mystical idea of the Church that the Cup is to be understood (cf. πνευματικὸς ποτός in x. 3). The resemblance to John 15¹ rests on little more than the figure of the vine for the Messianic Kingdom.

(17) Did. ix. 3 εὐχαριστοῦμέν σοι ... ὑπὲρ τῆς ζωῆς καὶ γνώσεως ἧς ἐγνώρισας ἡμῖν διὰ 'Ιησοῦ τοῦ παιδός σου. Cf. John 17³.

(18) Did. x. 3 ἡμῖν δὲ ἐχαρίσω πνευματικὴν τροφὴν καὶ ποτὸν καὶ ζωὴν αἰώνιον διὰ τοῦ παιδός σου. Cf. John 6⁴⁵⁻⁵⁵.

It is noticeable that the distinctive ideas of the manna and the identification of the bread with the body of Christ, are not found in the *Didache*. The point of closest resemblance is that the *Didache*, like the Fourth Gospel, does not connect the spiritual food with the specific ideas of the institution, as is done in the Synoptic narrative.

3. THE ESCHATOLOGICAL CHAPTER.

GOSPELS.

The Synoptic Tradition.

(19)   Did. xvi. 1.

γρηγορεῖτε ὑπὲρ τῆς ζωῆς ὑμῶν· οἱ λύχνοι ὑμῶν μὴ σβεσθήτωσαν καὶ οἱ ὀσφύες ὑμῶν μὴ ἐκλυέσθωσαν, ἀλλὰ

Matt. 24⁴², ⁴⁴.

γρηγορεῖτε οὖν, ὅτι οὐκ οἴδατε ποία ἡμέρᾳ ὁ κύριος ὑμῶν ἔρχεται ... καὶ ὑμεῖς γίνεσθε ἕτοιμοι· ὅτι ᾗ ὥρᾳ οὐ

γίνεσθε ἕτοιμοι· οὐ γὰρ οἴδατε τὴν ὥραν
ἐν ᾗ ὁ κύριος ἡμῶν ἔρχεται.

δοκεῖτε ὁ υἱὸς τοῦ ἀνθρώπου ἔρχεται.
Cf. 25¹³.

Luke 12³⁵.

ἔστωσαν ὑμῶν αἱ ὀσφύες περιεζωσ-
μέναι καὶ οἱ λύχνοι καιόμενοι. Cf. 12⁴⁰.

Matt. 24⁴² ἡμέρᾳ] ὥρᾳ LΓΚΠ al. pler. lat-vet. syr^sin pesh. Tat^ar·
Orig. Ath.

There is a marked parallel to Luke 12³⁵, where alone ὀσφύες
and λύχνοι occur in the same combination; but it is in Matt.
that γρηγορεῖτε goes with οὐκ οἴδατε ποίᾳ ἡμέρᾳ [ὥρᾳ] ὁ κύριος
ὑμῶν ἔρχεται, and with ἡμέραν οὐδὲ τὴν ὥραν in 25¹³.

(20)   Did. xvi. 3-5.

ἐν γὰρ ταῖς ἐσχάταις ἡμέραις πληθυν-
θήσονται οἱ ψευδοπροφῆται καὶ οἱ φθο-
ρεῖς καὶ στραφήσονται τὰ πρόβατα εἰς
λύκους καὶ ἡ ἀγάπη στραφήσεται εἰς
μῖσος. αὐξανούσης γὰρ τῆς ἀνομίας μισή-
σουσιν ἀλλήλους καὶ διώξουσι καὶ παραδώσουσι, καὶ τότε φανήσεται ὁ κοσμοπλάνος ὡς υἱὸς Θεοῦ καὶ ποιήσει σημεῖα
καὶ τέρατα, καὶ ἡ γῆ παραδοθήσεται εἰς
χεῖρας αὐτοῦ καὶ ποιήσει ἀθέμιτα ἃ
οὐδέποτε γέγονεν ἐξ αἰῶνος· τότε ἥξει
ἡ κτίσις τῶν ἀνθρώπων εἰς τὴν πύρωσιν
τῆς δοκιμασίας καὶ σκανδαλισθήσονται
πολλοὶ καὶ ἀπολοῦνται οἱ δὲ ὑπομεί-
ναντες ἐν τῇ πίστει αὐτῶν σωθήσονται
ὑπ᾽ αὐτοῦ τοῦ καταθέματος.

Matt. 24¹⁰⁻¹³.

καὶ τότε σκανδαλισθήσονται πολλοί,
καὶ ἀλλήλους παραδώσουσι, καὶ μισή-
σουσιν ἀλλήλους· καὶ πολλοὶ ψευδοπροφῆται ἐγερθήσονται καὶ πλανήσουσι
πολλούς· καὶ διὰ τὸ πληθυνθῆναι τὴν
ἀνομίαν ψυγήσεται ἡ ἀγάπη τῶν πολ-
λῶν· ὁ δὲ ὑπομείνας εἰς τέλος οὗτος
σωθήσεται. Cf. Matt. 7¹⁵, 24²⁴ and
Mark 13¹³.

There are several points of connexion with Matt. 24¹⁰⁻¹³,
but this may not represent more than a common oral basis
containing a good many conventional Apocalyptic ideas. It
is to be noted that there is nothing in Matthew analogous to
ὁ κοσμοπλάνος κτλ. and to ὑπ᾽ αὐτοῦ τοῦ καταθέματος, parallels
to which are rather to be found in *Ascensio Isaiae*, iv. 2 ff.

(21)   Did. xvi. 6.

καὶ τότε φανήσεται τὰ σημεῖα τῆς
ἀληθείας· πρῶτον σημεῖον ἐκπετάσεως ἐν
οὐρανῷ, εἶτα σημεῖον φωνῆς σάλπιγγος,
καὶ τὸ τρίτον ἀνάστασις νεκρῶν.

Matt. 24³⁰ f.

καὶ τότε φανήσεται τὸ σημεῖον τοῦ
υἱοῦ τοῦ ἀνθρώπου ἐν τῷ οὐρανῷ . . . καὶ
ἀποστελεῖ τοὺς ἀγγέλους αὐτοῦ μετὰ
σάλπιγγος φωνῆς μεγάλης.

The parallelism is insufficient to warrant any sure inference.
The scheme in the *Didache* is rather that of 1 Thess. 4¹⁴⁻¹⁶,
where we have (1) the revelation of the Lord from Heaven

with angels of power, (2) the archangel's trumpet call, (3) the resurrection. Cf. too the σήματα τρισσά of the *Sibylline Oracles*, ii. 188 (ῥομφαία, σάλπιγξ, ἀνάστασις, cf. iv. 173 ff.), and the description of the παρουσία in the *Ascensio Isaiae*, chap. iv. For heavenly portents, cf. Josephus's account of signs before the war; and for the meaning of ἐκπέτασις, cf. *Sib. Orac.* viii. 302 and Isa. 65³ (in which Barnabas sees a reference to the Crucifixion). Apparently this idea was a more specific form given to 'the sign of the Son of Man,' which originally pointed simply to Dan. 7¹³ and its imagery.

On the whole, we notice that this section (1) contains features not found in our Synoptic tradition, and represents a more specific and personal doctrine of Antichrist, more closely resembling that found in 2 Thess. 2; Barn. iv; *Asc. Isaiae*, iv: (2) agrees far more fully with Matthew than with any other single Synoptic, though it has certain points peculiar to Luke, cf. (19): but (3) cannot be said to prove its author's knowledge of our Matthew, as distinct from the tradition lying behind it, which may well have been that of the region in which the *Didache* itself was compiled. While, then, use of our Synoptic tradition is highly probable, the verdict in relation to the individual gospels must remain doubtful.

4. THE INTERPOLATION IN THE 'TWO WAYS'

(i. 3–ii. 1).

EPISTLES.

D

1 *Peter*	**d**	
(22) Did. i. 4.		1 Pet. 2¹¹.
ἀπέχου τῶν σαρκικῶν καὶ σωματικῶν ἐπιθυμιῶν.		ἀπέχεσθαι τῶν σαρκικῶν ἐπιθυμιῶν.

The text of the *Didache*, as it stands, recalls 1 Pet. 2¹¹. The sentiment, however, is a natural one, and it is worth noticing that the conjunction of σωματικῶν and σαρκικῶν seems rather tautologous, and that σωματικῶν has been replaced in A. C. vii. 1 by κοσμικῶν. For the possibility that σωματικῶν originally stood alone, cf. 4 Macc. 1³² τῶν δὲ ἐπιθυμιῶν αἱ μέν εἰσι ψυχικαὶ αἱ δὲ σωματικαί. If this suggestion be right, σαρκικῶν would be a later gloss derived from 1 Peter and due to the same feeling as that which led to the substitution of κοσμικῶν in A. C. vii. 1 (possibly from Titus 2¹²). The context suggests that *Didache* has in view ἐπιθυμίαι that wrong one's neighbour, as in Matt. 5²⁷⁻³⁰.

(I) The Synoptic Gospels.

D

Matthew

(23)   Did. i. 5.

οὐκ ἐξελεύσεται ἐκεῖθεν μέχρις οὗ ἀποδῷ τὸν ἔσχατον κοδράντην.

Matt. 5²⁶.

οὐ μὴ ἐξέλθῃς ἐκεῖθεν ἕως ἂν ἀποδῷς τὸν ἔσχατον κοδράντην. Cf Luke 12⁵⁹, which has λεπτὸν ἀποδῷς.

The wording of the *Didache* is closer to Matthew than it is to Luke, especially in the use of κοδράντην and not λεπτόν. But the context is quite different, and it would be hazardous to lay much stress on a phrase which must have been a familiar one. See further under (25), (26).

Luke

(24) See under the next section.

(II) The Synoptic Tradition.

(25)   Did. i. 3.

εὐλογεῖτε τοὺς καταρωμένους ὑμῖν καὶ προσεύχεσθε ὑπὲρ τῶν ἐχθρῶν ὑμῶν, νηστεύετε δὲ ὑπὲρ τῶν διωκόντων ὑμᾶς. ποία γὰρ χάρις ἐὰν ἀγαπᾶτε τοὺς ἀγαπῶντας ὑμᾶς, οὐχὶ καὶ τὰ ἔθνη τὸ αὐτὸ ποιοῦσιν, ὑμεῖς δὲ ἀγαπᾶτε τοὺς μισοῦντας ὑμᾶς καὶ οὐχ ἕξετε ἐχθρόν.

Matt. 5⁴⁴⁻⁴⁷.

ἀγαπᾶτε τοὺς ἐχθροὺς ὑμῶν, καὶ προσεύχεσθε ὑπὲρ τῶν διωκόντων ὑμᾶς . . . ἐὰν γὰρ ἀγαπήσητε τοὺς ἀγαπῶντας ὑμᾶς, τίνα μισθὸν ἔχετε; οὐχὶ καὶ οἱ τελῶναι τὸ αὐτὸ ποιοῦσι κτλ.

Luke 6²⁷⁻³³.

ἀγαπᾶτε τοὺς ἐχθροὺς ὑμῶν, καλῶς ποιεῖτε τοῖς μισοῦσιν ὑμᾶς, εὐλογεῖτε τοὺς καταρωμένους ὑμῖν, προσεύχεσθε ὑπὲρ τῶν ἐπηρεαζόντων ὑμᾶς . . . καὶ εἰ ἀγαπᾶτε τοὺς ἀγαπῶντας ὑμᾶς, ποία ὑμῖν χάρις ἐστί, . . . καὶ γὰρ οἱ ἁμαρτωλοὶ τὸ αὐτὸ ποιοῦσι.

In Matt. *post* ἐχθροὺς ὑμῶν *add.* εὐλογεῖτε τοὺς καταρωμένους ὑμᾶς DLKΠ c f h pesh et mss. vss pp recen. *ante* καὶ προσεύχ *add* καλῶς ποιεῖτε τοὺς μισοῦντας ὑμᾶς D lat. pler. (non k) pesh. mss. vss pp. recen. *ante* διωκόντων *add.* ἐπηρεαζόντων ὑμᾶς καὶ D lat. pler. (non k) pesh. mss. vss. pp. recen.

It seems impossible to decide whether the occurrence of Matthaean and Lucan features, e. g. ποία χάρις (cf. Luke 6³²) and τὰ ἔθνη (cf. Matt. 5⁴⁷), be due (1) to a blending of the two Gospels, (2) or to the knowledge of another Greek source nearer to the Λόγια, which are generally supposed to be the source of this section of the matter common to the first and third evangelists, (3) or to oral tradition, (4) or to an early harmony (e. g. the Diatessaron).

With regard to the second possibility, it may be noted that the emphasis on fasting, which seems to be represented as a climax, is in keeping with a tendency discernible in later Jewish literature (cf. Tobit 12⁸) and which assumes prominence in 2 Clement 16⁴, but it is not found in the N. T.[1] It is therefore unlikely that it appeared in a source earlier than the Canonical Gospels. οὐχ ἕξετε ἐχθρόν at the end of a paragraph, if an addition of a redactor, cannot be very late, see *Didasc.* i. 1, and cf. *Apol. Aristidis* 15, Justin, *Apol.* i. 14.

(26) Did. i 4–6.

(1) ἐάν τίς σοι δῷ ῥάπισμα εἰς τὴν δεξιὰν σιαγόνα, στρέψον αὐτῷ καὶ τὴν ἄλλην καὶ ἔσῃ τέλειος. (2) ἐὰν ἀγγαρεύσῃ σέ τις μίλιον ἕν, ὕπαγε μετ' αὐτοῦ δύο. (3) ἐὰν ἄρῃ τις τὸ ἱμάτιόν σου, δὸς αὐτῷ καὶ τὸν χιτῶνα (4) ἐὰν λάβῃ τις ἀπὸ σοῦ τὸ σόν, μὴ ἀπαίτει, οὐδὲ γὰρ δύνασαι. (5) παντὶ τῷ αἰτοῦντί σε δίδου καὶ μὴ ἀπαίτει.

Matt. 5³⁹⁻⁴².

ὅστις σε ῥαπίζει εἰς τὴν δεξιάν σου σιαγόνα, στρέψον αὐτῷ καὶ τὴν ἄλλην· καὶ τῷ θέλοντί σοι κριθῆναι καὶ τὸν χιτῶνά σου λαβεῖν ἄφες αὐτῷ καὶ τὸ ἱμάτιον· καὶ ὅστις σε ἀγγαρεύσει μίλιον ἕν, ὕπαγε μετ' αὐτοῦ δύο· τῷ αἰτοῦντί σε δίδου, καὶ τὸν θέλοντα ἀπὸ σοῦ δανείσασθαι μὴ ἀποστραφῇς.

Luke 6²⁹⁻³⁰.

τῷ τύπτοντί σε ἐπὶ τὴν σιαγόνα πάρεχε καὶ τὴν ἄλλην· καὶ ἀπὸ τοῦ αἴροντός σου τὸ ἱμάτιον καὶ τὸν χιτῶνα μὴ κωλύσῃς· παντὶ αἰτοῦντί σε δίδου, καὶ ἀπὸ τοῦ αἴροντος τὰ σὰ μὴ ἀπαίτει.

The resemblance of this passage to Matthew and Luke is obvious. It should however be observed that, if we take the five cases as arranged and numbered above in the *Didache*, Matthew has 1, 3, 2, 5, omitting 4, while Luke has 1, 3, 5, 4, omitting 2. Going outside the Canonical Gospels, Tatian's *Diatessaron* (according to the reconstruction made by Zahn in

---

[1] But notice in this connexion the quite early addition in Mark 9²⁹ of καὶ νηστείᾳ to προσευχῇ, which is found in syr^sin and almost all late authorities.

his *Forschungen*, i. 17) had 1, 2, 3, 4, omitting 5, and Justin's *Apology*, i. 16, cites only 1, 3, and 2 a line later. It is hard to draw any more definite conclusion from these facts, than that the resemblance to our Gospels may be explained in any one of the four ways mentioned in the preceding note. It should be added that the addition of the phrases καὶ ἔσῃ τέλειος and οὐδὲ γὰρ δύνασαι shows the freedom with which the redactor is handling his material, whencesoever derived. It is useless to analyse closely the exact verbal correspondences with Matthew and Luke; for in a passage in which so many possibilities are open, only the closest verbal resemblances would be sufficient to prove literary dependence.

CLEMENT OF ROME

INTRODUCTION.

Standard of Accuracy in quotations. The quotations from the Old Testament seem for the most part to be made with great exactness, especially in the case of the citation of longer passages. Occasional variations from the text of the Septuagint occur; but these are usually very slight, and may possibly represent readings of the text differing from those in the principal MSS.: see also p. 124. The quotations from the N. T. are clearly made in a different way. Even in the case of N. T. works which as it appears to us were certainly known and used by Clement, such as Romans and 1 Corinthians, the citations are loose and inexact. This is not the place to discuss the causes of this difference in method; it is sufficient to point out that this fact makes it in the highest degree precarious to argue from the inexactness of possible quotations of other works in the N. T., that Clement did not know, and was not using these works.

Formulae of Citation. Passages from the O. T. are frequently introduced by the phrases γέγραπται, τὸ γεγραμμένον, ἡ γραφή.

EPISTLES, ACTS, AND APOCALYPSE.

A

Romans   **a**

(1)   Clem. xxxv. 5, 6.   Rom. 1[29—32].

ἀπορρίψαντες ἀφ᾽ ἑαυτῶν πᾶσαν ἀδικίαν καὶ ἀνομίαν, πλεονεξίαν, ἔρεις, κακοηθείας τε καὶ δόκους, ψιθυρισμούς τε καὶ καταλαλιάς, θεοστυγίαν, ὑπερηφανίαν τε καὶ ἀλαζονείαν, κενοδοξίαν τε καὶ ἀφιλοξενίαν.

πεπληρωμένους πάσῃ ἀδικίᾳ, πονηρίᾳ, πλεονεξίᾳ, κακίᾳ, μεστοὺς φθόνου, φόνου, ἔριδος, δόλου, κακοηθείας, ψιθυριστάς, καταλάλους, θεοστυγεῖς, ὑβριστάς, ὑπερηφάνους, ἀλαζόνας, ἐφευρετὰς κακῶν, γονεῦσιν ἀπειθεῖς, ταῦτα γὰρ οἱ πράσσοντες στυγη- τοὶ τῷ Θεῷ ὑπάρχουσιν· οὐ μόνον δὲ οἱ πράσσοντες αὐτά, ἀλλὰ καὶ οἱ συν- ευδοκοῦντες αὐτοῖς.

ἀσυνέτους, ἀσυνθέτους, ἀστόργους, ἀνελεήμονας, οἵτινες τὸ δικαίωμα τοῦ Θεοῦ ἐπιγνόντες, ὅτι τὰ τοιαῦτα πράσ- σοντες ἄξιοι θανάτου εἰσίν, οὐ μόνον αὐτὰ ποιοῦσιν, ἀλλὰ καὶ συνευδοκοῦσι τοῖς πράσσουσι.

An examination of this passage makes it practically certain that Clement is influenced by the recollection of the passage in the Epistle to the Romans. This judgement is founded upon—

1. The remarkable coincidence of the vices which are mentioned: this seems too detailed to have occurred by chance.

2. The character of the concluding sentences in the two passages: it would be very difficult to imagine that Clement is here independent of St. Paul.

b

(2)   Clem. xxxiii. 1.

τί οὖν ποιήσωμεν, ἀδελφοί, ἀργή- σωμεν ἀπὸ τῆς ἀγαθοποιίας καὶ ἐγ- καταλίπωμεν τὴν ἀγάπην, μηθαμῶς τοῦτο ἐάσαι ὁ δεσπότης ἐφ' ἡμῖν γε γενηθῆναι, ἀλλὰ σπεύσωμεν μετὰ ἐκτενείας καὶ προθυμίας πᾶν ἔργον ἀγαθὸν ἐπιτελεῖν.

Rom. 6¹.

τί οὖν ἐροῦμεν, ἐπιμένωμεν τῇ ἁμαρτίᾳ, ἵνα ἡ χάρις πλεονάσῃ, μὴ γένοιτο.

It seems most probable that Clement is here writing under the impression of the passage in the Romans. It is true that there is little verbal coincidence between the passages, but their thought is closely related. The impression produced by this is very much strengthened when the context of the two passages is observed. In the last section of the previous chapter Clement has stated that we are justified by means of faith.

c

(3)   Clem. xxxii. 2.

ἐξ αὐτοῦ (Ἰακὼβ) ὁ Κύριος Ἰησοῦς τὸ κατὰ σάρκα.

Rom. 9⁵.

ἐξ ὧν (τῶν πατέρων) ὁ Χριστὸς τὸ κατὰ σάρκα.

It seems probable that the sentence in Clement was

suggested by that in Romans. The phrase τὸ κατὰ σάρκα is not a very obvious one.

(4) Clem. l. 6, 7.	Rom. 4[7–9].	Ps. 31 (32)[1, 2].
γέγραπται γάρ· Μα-κάριοι ὧν ἀφέθησαν αἱ ἀνομίαι καὶ ὧν ἐπεκα-λύφθησαν αἱ ἁμαρτίαι· μακάριος ἀνὴρ ᾧ οὐ μὴ λογίσηται Κύριος ἁμαρ-τίαν, οὐδέ ἐστιν ἐν τῷ στόματι αὐτοῦ δόλος. οὗτος ὁ μακαρισμὸς ἐγέ-νετο ἐπὶ τοὺς ἐκλελεγ-μένους ὑπὸ τοῦ Θεοῦ διὰ Ἰησοῦ Χριστοῦ τοῦ Κυρίου ἡμῶν.	μακάριοι ὧν ἀφέθησαν αἱ ἀνομίαι, καὶ ὧν ἐπε-καλύφθησαν αἱ ἁμαρ-τίαι· μακάριος ἀνὴρ ᾧ οὐ μὴ λογίσηται Κύριος ἁμαρτίαν. ὁ μακαρισμὸς οὖν οὗτος ἐπὶ τὴν περι-τομήν; ἢ καὶ ἐπὶ τὴν ἀκροβυστίαν,	μακάριοι ὧν ἀφέθησαν αἱ ἀνομίαι, καὶ ὧν ἐπε-καλύφθησαν αἱ ἁμαρτίαι. μακάριος ἀνὴρ οὗ οὐ μὴ λογίσηται Κύριος ἁμαρ-τίαν, οὐδέ ἐστιν ἐν τῷ στόματι αὐτοῦ δόλος.

It is clear that Clement intends to quote the Psalm; he introduces the quotation with the word γέγραπται, and we have not found any clear case where he has done this in the case of a passage from the N. T. This seems also evident from his concluding the quotation with words which are in the Psalm, but not in Romans. But it must also be recognized that the words οὗτος ὁ μακαρισμός suggest strongly that he was influenced by his recollection of the same words in the Romans.

d

(5) Clem. xxxvi. 2.	Rom. 1[21].
ἡ ἀσύνετος καὶ ἐσκοτωμένη διάνοια ἡμῶν.	καὶ ἐσκοτίσθη ἡ ἀσύνετος αὐτῶν καρδία.

Clem. li. 5.	Eph. 4[18].
τὰς ἀσυνέτους καρδίας.	ἐσκοτισμένοι τῇ διανοίᾳ.

The phrases in Clement may have been suggested by the Romans, but there is a similar phrase in Eph. 4[18] : see (37).

(6) Clem. xxxviii. 1.	Rom. 12[4].
σωζέσθω οὖν ἡμῶν ὅλον τὸ σῶμα ἐν Χριστῷ Ἰησοῦ, καὶ ὑποτασσέσθω ἕκαστος τῷ πλησίον αὐτοῦ.	καθάπερ γὰρ ἐν ἑνὶ σώματι πολλὰ μέλη ἔχομεν, τὰ δὲ μέλη πάντα οὐ τὴν αὐτὴν ἔχει πρᾶξιν· οὕτως οἱ πολλοὶ ἓν σῶμά ἐσμεν ἐν Χριστῷ.

Clem. xlvi. 7.	1 Cor. 6[15].
ἱνατί διέλκομεν καὶ διασπῶμεν τὰ μέλη τοῦ Χριστοῦ καὶ στασιάζομεν πρὸς τὸ σῶμα τὸ ἴδιον.	τὰ σώματα ὑμῶν μέλη Χριστοῦ ἐστιν.

1 Cor. 12¹².

καθάπερ γὰρ τὸ σῶμα ἕν ἐστι, καὶ
μέλη πολλὰ ἔχει, πάντα δὲ τὰ μέλη
τοῦ σώματος πολλὰ ὄντα ἕν ἐστι
σῶμα, οὕτω καὶ ὁ Χριστός.

Eph. 4⁴.

ἓν σῶμα καὶ ἓν πνεῦμα.

Eph. 4²⁵.

ὅτι ἐσμὲν ἀλλήλων μέλη.

Eph. 5³⁰.

ὅτι μέλη ἐσμὲν τοῦ σώματος αὐτοῦ.

It is hardly possible to say here whether Clement is
influenced by the Romans or the other Epistles.

1 Corinthians   a

(7)   Clem. xxxvii. 5.

λάβωμεν τὸ σῶμα ἡμῶν· ἡ κεφαλὴ
δίχα τῶν ποδῶν οὐδέν ἐστιν, οὕτως
οὐδὲ οἱ πόδες δίχα τῆς κεφαλῆς· τὰ
δὲ ἐλάχιστα μέλη τοῦ σώματος ἡμῶν
ἀναγκαῖα καὶ εὔχρηστά εἰσιν ὅλῳ τῷ
σώματι· ἀλλὰ πάντα συνπνεῖ καὶ ὑποταγῇ μιᾷ χρῆται εἰς τὸ σῴζεσθαι ὅλον
τὸ σῶμα.

xxxviii. 1.

σωζέσθω οὖν ἡμῶν ὅλον τὸ σῶμα
ἐν Χριστῷ Ἰησοῦ, καὶ ὑποτασσέσθω
ἕκαστος τῷ πλησίον αὐτοῦ, καθὼς καὶ
ἐτέθη ἐν τῷ χαρίσματι αὐτοῦ.

1 Cor. 12¹² ff·

καθάπερ γὰρ τὸ σῶμα ἕν ἐστι, καὶ
μέλη πολλὰ ἔχει, πάντα δὲ τὰ μέλη
τοῦ σώματος πολλὰ ὄντα ἕν ἐστι
σῶμα, οὕτω καὶ ὁ Χριστός . . .
¹⁴ καὶ γὰρ τὸ σῶμα οὐκ ἔστιν ἓν
μέλος, ἀλλὰ πολλά . . .
²¹ οὐ δύναται δὲ ὁ ὀφθαλμὸς
εἰπεῖν τῇ χειρί, Χρείαν σου οὐκ ἔχω·
ἢ πάλιν ἡ κεφαλὴ τοῖς ποσί, Χρείαν
ὑμῶν οὐκ ἔχω. ἀλλὰ πολλῷ μᾶλλον
τὰ δοκοῦντα μέλη τοῦ σώματος ἀσθενέ-
στερα ὑπάρχειν ἀναγκαῖά ἐστι.

Cf. 1 Clem. xlvi. 7 and 1 Cor. 6¹⁵.

It would appear to be certain that Clement is here influenced by the First Epistle to the Corinthians. The
metaphor of the body and its members is indeed found also
in Romans and Ephesians, but the details are taken from the
passage in Corinthians.

(8)   Clem. xlvii. 1.

ἀναλάβετε τὴν ἐπιστολὴν τοῦ μακαρίου Παύλου τοῦ ἀποστόλου. 2 τί
πρῶτον ὑμῖν ἐν ἀρχῇ τοῦ εὐαγγελίου
ἔγραψεν; 3 ἐπ' ἀληθείας πνευμα-

1 Cor. 1¹¹⁻¹³.

ἐδηλώθη γάρ μοι περὶ ὑμῶν, ἀδελφοί μου, ὑπὸ τῶν Χλόης, ὅτι ἔριδες ἐν
ὑμῖν εἰσι. λέγω δὲ τοῦτο, ὅτι ἕκαστος
ὑμῶν λέγει, Ἐγὼ μέν εἰμι Παύλου,

τικῶς ἐπέστειλεν ὑμῖν περὶ ἑαυτοῦ τε
καὶ Κηφᾶ τε καὶ Ἀπολλώ, διὰ τὸ καὶ
τότε προσκλίσεις ὑμᾶς πεποιῆσθαι·

Ἐγὼ δὲ Ἀπολλώ, Ἐγὼ δὲ Κηφᾶ,
Ἐγὼ δὲ Χριστοῦ.

It cannot be doubted that this passage refers to the First
Epistle to the Corinthians; the references to Cephas and
Apollos and the trouble in the Church seem to make this
plain, and the conclusion is borne out by actual quotations
from the Epistle.

It is important to ask whether the mode of referring to this
letter implies that Clement had no knowledge of our second
letter. Dr. Lightfoot, in his note on the passage, cites
parallels which seem to make it plain that such a conclusion
would be unwarranted.

(9)   Clem. xlix. 5.

ἀγάπη πάντα ἀνέχεται, πάντα μακρο-
θυμεῖ· οὐδὲν βάναυσον ἐν ἀγάπῃ,
οὐδὲν ὑπερήφανον· ἀγάπη σχίσμα οὐκ
ἔχει, ἀγάπη οὐ στασιάζει, ἀγάπη πάντα
ποιεῖ ἐν ὁμονοίᾳ·

1 Cor. 13⁴⁻⁷.

ἡ ἀγάπη μακροθυμεῖ, χρηστεύεται·
ἡ ἀγάπη οὐ ζηλοῖ· ἡ ἀγάπη οὐ
περπερεύεται, οὐ φυσιοῦται, οὐκ ἀσχη-
μονεῖ, οὐ ζητεῖ τὰ ἑαυτῆς, οὐ παρ-
οξύνεται, οὐ λογίζεται τὸ κακόν, οὐ
χαίρει ἐπὶ τῇ ἀδικίᾳ, συγχαίρει δὲ
τῇ ἀληθείᾳ, πάντα στέγει, πάντα
πιστεύει, πάντα ἐλπίζει, πάντα ὑπομένει.

It can hardly be doubted that many of the phrases in
Clement were suggested by the recollection of the passage in
Corinthians.

b

(10)   Clem. xxiv. 1.

κατανοήσωμεν, ἀγαπητοί, πῶς ὁ
δεσπότης ἐπιδείκνυται διηνεκῶς ἡμῖν
τὴν μέλλουσαν ἀνάστασιν ἔσεσθαι, ἧς
τὴν ἀπαρχὴν ἐποιήσατο τὸν Κύριον
Ἰησοῦν ἐκ νεκρῶν ἀναστήσας.

1 Cor. 15²⁰.

νυνὶ δὲ Χριστὸς ἐγήγερται ἐκ
νεκρῶν, ἀπαρχὴ τῶν κεκοιμημένων.

1 Cor. 15²³.

ἀπαρχὴ Χριστός.

This would appear to be almost certainly a reminiscence.
The word ἀπαρχή, used in this sense of our Lord, in reference
to the resurrection, seems to make this plain.

(11)   Clem. xxiv. 4, 5.

λάβωμεν τοὺς καρπούς· ὁ σπόρος
πῶς καὶ τίνα τρόπον γίνεται; ἐξῆλθεν
ὁ σπείρων καὶ ἔβαλεν εἰς τὴν γῆν

1 Cor. 15³⁶, ³⁷.

ἄφρων, σὺ ὃ σπείρεις οὐ ζωοποιεῖ-
ται, ἐὰν μὴ ἀποθάνῃ· καὶ ὃ σπείρεις,
οὐ τὸ σῶμα τὸ γενησόμενον σπείρεις

ἕκαστον τῶν σπερμάτων· ἅτινα πε- | ἀλλὰ γυμνὸν κόκκον, εἰ τύχοι, σίτου, ἤ
σόντα εἰς τὴν γῆν ξηρὰ καὶ γυμνὰ | τινος τῶν λοιπῶν· ὁ δὲ Θεὸς δίδωσιν
διαλύεται, εἶτ᾽ ἐκ τῆς διαλύσεως ἡ | αὐτῷ σῶμα καθὼς ἠθέλησε, καὶ ἑκάστῳ
μεγαλειότης τῆς προνοίας τοῦ δεσπότου | τῶν σπερμάτων ἴδιον σῶμα.
ἀνίστησιν αὐτά, καὶ ἐκ τοῦ ἑνὸς πλείονα
αὔξει καὶ ἐκφέρει καρπόν.

It seems most probable that the thought of this passage is
suggested by that in Corinthians. It is true that the develop-
ment of the conception is different, but there is nothing
surprising in this, if, as seems probable, Clement's references
to the N. T. are usually made from memory.

c

(12)   Clem. xlviii. 5.   1 Cor. 12⁸, ⁹.

ἤτω τις πιστός, ἤτω δυνατὸς γνῶσιν | ᾧ μὲν γὰρ διὰ τοῦ Πνεύματος δίδο-
ἐξειπεῖν, ἤτω σοφὸς ἐν διακρίσει | ται λόγος σοφίας, ἄλλῳ δὲ λόγος
λόγων, ἤτω ἁγνὸς ἐν ἔργοις. | γνώσεως κατὰ τὸ αὐτὸ Πνεῦμα, ἑτέρῳ
| πίστις ἐν τῷ αὐτῷ Πνεύματι.

It is noticeable that though the form of Clement's phrase
is quite different from that of St. Paul, he groups together the
same three qualities or gifts, πιστός—πίστις, γνῶσις—λογός
γνώσεως, σοφὸς ἐν διακρίσει λόγων—λόγος σοφίας. In view of
this it would seem probable that we have here a reminiscence
of St. Paul's words.

d

(13)   Clem. v. 1, 5.   1 Cor. 9²⁴.

ἀθλητάς· . . . βραβεῖον.   οὐκ οἴδατε, ὅτι, οἱ ἐν σταδίῳ τρέ-
                              χοντες πάντες μὲν τρέχουσιν, εἰς δὲ
                              λαμβάνει τὸ βραβεῖον,

Cf. Phil. 3¹⁴.

(14) Clem. xxxiv. 8. | 1 Cor. 2⁹. | Isa. 64⁴.

λέγει γάρ· ¹ὀφθαλμὸς | ἀλλὰ καθὼς γέγραπται, | ἀπὸ τοῦ αἰῶνος οὐκ
οὐκ εἶδεν καὶ οὖς οὐκ | ˮΑ ὀφθαλμὸς οὐκ εἶδε, | ἠκούσαμεν οὐδὲ οἱ ὀ-
ἤκουσεν, καὶ ἐπὶ καρδίαν | καὶ οὖς οὐκ ἤκουσε, καὶ | φθαλμοὶ ἡμῶν εἶδον θεὸν
ἀνθρώπου οὐκ ἀνέβη, ὅσα | ἐπὶ καρδίαν ἀνθρώπου | πλὴν σοῦ, καὶ τὰ ἔργα
² ἡτοίμασεν τοῖς ὑπομέ- | οὐκ ἀνέβη, ὅσα ἡτοίμα- | σου ἃ ποιήσεις τοῖς ὑπο-
νουσιν ³ αὐτόν. | σεν ὁ Θεὸς τοῖς ἀγαπῶ- | μένουσιν ἔλεον. Cf. 65¹⁶
| σιν αὐτόν. | οὐκ ἀναβήσεται αὐτῶν
| | ἐπὶ τὴν καρδίαν.

¹ Syr. Lat and Constant. insert ἃ.   ² Syr. Lat and Constant insert
ὁ κύριος.   ³ Constant. reads ἀγαπῶσιν, and Syr. supports this ; Lat. reads
sustinentibus, with Alexand.

The passages in Clement and 1 Corinthians are almost

verbally agreed, and it would at first sight seem natural to conclude that Clement is quoting from 1 Corinthians, while the relation of St. Paul's phrase to that of Isaiah is a difficult question. But a more careful examination of the passages shows clearly that the phenomena are very complex.

1. The context, and therefore the meaning of the passage in Clement, is entirely different from that in St. Paul. In Clement the things which eye hath not seen nor ear heard are the rewards promised to the servants of God. This is evident from the whole character of the chapter, and especially of the preceding sentence, εἰς τὸ μετόχους ἡμᾶς γενέσθαι τῶν μεγάλων καὶ ἐνδόξων ἐπαγγελιῶν αὐτοῦ. In 1 Corinthians the things which eye hath not seen nor ear heard are the hidden mysteries which are revealed to the believers by the Spirit of God. In Isaiah the meaning of the passage is like that of Clement, but the phrases are very different.

2. A. Resch (*Agrapha*, p. 102) has collected a great number of cases where the same phrase is quoted or referred to—

Hegesippus in Stephen Gobarus ap. Photium, cod. 232, col. 893; Hom. Clem. ii. 13; Clem. Alex. *Protrept.* x. 94; Origen, *in Ierem. Hom.* xviii. 15; *Apost. Const.* vii. 32 ; Athanasius, *De Virginitate*, 18 ; Epiph. *Haer.* lxiv. 69. We may add *Actus Petri*, 10, *Acts of Thomas*, Syriac, ed. Wright, p. 205, and 2 Clem. xi. 7.

In all these passages the phrase seems to be used in the same sense as in Clem. xxxiv. 8, that is as referring to the future rewards promised to the righteous.

3. Resch also points out that St. Jerome, *Comm. on Isaiah*, lib. xvii, says that the apocryphal *Ascension of Isaiah* contained this phrase, and (Ep. 57) that it was also contained in the *Apocalypse of Elias*; while Origen, *Comm. on Matt.* xxvii. 9, says that the phrase occurs ' in nullo regulari libro,' but ' in secretis Eliae prophetae.' The *Testamentum Iesu Christi*, xxviii (ed. Rahmani, Mainz, 1899), cites the passage as a saying of the Lord, but adds ' as Moses and other holy men have said.'

It seems then most probable that Clement and the other authors mentioned are not taking the phrase from St. Paul. It is impossible to think that they take it from Isaiah ; the form in which they cite the saying is wholly different from his, while it corresponds almost exactly with that of St. Paul. Accordingly it is probable that St. Paul, Clement, and the other writers are quoting from some unknown source, a pre-Christian work, to judge from Paul's use of it (with καθὼς γέγραπται).

(15)   Clem. xxxvii. 3.   1 Cor. 15²³.

ἀλλ' ἕκαστος ἐν τῷ ἰδίῳ τάγματι—   ἕκαστος δὲ ἐν τῷ ἰδίῳ τάγματι—

There is here an exact correspondence of words, but the phrase in Clement arises quite naturally from the context, and is of too obvious a character to demand explanation.

(16)   Clem. xxxviii. 2.   1 Cor. 16¹⁷.

ὁ δὲ πτωχὸς εὐχαριστείτω τῷ Θεῷ   χαίρω δὲ ἐπὶ τῇ παρουσίᾳ Στεφανᾶ
ὅτι ἔδωκεν αὐτῷ δι' οὗ ἀναπληρωθῇ   καὶ Φορτουνάτου καὶ Ἀχαϊκοῦ, ὅτι τὸ
αὐτοῦ τὸ ὑστέρημα.   ὑμῶν ὑστέρημα οὗτοι ἀνεπλήρωσαν.

Phil. 2³⁰.

παραβολευσάμενος τῇ ψυχῇ, ἵνα ἀνα-
πληρώσῃ τὸ ὑμῶν ὑστέρημα τῆς πρός
με λειτουργίας.

Cf. also 2 Cor. 9¹², 11⁹, and
Col. 1²⁴.

(17)   Clem. xl. 1.   1 Cor. 2¹⁰.

προδήλων οὖν ἡμῖν ὄντων τούτων,   τὸ γὰρ Πνεῦμα πάντα ἐρευνᾷ, καὶ τὰ
καὶ ἐγκεκυφότες εἰς τὰ βάθη τῆς θείας   βάθη τοῦ Θεοῦ.
γνώσεως.

Rom. 11³³.

ὦ βάθος πλούτου καὶ σοφίας καὶ
γνώσεως Θεοῦ.

(18)   Clem. xlviii. 6.   1 Cor. 10²⁴, ³³.

Cf. Phil. 2⁴.

Hebrews   a

(19)   Clem. xxxvi. 2–5.   Heb. 1.

διὰ τούτου (Ἰησοῦ Χριστοῦ) ἠθέλη-   πολυμερῶς καὶ πολυτρόπως πάλαι 1
σεν ὁ δεσπότης τῆς ἀθανάτου γνώσεως   ὁ Θεὸς λαλήσας τοῖς πατράσιν ἐν τοῖς
ἡμᾶς γεύσασθαι· ὃς ὢν ἀπαύγασμα τῆς   προφήταις ἐπ' ἐσχάτου τῶν ἡμερῶν τού- 2
μεγαλωσύνης αὐτοῦ, τοσούτῳ μείζων   των ἐλάλησεν ἡμῖν ἐν υἱῷ, ὃν ἔθηκε
ἐστὶν ἀγγέλων ὅσῳ διαφορώτερον   κληρονόμον πάντων, δι' οὗ καὶ ἐποίησε

ὄνομα κεκληρονόμηκεν¹. γέγραπται
γὰρ οὕτως· Ὁ ποιῶν τοὺς ἀγγέλους
αὐτοῦ πνεύματα καὶ τοὺς λειτουργοὺς
αὐτοῦ πυρὸς φλόγα. ἐπὶ δὲ τῷ υἱῷ
αὐτοῦ οὕτως εἶπεν ὁ δεσπότης· Υἱός
μου εἶ σύ, ἐγὼ σήμερον γεγέννηκά σε·
αἴτησαι παρ᾽ ἐμοῦ καὶ δώσω σοι ἔθνη
τὴν κληρονομίαν σου καὶ τὴν κατάσχεσίν σου τὰ πέρατα τῆς γῆς. καὶ
πάλιν λέγει πρὸς αὐτόν· Κάθου ἐκ
δεξιῶν μου, ἕως ἂν θῶ τοὺς ἐχθρούς
σου ὑποπόδιον τῶν ποδῶν σου.

τοὺς αἰῶνας· ὃς ὢν ἀπαύγασμα τῆς 3
δόξης καὶ χαρακτὴρ τῆς ὑποστάσεως
αὐτοῦ, φέρων τε τὰ πάντα τῷ ῥήματι
τῆς δυνάμεως αὐτοῦ, καθαρισμὸν τῶν
ἁμαρτιῶν ποιησάμενος ἐκάθισεν ἐν δεξιᾷ
τῆς μεγαλωσύνης ἐν ὑψηλοῖς, τοσούτῳ 4
κρείττων γενόμενος τῶν ἀγγέλων ὅσῳ
διαφορώτερον παρ᾽ αὐτοὺς κεκληρονόμηκεν ὄνομα. τίνι γὰρ εἶπέ ποτε τῶν 5
ἀγγέλων, Υἱός μου εἶ σύ, ἐγὼ σήμερον
γεγέννηκά σε; Καὶ πάλιν, Ἐγὼ ἔσομαι
αὐτῷ εἰς πατέρα, καὶ αὐτὸς ἔσται μοι
εἰς υἱόν, ὅταν δὲ πάλιν εἰσαγάγῃ τὸν 6
πρωτότοκον εἰς τὴν οἰκουμένην λέγει,
Καὶ προσκυνησάτωσαν αὐτῷ πάντες
ἄγγελοι Θεοῦ. Καὶ πρὸς μὲν τοὺς 7
ἀγγέλους λέγει, Ὁ ποιῶν τοὺς ἀγγέλους
αὐτοῦ πνεύματα, καὶ τοὺς λειτουργοὺς
αὐτοῦ πυρὸς φλόγα· πρὸς δὲ τὸν υἱόν, 8
Ὁ θρόνος σου, ὁ Θεός, εἰς τὸν αἰῶνα
τοῦ αἰῶνος, καὶ ἡ ῥάβδος τῆς εὐθύτητος
ῥάβδος τῆς βασιλείας σου· ἠγάπησας 9
δικαιοσύνην, καὶ ἐμίσησας ἀνομίαν·
διὰ τοῦτο ἔχρισέ σε ὁ Θεός, ὁ Θεός σου,
ἔλαιον ἀγαλλιάσεως παρὰ τοὺς μετόχους σου. καί, Σὺ κατ᾽ ἀρχάς, Κύριε, 10
τὴν γῆν ἐθεμελίωσας, καὶ ἔργα τῶν
χειρῶν σου εἰσὶν οἱ οὐρανοί· αὐτοὶ 11
ἀπολοῦνται, σὺ δὲ διαμένεις· καὶ
πάντες ὡς ἱμάτιον παλαιωθήσονται, καὶ 12
ὡσεὶ περιβόλαιον ἑλίξεις αὐτούς, ὡς
ἱμάτιον, καὶ ἀλλαγήσονται· σὺ δὲ ὁ
αὐτὸς εἶ, καὶ τὰ ἔτη σου οὐκ ἐκλείψουσι. 13
πρὸς τίνα δὲ τῶν ἀγγέλων εἴρηκέ ποτε,
Κάθου ἐκ δεξιῶν μου, ἕως ἂν θῶ τοὺς
ἐχθρούς σου ὑποπόδιον τῶν ποδῶν
σου, οὐχὶ πάντες εἰσὶ λειτουργικὰ 14
πνεύματα εἰς διακονίαν ἀποστελλόμενα
διὰ τοὺς μέλλοντας κληρονομεῖν σωτηρίαν;

Ps. 2⁷, ⁸ υἱός μου εἶ σύ, ἐγὼ σήμερον γεγέννηκά σε. αἴτησαι παρ᾽ ἐμοῦ,
καὶ δώσω σοι ἔθνη τὴν κληρονομίαν σου, καὶ τὴν κατάσχεσίν σου τὰ πέρατα
τῆς γῆς.
Ps. 103 (104)⁴ ὁ ποιῶν τοὺς ἀγγέλους αὐτοῦ πνεύματα, καὶ τοὺς
λειτουργοὺς αὐτοῦ πῦρ φλέγον².
Ps. 109 (110)¹ κάθου ἐκ δεξιῶν μου ἕως ἂν θῶ τοὺς ἐχθρούς σου ὑποπόδιον τῶν ποδῶν σου.

¹ C reads κεκληρονόμηκεν ὄνομα.
² Aᵃ read πυρὸς φλέγα.

There can be practically no doubt that in this passage we have a reminiscence of the first chapter of the Hebrews. The following are the most important points:—

1. Clement quotes the first words of Heb. 1³, and then Heb. 1⁴, omitting the intervening words, and with the following changes. Clement reads μεγαλωσύνης for δόξης, μείζων ἐστίν for κρείττων γενόμενος: he omits παρ' αὐτούς, and in the best texts transposes κεκληρονόμηκεν and ὄνομα. The substitution of μεγαλωσύνη for δόξα might easily be accounted for by the occurrence of the former at the end of Heb. 1³.

2. Clement then quotes, with the formula γέγραπται, Ps. 104⁴, in a form which corresponds exactly with Heb. 1⁷. It can hardly be doubted that Clement intends to quote the Psalm, but the form in which he does it is exactly the same as that in Hebrews, while it differs from the best text of the LXX in one particular. Clement reads πυρὸς φλόγα, while the LXX reads πῦρ φλέγον (Aᵃ πυρὸς φλέγα).

3. Clement then quotes Ps. 2⁷ and ⁸, while in Heb. 1⁵ only Ps. 2⁷ is quoted.

4. Clement then quotes Ps. 110¹, which is quoted in Heb. 1¹³.

We have then an almost verbal citation from the Hebrews, and the citation of a group of passages from the Psalms which would be difficult to explain except as suggested by the Hebrews. It may, indeed, be objected that the latter phenomenon might be explained as being due to the citation of some collection of Messianic passages in common use; but against this it must be observed that the passage quoted from Ps. 104⁴, which occurs naturally in the context in Heb. 1⁷, would not naturally be included in any collection of Messianic passages.

c

(20) Clem. xvii. 5.	Heb. 3².	Num. 12⁷.
Μωυσῆς πιστὸς ἐν ὅλῳ τῷ οἴκῳ αὐτοῦ ἐκλήθη.	Ἰησοῦν, πιστὸν ὄντα τῷ ποιήσαντι αὐτόν, ὡς καὶ Μωσῆς ἐν ὅλῳ τῷ οἴκῳ αὐτοῦ.	ὁ θεράπων μου Μωυσῆς· ἐν ὅλῳ τῷ οἴκῳ μου πιστός ἐστιν.

The passage might be based on Num. 12⁷, but the

substitution of αὐτοῦ for μοῦ suggests the influence of the Hebrews.
Cf. Clem. xliii. 1 and Heb. 3⁵.

(21)   Clem. xxxvi. 1.

Ἰησοῦν Χριστόν, τὸν ἀρχιερέα τῶν προσφορῶν ἡμῶν, τὸν προστάτην καὶ βοηθὸν τῆς ἀσθενείας ἡμῶν.

Heb. 2¹⁸, 3¹.

ἐν ᾧ γὰρ πέπονθεν αὐτὸς πειρασθείς, δύναται τοῖς πειραζομένοις βοηθῆσαι . . . κατανοήσατε τὸν ἀπόστολον καὶ ἀρχιερέα τῆς ὁμολογίας ἡμῶν Ἰησοῦν.

It seems probable that we have in this passage a reminiscence of the Hebrews. Cf. Clem. lxi. 3 and lxiv.

d

(22)   Clem. xvii. 1.

μιμηταὶ γενώμεθα κἀκείνων οἵτινες ἐν δέρμασιν αἰγείοις καὶ μηλωταῖς περιεπάτησαν κηρύσσοντες τὴν ἔλευσιν τοῦ Χριστοῦ· λέγωμεν δὲ Ἡλίαν καὶ Ἐλισαιέ, ἔτι δὲ καὶ Ἰεζεκιήλ, τοὺς προφήτας, πρὸς τούτοις καὶ τοὺς μεμαρτυρημένους.

Heb. 11³⁷, ³⁹.

περιῆλθον ἐν μηλωταῖς, ἐν αἰγείοις δέρμασιν, ὑστερούμενοι, θλιβόμενοι, κακουχούμενοι . . . καὶ οὗτοι πάντες, μαρτυρηθέντες διὰ τῆς πίστεως, οὐκ ἐκομίσαντο τὴν ἐπαγγελίαν.

It would at first sight appear that we have in the passage of Clement a probable reminiscence of the passage in the Hebrews, but against this it must be observed :—

1. That the author of the Hebrews is very possibly using some uncanonical source.

2. That it is, therefore, quite possible that the passage in Clement is founded upon this source rather than on Hebrews, and that the reference to Elijah, Isaiah, and Ezekiel points in this direction.

(23)   Clem. xix. 2.

πολλῶν οὖν καὶ μεγάλων καὶ ἐνδόξων μετειληφότες πράξεων ἀναδράμωμεν ἐπὶ τὸν ἐξ ἀρχῆς παραδεδομένον ἡμῖν τῆς εἰρήνης σκοπόν, καὶ ἀτενίσωμεν εἰς τὸν πατέρα καὶ κτίστην τοῦ σύμπαντος κόσμου, καὶ ταῖς μεγαλοπρεπέσι καὶ ὑπερβαλλούσαις αὐτοῦ δωρεαῖς τῆς εἰρήνης εὐεργεσίαις τε κολληθῶμεν.

Heb. 12¹.

τοιγαροῦν καὶ ἡμεῖς, τοσοῦτον ἔχοντες περικείμενον ἡμῖν νέφος μαρτύρων, ὄγκον ἀποθέμενοι πάντα καὶ τὴν εὐπερίστατον ἁμαρτίαν δι' ὑπομονῆς τρέχωμεν τὸν προκείμενον ἡμῖν ἀγῶνα, ἀφορῶντες εἰς τὸν τῆς πίστεως ἀρχηγὸν καὶ τελειωτὴν Ἰησοῦν.

There is little correspondence in phrase, but a strong
similarity in general conception.   But if the preceding passage
is founded upon some uncanonical document, the influence of the
document might also extend to the present one.

(24)   Clem. xxi. 9.   Heb. 4¹².

ἐρευνητὴς γάρ ἐστιν ἐννοιῶν καὶ   ζῶν γὰρ ὁ λόγος τοῦ Θεοῦ, καὶ
ἐνθυμήσεων· οὗ ἡ πνοὴ αὐτοῦ ἐν ἡμῖν   ἐνεργής . . . καὶ κριτικὸς ἐνθυμήσεων
ἐστίν, καὶ ὅταν θέλῃ ἀνελεῖ αὐτήν.   καὶ ἐννοιῶν καρδίας.

It seems possible that we have here a reminiscence of the
Hebrews, but it must be noticed :—

1. We have ἐρευνητής instead of κριτικός.

2. The subject of the sentence is not the same ; in Hebrews
it is the Word of God, in Clement it seems to be the Fear of
God.

3. The conception is found also in Philo 'Quis rer. div.
heres,' 26, 27.

(25)   Clem. xxvii. 1.   Heb. 10²³.

ταύτῃ οὖν τῇ ἐλπίδι προσδεδέ-   πιστὸς γὰρ ὁ ἐπαγγειλάμενος.
σθωσαν αἱ ψυχαὶ ἡμῶν τῷ πιστῷ ἐν
ταῖς ἐπαγγελίαις καὶ τῷ δικαίῳ ἐν   Heb. 11¹¹.
τοῖς κρίμασιν.
                                         ἐπεὶ πιστὸν ἡγήσατο τὸν ἐπαγ-
                                         γειλάμενον.

(26)   Clem. xxvii. 2.   Heb. 6¹⁸.

οὐδὲν γὰρ ἀδύνατον παρὰ τῷ θεῷ   ἐν οἷς ἀδύνατον ψεύσασθαι Θεόν.
εἰ μὴ τὸ ψεύσασθαι.

(27) Clem. lvi. 4.   Heb. 12⁶.   Prov. 3¹².

ὃν γὰρ ἀγαπᾷ Κύριος   ὃν γὰρ ἀγαπᾷ Κύριος   ὃν γὰρ ἀγαπᾷ Κύριος
παιδεύει, μαστιγοῖ δὲ   παιδεύει, μαστιγοῖ δὲ   ἐλέγχει¹ μαστιγοῖ δὲ
πάντα υἱὸν ὃν παρα-   πάντα υἱὸν ὃν παρα-   πάντα υἱὸν ὃν παρα-
δέχεται . . .   δέχεται.   δέχεται.

                                         ¹ אA read παιδεύει.

C
Acts   c
(28)   Clem. xviii. 1.   Acts 13²².

τί δὲ εἴπωμεν ἐπὶ τῷ μεμαρτυρη-   ἤγειρε τὸν Δαβὶδ αὐτοῖς εἰς βασιλέα,
μένῳ Δαυίδ ; πρὸς ὃν εἶπεν ὁ Θεός·   ᾧ καὶ εἶπε μαρτυρήσας, Εὗρον Δαβὶδ
Εὗρον ἄνδρα κατὰ τὴν καρδίαν μου,   τὸν τοῦ Ἰεσσαί, ἄνδρα κατὰ τὴν
Δαυὶδ τὸν τοῦ Ἰεσσαί· ἐν ἐλέει   καρδίαν μου, ὃς ποιήσει πάντα τὰ
αἰωνίῳ ἔχρισα αὐτόν.   θελήματά μου.

Ps. 88 (89) [21].   1 Sam. 13[14].

εὗρον Δαυεὶδ τὸν δοῦλόν μου, ἐν   καὶ ζητήσει Κύριος ἑαυτῷ ἄνθρωπον
ἐλέει [1] ἁγίῳ ἔχρισα αὐτόν.   κατὰ τὴν ͚καρδίαν αὐτοῦ.

[1] Bᵃ ελεω (R ?), BᵇℵA(R ?)T ελαιω.

It is to be noticed in the passages that:—

1. Clement and the author of the Acts combine phrases from the Psalm and from 1 Samuel.

2. Clement and the Acts both insert the words τὸν τοῦ Ἰεσσαί, which are not read either in the Psalm or in 1 Samuel.

3. Clement and Acts agree in reading ἄνδρα, Ps. 88[21] reads δοῦλον, and 1 Sam. 13[14] reads ἄνθρωπον.

There are, however, certain differences between Clement and the Acts:—

1. Clement finishes the quotation with the words ἐν ἐλέει αἰωνίῳ ἔχρισα αὐτόν, agreeing with the Psalm.

2. Acts concludes the quotation with ὃς ποιήσει πάντα τὰ θελήματά μου (cf. Isa. 44[28]), for which there is no authority either in the LXX, or in the Hebrew of the Psalm, or of 1 Sam. 13[14].

The phenomena of the passages are thus somewhat complicated; the conclusion to which we incline is that Clement intended to quote Ps. 88[21]—this would seem to be indicated by the conclusion of the passage—but that he has possibly been influenced by a recollection of the passage as it is quoted in Acts 13[22]. It seems difficult otherwise to account for the combination of the passages from the Psalm and from 1 Samuel, and for the addition of the words τὸν τοῦ Ἰεσσαί, which is found both in Acts and in Clement.

It must, however, be observed that these suggestions do not account for the conclusion of the quotation in the Acts. It may be suggested that this is simply an example of the inaccuracy which may be due to quotation from memory. But it may also be suggested that the form of the quotation in Acts may be due to some other cause, e.g. the possible influence of some collection of Davidic or Messianic passages. It is possible that such collections of O.T. passages may have been current in Apostolic times. Such a collection might explain the phenomena presented by the passages in Clement

and in the Acts without requiring any direct dependence of
the one upon the other.

d

(29)   Clem. ii. 1.   Acts 20³⁵.

πάντες τε ἐταπεινοφρονεῖτε μηδὲν   μνημονεύειν τε τῶν λόγων τοῦ
ἀλαζονευόμενοι, ὑποτασσόμενοι μᾶλλον   Κυρίου Ἰησοῦ, ὅτι αὐτὸς εἶπε, Μακά-
ἢ ὑποτάσσοντες, ἥδιον διδόντες ἢ   ριόν ἐστι μᾶλλον διδόναι ἢ λαμβάνειν.
λαμβάνοντες, τοῖς ἐφοδίοις τοῦ Θεοῦ
ἀρκούμενοι.

The phrase in Clement finds a parallel in the words of our
Lord quoted by St. Paul, but we do not feel that the circumstances are such that we are compelled to think that Clement
has the passage in the Acts in his mind.

1. St. Paul is quoting an otherwise unrecorded saying of
our Lord's, which may have been known to Clement simply
as a saying of our Lord current among Christian men.

2. It is possible that the phrase in Clement has no direct
relation to any particular saying of our Lord, but represents
a conception current among Christians.

(30)   Clem. lix. 2.   Acts 26¹⁸.

ἐκάλεσεν ἡμᾶς ἀπὸ σκότους εἰς φῶς.   ἐπιστρέψαι ἀπὸ σκότους εἰς φῶς.

Cf. Col. 1¹³ and 1 Peter 2⁹, under (42) and (49).

Titus   **c**

(31)   Clem. i. 3.   Titus 2⁴, ⁵.

γυναιξίν τε ἐν ἀμώμῳ καὶ σεμνῇ   ἵνα σωφρονίζωσι τὰς νέας φιλάν-
καὶ ἁγνῇ συνειδήσει πάντα ἐπιμελεῖν   δρους εἶναι, φιλοτέκνους, σώφρονας,
παρηγγέλλετε, στεργούσας καθηκόντως   ἁγνάς, οἰκουργούς², ἀγαθάς, ὑπο-
τοὺς ἄνδρας ἑαυτῶν· ἔν τε τῷ κανόνι   τασσομένας τοῖς ἰδίοις ἀνδράσιν, ἵνα
τῆς ὑποταγῆς ὑπαρχούσας τὰ κατὰ τὸν   μὴ ὁ λόγος τοῦ Θεοῦ βλασφημῆται·
οἶκον σεμνῶς οἰκουργεῖν¹ ἐδιδάσκετε,
πάνυ σωφρονούσας.

¹ L. regere ; S. curam gerentes ; C. (e rasura) οἰκουρεῖν.   ² אᵃD οἰκουρούς.

The passage in Clement contains a number of phrases
which correspond with those of Titus.

ἁγνῇ συνειδήσει.   ἁγνάς.
στεργούσας καθηκόντως τοὺς ἄνδρας
    ἑαυτῶν.   φιλάνδρους.

ἔν τε τῷ κανόνι τῆς ὑποταγῆς ὑπαρχούσας.

ὑποτασσομένας τοῖς ἰδίοις ἀνδράσιν.

οἰκουργεῖν.

οἰκουργούς.

πάνυ σωφρονούσας.

σώφρονας.

There is a parallel list in Philo, *De Execr.* γυναῖκας σώφρονας οἰκουροὺς καὶ φιλάνδρους.

The Committee is inclined to think that the correspondence of phrases, and especially of οἰκουργεῖν and οἰκουργούς, cannot well be accounted for by chance, and makes it probable that the one writer is dependent on the other: they have, therefore, with some hesitation, decided to place the passage in Class C.

(I am inclined to think that the correspondence of the two passages may be accounted for by the conjecture that the author of Titus and Clement are both using some manual of directions for the moral life.—A. J. C.)

d

(32) Clem. ii. 7.

ἕτοιμοι εἰς πᾶν ἔργον ἀγαθόν.

Clem. xxiv. 4.

μὴ ἀργοὺς μηδὲ παρειμένους εἶναι ἐπὶ πᾶν ἔργον ἀγαθόν.

Titus 3[1].

πρὸς πᾶν ἔργον ἀγαθὸν ἑτοίμους εἶναι.

2 Tim. 2[21].

εἰς πᾶν ἔργον ἀγαθὸν ἡτοιμασμένον.

2 Tim. 3[17].

πρὸς πᾶν ἔργον ἀγαθὸν ἐξηρτισμένος.

2 Cor. 9[8].

ἵνα ... περισσεύητε εἰς πᾶν ἔργον ἀγαθόν.

D

2 *Corinthians* d

(33) Clem. xxxvi. 2.

διὰ τούτου ἀτενίζομεν εἰς τὰ ὕψη τῶν οὐρανῶν· διὰ τούτου ἐνοπτριζόμεθα τὴν ἄμωμον καὶ ὑπερτάτην ὄψιν αὐτοῦ.

2 Cor. 3[18].

ἡμεῖς δὲ πάντες ἀνακεκαλυμμένῳ προσώπῳ τὴν δόξαν Κυρίου κατοπτριζόμενοι τὴν αὐτὴν εἰκόνα μεταμορφούμεθα ἀπὸ δόξης εἰς δόξαν, καθάπερ ἀπὸ Κυρίου Πνεύματος.

The form of the two passages is very different, and there is little correspondence between the conceptions; but the phrases ἐνοπτριζόμεθα and κατοπτριζόμενοι might seem to suggest some connexion.

Dr. Lightfoot has, however, pointed out in his note that there is a parallel phrase in Philo, *Leg. Alleg.* iii. 33 μηδὲ κατοπτρισαίμην ἐν ἄλλῳ τινὶ τὴν σὴν ἰδέαν ἢ ἐν σοὶ τῷ Θεῷ. It would appear that the phrase is not distinctive enough to enable us to infer that Clement knew this Epistle.

UNCLASSED

(34)   Clem. v. 5, 6.   2 Cor. 11²³⁻²⁷.

Clement's enumeration of St. Paul's sufferings might at first sight seem to suggest this Epistle; but these would probably be known to Clement apart from the account in the Epistle, and one of his statements, ἑπτάκις δεσμὰ φορέσας, is obviously not derived from the Epistle.

Galatians   **d**

(35) Clem. ii. 1.   Gal. 3¹.   Deut. 28⁶⁶.

καὶ τὰ παθήματα αὐτοῦ   οἷς κατ᾽ ὀφθαλμοὺς   καὶ ἔσται ἡ ζωή σου
ἦν πρὸ ὀφθαλμῶν ὑμῶν.   Ἰησοῦς Χριστὸς προ-   κρεμαμένη ἀπέναντι τῶν
                          εγράφη ἐσταυρωμένος.   ὀφθαλμῶν σου.

It has been suggested that St. Paul has been influenced by Deuteronomy, and that Clement is affected both by Deuteronomy and by St. Paul.

But the coincidence appears to be too uncertain to serve as the foundation for the conclusion that Clement was acquainted with Galatians.

(36)   Clem. v. 2.   Gal. 2⁹.

The word στῦλοι is used in both passages in connexion with the Apostles and leading men in the Church.

Dr. Lightfoot, however, has pointed out in his note that the use of the word seems to have been very common in this sense in Jewish writers.

Ephesians   **d**

(37)   Clem. xxxvi. 2.   Eph. 4¹⁸.

These passages have already been considered in connexion with Rom. 1²¹, see (5). It should be observed that Clement's ἐσκοτωμένη διάνοια corresponds with Ephesians ἐσκοτισμένοι (אAB, W. & H. ἐσκοτωμένοι) τῇ διανοίᾳ.

(38)　　Clem. xlvi. 6.

ἢ οὐχὶ ἕνα θεὸν ἔχομεν καὶ ἕνα
Χριστὸν καὶ ἐν πνεῦμα τῆς χάριτος
τὸ ἐκχυθὲν ἐφ' ἡμᾶς; καὶ μία κλῆσις
ἐν Χριστῷ;

Eph. 4⁴⁻⁶.

ἐν σῶμα καὶ ἐν Πνεῦμα, καθὼς καὶ
ἐκλήθητε ἐν μιᾷ ἐλπίδι τῆς κλήσεως
ἡμῶν, εἷς Κύριος, μία πίστις, ἐν βάπτισμα, εἷς Θεὸς καὶ πατὴρ πάντων,
ὁ ἐπὶ πάντων καὶ διὰ πάντων καὶ ἐν
πᾶσιν. ἐνὶ δὲ ἐκάστῳ ἡμῶν ἐδόθη ἡ
χάρις κατὰ τὸ μέτρον τῆς δωρεᾶς τοῦ
Χριστοῦ.

It is noticeable that there is not only a general resemblance
between these two passages, but a close correspondence in
phrase—

Clem.	Eph.
1. ἕνα Θεόν.	1. εἷς Θεός.
2. ἕνα Χριστόν.	2. εἷς Κύριος.
3. ἐν πνεῦμα τῆς χάριτος τὸ ἐκ-χυθὲν ἐφ' ἡμᾶς.	3. ἐν Πνεῦμα and ἐνὶ δὲ ἐκάστῳ ἡμῶν ἐδόθη ἡ χάρις κατὰ τὸ μέτρον τῆς δωρεᾶς τοῦ Χριστοῦ.
4. μία κλῆσις ἐν Χριστῷ.	4. ἐκλήθητε ἐν μιᾷ ἐλπίδι τῆς κλήσεως.

Cf. Hermas, *Sim.* ix. 13, 5, and 18, 4.

At first sight it would appear probable that Clement has
the passage in Ephesians in his mind; but we must remember
that the passages both in Ephesians and in Clement are
very possibly founded upon some liturgical forms, and it
thus seems impossible to establish any dependence of Clement
upon Ephesians.

(39)　　Clem. lix. 3.

ἀνοίξας τοὺς ὀφθαλμοὺς τῆς καρδίας
ὑμῶν.

Eph. 1¹⁸.

πεφωτισμένους τοὺς ὀφθαλμοὺς τῆς
καρδίας ὑμῶν.

Cf. Clem. xxxvi. 2.

The phrase is noticeable, and it should be observed that the
preceding sentences in Clement have considerable affinity
with Eph. 1⁴⁻⁶, ¹⁷.

Philippians　　　　　d

(40)　　Clem. iii. 4.

μηδὲ . . . πορεύεσθαι μηδὲ πολι-
τεύεσθαι κατὰ τὸ καθῆκον τῷ Χριστῷ.

Phil. 1²⁷.

μόνον ἀξίως τοῦ εὐαγγελίου τοῦ
Χριστοῦ πολιτεύεσθε.

Clem. xxi. 1.

ἐὰν μὴ ἀξίως αὐτοῦ πολιτευόμενοι . . .

A possible reminiscence, but the metaphorical use of the

phrases of citizenship in connexion with the moral and spiritual life was probably common.

(41)   Clem. xlvii. 1, 2.

'Αναλάβετε τὴν ἐπιστολὴν τοῦ μακαρίου Παύλου τοῦ ἀποστόλου. τί πρῶτον ὑμῖν ἐν ἀρχῇ τοῦ εὐαγγελίου ἔγραψεν;

Phil. 4[15].

οἴδατε δὲ καὶ ὑμεῖς Φιλιππήσιοι ὅτι ἐν ἀρχῇ τοῦ εὐαγγελίου, ὅτε ἐξῆλθον ἀπὸ Μακεδονίας.

The phrase ἐν ἀρχῇ, &c., is peculiar, and it seems clear that Clement is using it in the same sense as St. Paul.

But it would scarcely appear that this is enough to prove that Clement takes the phrase from Philippians.

Colossians   **d**

(42)   Clem. lix. 2.

δι' οὗ ἐκάλεσεν ἡμᾶς ἀπὸ σκότους εἰς φῶς, ἀπὸ ἀγνωσίας εἰς ἐπίγνωσιν δόξης ὀνόματος αὐτοῦ.

Col. 1[12, 13].

εὐχαριστοῦντες τῷ πατρὶ τῷ ἱκανώσαντι ἡμᾶς εἰς τὴν μερίδα τοῦ κλήρου τῶν ἁγίων ἐν τῷ φωτί· ὃς ἐρρύσατο ἡμᾶς ἐκ τῆς ἐξουσίας τοῦ σκότους, καὶ μετέστησεν εἰς τὴν βασιλείαν τοῦ υἱοῦ τῆς ἀγάπης αὐτοῦ.

Cf. also Col. 1[9].

ἵνα πληρωθῆτε τὴν ἐπίγνωσιν τοῦ θελήματος αὐτοῦ ἐν πάσῃ σοφίᾳ ...

The metaphor of transference from darkness to light is worth observing, but it is also found in Acts 26[18] and 1 Peter 2[9], see (30) and (48).

We cannot, therefore, assert that Clement is dependent upon Colossians.

UNCLASSED

(43)   Clem. ii. 4.

ἀγὼν ἦν ὑμῖν ἡμέρας τε καὶ νυκτὸς ὑπὲρ πάσης τῆς ἀδελφότητος—

Col. 2[1].

θέλω γὰρ ὑμᾶς εἰδέναι ἡλίκον ἀγῶνα ἔχω ὑπὲρ ὑμῶν—

1 *Timothy*   **d**

(44)   Clem. lxi. 2.

σὺ γάρ, δέσποτα ἐπουράνιε, βασιλεῦ τῶν αἰώνων.

1 Tim. 1[17].

τῷ δὲ βασιλεῖ τῶν αἰώνων, ἀφθάρτῳ, ἀοράτῳ, μόνῳ Θεῷ ...

The phrase is striking, but Dr. Lightfoot has pointed out in his notes on the passage, that it is probably based upon

Jewish liturgical forms, and the phrase itself occurs in Tobit 13⁶, ¹⁰, and in Apoc. 15³ (א and C read αἰώνων; אᶜA and B read ἐθνῶν).

UNCLASSED

(45)   Clem. xxix. 1.   1 Tim. 2⁸.

προσέλθωμεν οὖν αὐτῷ ἐν ὁσιότητι   ἐπαίροντας ὁσίους χεῖρας χωρὶς
ψυχῆς, ἁγνὰς καὶ ἀμιάντους χεῖρας   ὀργῆς καὶ διαλογισμοῦ.
αἴροντες πρὸς αὐτόν.

The phrase appears to be used by many writers. Cf. Dr. Lightfoot's note.

1 Peter   d
(46)   Clem. vii. 2, 4.   1 Pet. 1¹⁸, ¹⁹.

διὸ ἀπολίπωμεν τὰς κενὰς καὶ   εἰδότες ὅτι οὐ φθαρτοῖς, ἀργυρίῳ ἢ
ματαίας φροντίδας, καὶ ἔλθωμεν ἐπὶ   χρυσίῳ, ἐλυτρώθητε ἐκ τῆς ματαίας
τὸν εὐκλεῆ καὶ σεμνὸν τῆς παραδόσεως ὑμῶν ἀναστροφῆς πατροπαραδότου, ἀλλὰ
ἡμῶν κανόνα, ... ἀτενίσωμεν εἰς τὸ   τιμίῳ αἵματι ὡς ἀμνοῦ ἀμώμου καὶ
αἷμα τοῦ Χριστοῦ καὶ γνῶμεν ὡς ἔστιν ἀσπίλου Χριστοῦ ...
τίμιον τῷ θεῷ τῷ πατρὶ αὐτοῦ, ὅτι διὰ
τὴν ἡμετέραν σωτηρίαν ἐκχυθὲν παντὶ
τῷ κόσμῳ μετανοίας χάριν ἐπήνεγκεν.

These passages present many points of correspondence of phrase and thought, but the conception of redemption through the blood of Christ is not peculiar to St. Peter's Epistles in the N.T., and may well be supposed to have been current among all Christians.

(47)   Clem. xxx. 1, 2.   1 Pet. 2¹, 5⁵.

'Ἁγίου οὖν μερὶς ὑπάρχοντες ποιή-   ἀποθέμενοι οὖν πᾶσαν κακίαν καὶ
σωμεν τὰ τοῦ ἁγιασμοῦ πάντα, φεύ-   πάντα δόλον καὶ ὑποκρίσεις καὶ φθόνους
γοντες καταλαλιάς, μιαράς τε καὶ   καὶ πάσας καταλαλιὰς ὡς ἀρτιγέννητα
ἀνάγνους συμπλοκάς, μέθας τε καὶ   βρέφη τὸ λογικὸν ἄδολον γάλα ἐπιποθή-
νεωτερισμοὺς καὶ βδελυκτὰς ἐπιθυμίας, σατε.
μυσερὰν μοιχείαν βδελυκτὴν ὑπερη-   1 Pet. 5⁵ ὅτι ὁ Θεὸς ὑπερηφανίαν. Θεὸς γάρ, φησίν, ὑπερηφάνοις φάνοις ἀντιτάσσεται, ταπεινοῖς δὲ
ἀντιτάσσεται, ταπεινοῖς δὲ δίδωσιν   δίδωσι χάριν.
χάριν.   Cf. Jas. 4⁶ διὸ λέγει, ὁ Θεὸς κτλ.

Prov. 3³⁴.

Κύριος ὑπερηφάνοις ἀντιτάσσεται, ταπεινοῖς δὲ δίδωσιν χάριν.

The correspondence of thought with 1 Peter is interesting, but the last words are probably quoted from Prov. 3³⁴, and the subject of Clement's passage is probably suggested by the quotation from Deuteronomy, contained in the previous chapter.

(48) Clem. xlix. 5.	1 Pet. 4[8].	Jas. 5[20].
ἀγάπη καλύπτει πλῆθος ἁμαρτιῶν.	ἀγάπη καλύπτει πλῆθος ἁμαρτιῶν.	ὁ ἐπιστρέψας ἁμαρτωλὸν ἐκ πλάνης ὁδοῦ αὐτοῦ σώσει ψυχὴν ἐκ θανάτου, καὶ καλύψει πλῆθος ἁμαρτιῶν.
Prov. 10[12] LXX.	Prov. 10[12], Heb.	
πάντας δὲ τοὺς μὴ φιλονεικοῦντας καλύπτει φιλία.	'But love covereth all transgressions.'	

1. Clement and 1 Peter agree exactly in the terms of the passage; they differ from the Hebrew text of Proverbs in reading 'a multitude' instead of 'all,' and they differ entirely from the LXX text of Proverbs. It would, therefore, at first sight seem probable that Clement is quoting the phrase from 1 Peter.

2. A. Resch (*Agrapha*, p. 248) has argued that this phrase was originally a saying of our Lord, and brings forward the following parallels.

Didasc. ii. 3.

ὅτι λέγει Κύριος· ἀγάπη καλύπτει πλῆθος ἁμαρτιῶν.

Clem. Alex. Paedagog. iii. 12.

ναὶ μὴν καὶ περὶ ἀγάπης· ἀγάπη, φησί, καλύπτει πλῆθος ἁμαρτιῶν· καὶ περὶ πολιτείας· ἀπόδοτε τὰ Καίσαρος Καίσαρι καὶ τὰ τοῦ θεοῦ τῷ θεῷ.

2 Clem. xvi. 4.

ἀγάπη δὲ καλύπτει πλῆθος ἁμαρτιῶν.

Resch urges that the author of the *Didascalia* clearly regards the phrase as a saying of our Lord's, but an examination of the context shows plainly that the author cites with the same formula, 'the Lord saith,' passages from the O. T. He also argues that the fact that Clement of Alexandria sets this phrase beside a well-known saying of our Lord, shows that he looked upon it as having been spoken by Him; but again an examination of the context makes it plain that Clement is citing indifferently phrases from the Old and New Testaments as embodying the instruction of the *Paedagogus*.

It appears, therefore, that these parallels do not justify the conclusion that 1 Peter and Clement are quoting a traditional saying of our Lord.

3. It may, however, be suggested that Clement and 1 Peter are both quoting from some unknown source, i. e. another Greek version of the passage in Proverbs, or some Apocryphal writing, and it does not seem therefore that we can say more than that it is possible that Clement is quoting the passage from 1 Peter.

(49)   Clem. lix. 2.   1 Pet. 2⁹.

See under Colossians (42).

UNCLASSED

(50)   Clem. Introduction.   1 Pet. 1¹, ².

There are some parallel phrases, but they are not sufficiently important or distinctive to require special discussion.

(51)   Clem. ii. 2.   1 Pet. 4¹⁹.

ἀγαθοποιίαν.   ἐν ἀγαθοποιίᾳ.

The word occurs in the N. T. only in 1 Peter, and is not found in the LXX or other Greek versions of the O. T. and Apocrypha; and apparently it does not occur in classical literature.

(52)   Clem. ii. 4.   1 Pet. 2¹⁷.

τῆς ἀδελφότητος.   τὴν ἀδελφότητα.

                                     1 Pet. 5⁹.

                                       τῇ ἀδελφότητι.

The word occurs in the N. T. only in 1 Peter; it is found in the LXX of 1 Macc. 12¹⁰, ¹⁷, but in the sense of 'brotherly affection.' It does not apparently occur in classical literature.

1 *John*   **d**

(53)   Clem. xlix. 5.   1 John 4¹⁸.

ἐν τῇ ἀγάπῃ ἐτελειώθησαν πάντες οἱ   ὁ δὲ φοβούμενος οὐ τετελείωται ἐν

ἐκλεκτοὶ τοῦ Θεοῦ.   τῇ ἀγάπῃ.

         Clem. l. 3.

ἀλλ' οἱ ἐν ἀγάπῃ τελειωθέντες . . .

There is a verbal similarity between the first passage in Clement and that in John, but the meaning is different; the meaning in the second passage may perhaps be the same as in John.

Apocalypse	d	
(54) Clem. xxxiv. 3.	Apoc. 22¹².	Isa 40¹⁰.

Apocalypse

(54) Clem. xxxiv. 3.

προλέγει γὰρ ἡμῖν·
'Ιδοὺ ὁ Κύριος, καὶ ὁ
μισθὸς αὐτοῦ πρὸ προσ-
ώπου αὐτοῦ, ἀποδοῦναι
ἑκάστῳ κατὰ τὸ ἔργον
αὐτοῦ.

d

Apoc. 22¹².

ἰδού, ἔρχομαι ταχύ,
καὶ ὁ μισθός μου μετ᾽
ἐμοῦ, ἀποδοῦναι ἑκάστῳ
ὡς τὸ ἔργον ἐστὶν αὐτοῦ.

Isa 40¹⁰.

ἰδοὺ Κύριος, Κύριος
μετὰ ἰσχύος ἔρχεται . . .
ἰδοὺ ὁ μισθὸς αὐτοῦ μετ᾽
αὐτοῦ, καὶ τὸ ἔργον ἐναν-
τίον αὐτοῦ.

Isa. 62¹¹.

ἰδοὺ ὁ σωτήρ σοι
παραγέγονεν ἔχων τὸν
ἑαυτοῦ μισθόν, καὶ τὸ
ἔργον αὐτοῦ πρὸ προσ-
ώπου αὐτοῦ.

Prov. 24¹².

καὶ ὁ πλάσας πνοὴν
πᾶσιν αὐτὸς οἶδεν πάντα,
ὃς ἀποδίδωσιν ἑκάστῳ
κατὰ τὰ ἔργα αὐτοῦ.

The passages in Clement and the Apocalypse seem to be made up of a combination of phrases from Isaiah and Proverbs. The combination is noticeable, but may perhaps be accounted for by the hypothesis that it may have been made in some earlier Apocalyptic work. Cf. Barnabas (27).

GOSPELS.

The Synoptic Tradition.

(55) Clem. xiii. 1 f.

μάλιστα μεμνημένοι
τῶν λόγων τοῦ κυρίου
'Ιησοῦ, οὓς ἐλάλησεν
διδάσκων ἐπιείκειαν καὶ
μακροθυμίαν. οὕτως γὰρ
1 εἶπεν· 'Ελεᾶτε ἵνα ἐλεη-
2 θῆτε, ἀφίετε ἵνα ἀφεθῇ
3 ὑμῖν· ὡς ποιεῖτε, οὕτω
4 ποιηθήσεται ὑμῖν· ὡς
δίδοτε, οὕτως δοθήσεται
5 ὑμῖν· ὡς κρίνετε, οὕτως

Matt. 5⁷, &c.

5⁷ μακάριοι οἱ ἐλεή-
μονες· ὅτι αὐτοὶ ἐλεηθή-
σονται.

6¹² καὶ ἄφες ἡμῖν
τὰ ὀφειλήματα ἡμῶν, ὡς
καὶ ἡμεῖς ἀφήκαμεν τοῖς
ὀφειλέταις ἡμῶν.

6¹⁴ ἐὰν γὰρ ἀφῆτε
τοῖς ἀνθρώποις τὰ παρα-
πτώματα αὐτῶν, ἀφήσει
καὶ ὑμῖν ὁ πατὴρ ὑμῶν ὁ

Luke 6³¹, ³⁶⁻³⁸.

6³¹ καὶ καθὼς θέλετε
ἵνα ποιῶσιν ὑμῖν οἱ ἄν
θρωποι, καὶ ὑμεῖς ποιεῖτε
αὐτοῖς ὁμοίως.

6³⁶ γίνεσθε οἰκτίρ-
μονες, καθὼς ὁ πατὴρ
ὑμῶν οἰκτίρμων ἐστί.
καὶ μὴ κρίνετε καὶ οὐ μὴ
κριθῆτε , καὶ μὴ κατα-
δικάζετε, καὶ οὐ μὴ κατα-
δικασθῆτε· ἀπολύετε, καὶ

6 κριθήσεσθε· ὡς χρη-
στεύεσθε, οὕτως χρη-
7 στευθήσεται ὑμῖν[1]· ᾧ
μέτρῳ μετρεῖτε, ἐν αὐτῷ
μετρηθήσεται[2] ὑμῖν.

[1] Lat. omits the clause.
[2] Lat. reads remetietur.

οὐράνιος, ἐὰν δὲ μὴ ἀφῆτε
τοῖς ἀνθρώποις τὰ παρα-
πτώματα αὐτῶν, οὐδὲ ὁ
πατὴρ ὑμῶν ἀφήσει τὰ
παραπτώματα ὑμῶν.

7[1] μὴ κρίνετε, ἵνα
μὴ κριθῆτε· ἐν ᾧ γὰρ κρί-
ματι κρίνετε κριθήσεσθε,
καὶ ἐν ᾧ μέτρῳ μετρεῖτε
μετρηθήσεται ὑμῖν.

7[12] πάντα οὖν ὅσα
ἂν θέλητε ἵνα ποιῶ-
σιν ὑμῖν οἱ ἄνθρωποι,
οὕτω καὶ ὑμεῖς ποιεῖτε
αὐτοῖς· οὗτος γάρ ἐστιν
ὁ νόμος καὶ οἱ προφῆται.

ἀπολυθήσεσθε· δίδοτε καὶ
δοθήσεται ὑμῖν· μέτρον
καλόν, πεπιεσμένον, σε-
σαλευμένον ὑπερεκχυνό-
μενον, δώσουσιν εἰς τὸν
κόλπον ὑμῶν ᾧ γὰρ
μέτρῳ μετρεῖτε, ἀντι-
μετρηθήσεται ὑμῖν.

Clem. Alex. Stromata, ii. 18, 91.

ἐλεᾶτε, φησὶν ὁ Κύριος,
ἵνα ἐλεηθῆτε· ἀφίετε, ἵνα
ἀφεθῇ ὑμῖν· ὡς ποιεῖτε,
οὕτως ποιηθήσεται ὑμῖν·
ὡς δίδοτε οὕτως δοθή-
σεται ὑμῖν· ὡς κρίνετε,
οὕτως κριθήσεσθε· ὡς
χρηστεύεσθε, οὕτως χρη-
στευθήσεται ὑμῖν· ᾧ μέ-
τρῳ μετρεῖτε, ἀντιμετρη-
θήσεται ὑμῖν.

Polycarp ii. 3.

μνημονεύοντες δὲ ὧν
εἶπεν ὁ Κύριος διδάσκων
μὴ κρίνετε ἵνα μὴ κριθῆτε·
ἀφίετε, καὶ ἀφεθήσεται
ὑμῖν· ἐλεᾶτε, ἵνα [1] ἐλεηθῆτε, ᾧ μέτρῳ μετρεῖτε,
ἀντιμετρηθήσεται ὑμῖν.

[1] Lat. et.

Didasc. ii 21.

ὁδὸς δὲ εἰρήνης ἐστὶν
ὁ σωτὴρ ἡμῶν ['Ιησοῦς ὁ
Χριστός], ὃς καὶ εἶπεν·
ἄφετε καὶ ἀφεθήσεται
ὑμῖν· [δίδοτε καὶ δοθή-
σεται ὑμῖν][2].

[2] Syr. Lat. omit δίδοτε
... ὑμῖν.

Didasc. ii. 42.

ὅτι λέγει ὁ Κύριος· ᾧ κρίματι κρίνετε, κριθήσεσθε, καὶ ὡς καταδικάζετε, καταδικασθήσεσθε.

Macarius Aegypt., Hom. xxxvii. 3.

καθὼς ἐνετείλατο, ἄφετε καὶ ἀφεθήσεται ὑμῖν.

The phenomena of the passage are very complex.

I. The passage numbered 1 has no phrase directly corresponding to it in any of our Gospels, but might be founded on
Matt. 5[7].

The passage numbered 2 has no proper parallel in St.
Matthew, but is near Luke ἀπολύετε, &c.

No. 3 has no proper parallel in our Gospels, but may be
compared with Matt. 7[12] and Luke 6[31].

No. 4 has no parallel in Matthew, but is very near Luke 6[38],
only Clement has ὡς and οὕτως, while Luke has καί.

No. 5 is parallel to Matt. 7^1 and Luke 6^{37}, but Clement has ὡς and οὕτως, while Matthew has μή and ἵνα μὴ κριθῆτε, and Luke μή and καὶ οὐ μὴ κριθῆτε.

No. 6 has no parallel in either Gospel.

No. 7 is parallel to Matt. 7^1 and Luke 6^{36}, but Matthew has ἐν ᾧ for ᾧ, and Luke inserts γάρ after ᾧ, and reads ἀντι-μετρηθήσεται.

II. Resch (*Agrapha*, p. 136) has collected a number of parallels.

Clement of Alexandria has the passage exactly as in Clement with a few unimportant variations.

Clement of Alexandria's use of Clement of Rome is well established, and this fact, therefore, requires no special explanation.

In Polycarp some of Clement's phrases recur, cf. (75).

No. 1 is exactly the same, but Lat. reads *et*.

No. 2 is in Polycarp, but he reads καὶ ἀφεθήσεται instead of ἵνα ἀφεθῇ.

Nos. 3 and 4 are not in Polycarp.

No. 5 is found in Polycarp, but in the same form as in St. Matthew, not in Clement's form.

No. 6 is not in Polycarp.

No. 7 is found in Polycarp, but he omits Clement's ἐν αὐτῷ, and reads ἀντιμετρηθήσεται like Luke, yet he omits Luke's γάρ.

Didasc. ii. 21.

No. 2 is in the same form as in Polycarp.

No. 4 reads exactly as in Luke (but see critical note to text), omitting Clement's ὡς and οὕτως.

Didasc. ii. 42.

No. 5 occurs in the form of Matthew, while the clause καὶ ὡς καταδικάζετε, &c., is parallel to Luke.

Macarius, Hom. xxxvii. 3.

No. 2 reads as Polycarp.

III. To sum up these phenomena—

No. 1 is found in Clem. Alex. and Polycarp.

No. 2 is in Clem. Alex., Polycarp, Didasc., and Macarius.

No. 3 is found only in Clem. Alex.

No. 4 is found in Clem. Alex. and Didasc., but in the latter in the form of Luke.

No. 5 is found in Clem. Alex. and Polycarp, but in the latter in the form of Matthew.

No. 6 is found only in Clem. Alex.

No. 7 is found in Clem. Alex. and Polycarp, but in the latter in a form which approaches nearer to that of Matthew and Luke than that of Clem. Rom.

It must also be observed that except by Clem. Alex. the passage of Clem. Rom. is only partially reproduced, and so far as it is reproduced by Polycarp, it is in a totally different order.

IV. The Committee concludes that in the circumstances it is impossible to say with any confidence what is the source of Clement's quotations. It may be urged that they represent an inaccurate quotation of Matthew and Luke made from memory, but the recurrence in Polycarp of the phrase marked 1, and in Polycarp, Didasc., and Macarius of that marked 2, makes this less probable. On the other hand, the fact that the series of phrases as it is found in Polycarp and the Didasc is incomplete, and not in the same order as in Clem. Rom., seems to show that there is no one documentary source common to all these writers.

We incline to think that we have in Clem. Rom. a citation from some written or unwritten form of 'Catechesis' as to our Lord's teaching, current in the Roman Church, perhaps a local form which may go back to a time before our Gospels existed.

(56) Clem. xlvi. 7, 8.

μνήσθητε τῶν λόγων Ἰησοῦ τοῦ Κυρίου ἡμῶν· εἶπεν γάρ· Οὐαὶ τῷ ἀνθρώπῳ ἐκείνῳ· καλὸν ἦν αὐτῷ εἰ μὴ ἐγεννήθη, ἢ ἕνα τῶν ἐκλεκτῶν μου σκανδαλίσαι· κρεῖττον ἦν

Matt. 26²⁴.

οὐαὶ δὲ τῷ ἀνθρώπῳ ἐκείνῳ δι' οὗ ὁ υἱὸς τοῦ ἀνθρώπου παραδίδοται· καλὸν ἦν αὐτῷ, εἰ οὐκ ἐγεννήθη ὁ ἄνθρωπος ἐκεῖνος.

18⁶ f.

ὃς δ' ἂν σκανδαλίσῃ ἕνα τῶν μι-

Mark 14²¹.

ὅτι ὁ μὲν υἱὸς τοῦ ἀνθρώπου ὑπάγει, καθὼς γέγραπται περὶ αὐτοῦ· οὐαὶ δὲ τῷ ἀνθρώπῳ ἐκείνῳ, δι' οὗ ὁ υἱὸς τοῦ ἀνθρώπου παραδίδοται· καλὸν ἦν αὐτῷ, εἰ οὐκ ἐγεννήθη ὁ ἄνθρωπος ἐκεῖνος.

Luke 17¹, ².

Ἀνένδεκτόν ἐστι τοῦ τὰ σκάνδαλα μὴ ἐλθεῖν· πλὴν οὐαὶ δι' οὗ ἔρχεται. λυσιτελεῖ αὐτῷ εἰ λίθος μυλικὸς περίκειται περὶ τὸν τράχηλον αὐτοῦ, καὶ ἔρριπται εἰς τὴν θάλασσαν, ἢ ἵνα σκανδαλίσῃ

αὐτῷ περιτεθῆναι μύ-
λον καὶ καταποντι-
σθῆναι εἰς τὴν θά-
λασσαν, ἢ ἕνα τῶν
μικρῶν μου σκανδα-
λίσαι[1].

[1] ἐκλεκτῶν μου δια-
στρέψαι, Clem. Alex.,
Syr., Lat.

κρῶν τούτων τῶν
πιστευόντων εἰς ἐμέ,
συμφέρει αὐτῷ, ἵνα
κρεμασθῇ μύλος ὀνικὸς
περὶ τὸν τράχηλον
αὐτοῦ, καὶ καταπον-
τισθῇ ἐν τῷ πελά-
γει τῆς θαλάσσης.
. . . πλὴν οὐαὶ τῷ
ἀνθρώπῳ ἐκείνῳ, δι'
οὗ τὸ σκάνδαλον ἔρ-
χεται.

9[42].
καὶ ὃς ἂν σκανδα-
λίσῃ ἕνα τῶν μικρῶν
τούτων τῶν πιστευ-
όντων εἰς ἐμέ, καλόν
ἐστιν αὐτῷ μᾶλλον
εἰ περίκειται μύλος
ὀνικὸς περὶ τὸν τρά-
χηλον αὐτοῦ, καὶ βέ-
βληται εἰς τὴν θά-
λασσαν.

τῶν μικρῶν τούτων
ἕνα.

We have here the combination of the words spoken by our
Lord with regard to Judas, recorded by Matthew and Mark,
with a saying which is recorded in another connexion in
the three Synoptic Gospels. It is not impossible that Clement,
quoting from memory, might have combined some words from
the one context with the more general saying, and that he may
thus be quoting from one or other of the Gospels. But it is
just as probable that we have here, as in Clem. xiii, a
quotation from some form of catechetical instruction in our
Lord's doctrine.

(57)   Clem. xxiv. 5.
ἐξῆλθεν ὁ σπείρων.

Matt. 13[3]; Mark 4[3]; Luke 8[5].
ἐξῆλθεν ὁ σπείρων.

(58) Clem. xv. 2.
λέγει γάρ που ; οὗτος
ὁ λαὸς τοῖς χείλεσίν με
τιμᾷ, ἡ δὲ καρδία αὐτῶν
πόρρω ἄπεστιν ἀπ' ἐμοῦ.

Matt. 15[8].
καλῶς προεφήτευσε
περὶ ὑμῶν Ἡσαίας
λέγων, ὁ λαὸς οὗτος τοῖς
χείλεσί με τιμᾷ, ἡ δὲ
καρδία αὐτῶν πόρρω
ἀπέχει ἀπ' ἐμοῦ.

Mark 7[6].
Practically   the
same.

Isa. 29[13].
καὶ εἶπεν Κύριος, ἐγ-
γίζει μοι ὁ λαὸς οὗτος
ἐν τῷ στόματι αὐτοῦ, καὶ
ἐν τοῖς χείλεσιν αὐτῶν
τιμῶσίν με, ἡ δὲ καρδία
αὐτῶν πόρρω ἀπέχει ἀπ'
ἐμοῦ·

The quotation is probably from Isaiah, but the form of the
quotation in Clement is the same as that in the Gospels : cf.
2 Clem. (33).

IGNATIUS

INTRODUCTION.

BESIDES his references to books of N. T., none of which stands as a direct quotation, Ignatius occasionally quotes from, or refers to, books of O. T. The passages are these:—

(a)   Eph. v. 3.   Prov. 3³⁴.

γέγραπται γάρ· Ὑπερηφάνοις ὁ   Κύριος ὑπερηφάνοις ἀντιτάσσεται.
Θεὸς ἀντιτάσσεται.

This quotation is discussed below (76). Ignatius deviates from the order of the words, besides substituting Θεός for Κύριος.

(b)   Eph. xv. 1.   Ps. 33⁹.

εἶπεν καὶ ἐγένετο.   εἶπεν καὶ ἐγεννήθησαν.

Here ἐγένετο is a better translation of the original than ἐγεννήθησαν; but we need not suppose that Ignatius had access to the Hebrew text.

(c)   Magn. x. 3.   Isa. 66¹⁸.

ᾧ πᾶσα γλῶσσα πιστεύσασα εἰς   συναγαγεῖν πάντα τὰ ἔθνη καὶ τὰς
Θεὸν συνήχθη.   γλώσσας.

A loose reference.

(d)   Magn. xii. 1.   Prov. 18¹⁷.

ὁ δίκαιος ἑαυτοῦ κατήγορος.   δίκαιος ἑαυτοῦ κατήγορος.

Ignatius here follows the LXX. The Hebrew gives quite a different sense: 'the first man is upright in his suit; his neighbour then cometh and searcheth him out' (Lightfoot).

(e)   Magn. xiii. 1.   Ps. 1³.

ἵνα πάντα ὅσα ποιεῖτε κατευοδω-   πάντα ὅσα ἂν ποιῇ κατευοδω-
θῆτε.   θήσεται.

(f)   Trall. viii. 2.   Isa. 52⁵.

οὐαὶ γὰρ δι' οὗ ἐπὶ ματαιότητι τὸ   ὀλολύζετε· τάδε λέγει ὁ Κύριος,
ὄνομά μου ἐπί τινων βλασφημεῖται.   δι' ὑμᾶς διὰ παντὸς τὸ ὄνομά μου
                                             βλασφημεῖται ἐν τοῖς ἔθνεσιν.

The words are also quoted indirectly by St. Paul (Rom. 2²⁴).

Polycarp (Phil. x. 3) quotes them similarly to Ignatius, and so do the Apostolical Constitutions in two places. Both these last are probably borrowing directly from Ignatius.

(g)   Smyrn. i. 2.   Isa. 49²², 62¹⁰.

ἵνα ἄρῃ σύσσημον εἰς τοὺς αἰῶνας.

Cf. also Isa. 5²⁶. LXX has αἴρειν σύσσημον.

A comparison of these references, and of those in Class B from N. T., will show that Ignatius always quotes from memory; that he is inexact even as compared with his contemporaries; and that he appears sometimes to have a vague recollection of a phrase when he is not thinking of, or wishing to remind his readers of, the original context.

EPISTLES AND ACTS.

A

1 *Corinthians*	**b**	
(1) Eph. xvi. 1.		1 Cor. 6⁹, ¹⁰.

μὴ πλανᾶσθε, ἀδελφοί μου· οἱ οἰκοφθόροι βασιλείαν Θεοῦ οὐ κληρονομήσουσιν.

μὴ πλανᾶσθε· οὔτε πόρνοι, . . . οὔτε μοιχοί . . . βασιλείαν Θεοῦ κληρονομήσουσι.

Cf. also Philad. iii Μὴ πλανᾶσθε, ἀδελφοί μου· εἴ τις σχίζοντι ἀκολουθεῖ, βασιλείαν θεοῦ οὐ κληρονομεῖ. These passages also resemble Gal. 5²¹ (43), where διχοστασίαι and αἱρέσεις are mentioned (cf. σχίζοντι in Philad. iii). οἰκοφθόροι in Ignatius probably means 'seducers,' especially μοιχοί: if, however, we understand the 'house' to be the *Church* (so Hilgenfeld), we may also compare 1 Cor. 3¹⁷ εἴ τις τὸν ναὸν τοῦ Θεοῦ φθείρει, φθερεῖ τοῦτον ὁ Θεός.

(2)   Eph. xviii. 1.   1 Cor. 1¹⁸, ²⁰.

σταυροῦ, ὅ ἐστι σκάνδαλον τοῖς ἀπιστοῦσιν, ἡμῖν δὲ σωτηρία καὶ ζωὴ αἰώνιος. ποῦ σοφός; ποῦ συζητητής; ποῦ καύχησις τῶν λεγομένων συνετῶν;

ὁ λόγος γὰρ τοῦ σταυροῦ τοῖς μὲν ἀπολλυμένοις μωρία ἐστίν, τοῖς δὲ σωζομένοις ἡμῖν δύναμις Θεοῦ ἐστίν... ποῦ σοφός; ποῦ γραμματεύς; ποῦ συζητητὴς τοῦ αἰῶνος τούτου;

St. Paul's words (ποῦ σοφός, &c.) are a paraphrase of Isa. 33¹⁸; cf. also 19¹¹ sq. That Ignatius is quoting St. Paul is made more certain by the echo of 1 Cor. 1¹⁸ in the preceding sentence. The phrase σκάνδαλον τοῦ σταυροῦ occurs Gal. 5¹¹ (44).

(3)   Magn. x. 3.

ὑπέρθεσθε οὖν τὴν κακὴν ζύμην τὴν παλαιωθεῖσαν καὶ ἐνοξίσασαν, καὶ μεταβάλεσθε εἰς νέαν ζύμην, ὅς ἐστιν Ἰησοῦς Χριστός.

1 Cor. 5⁷.

ἐκκαθάρατε τὴν παλαιὰν ζύμην, ἵνα ἦτε νέον φύραμα.

A free quotation; but there can be little doubt that Ignatius had this passage in his mind.

(4)   Rom. v. 1.

ἀλλ' οὐ παρὰ τοῦτο δεδικαίωμαι.

1 Cor. 4⁴.

ἀλλ' οὐκ ἐν τούτῳ δεδικαίωμαι.

Ignatius quotes from memory; there is no difference in meaning between παρὰ τοῦτο and ἐν τούτῳ.

(5)   Rom. ix. 2.

ἐγὼ γὰρ αἰσχύνομαι ἐξ αὐτῶν λέγεσθαι· οὐδὲ γὰρ ἄξιός εἰμι, ὧν ἔσχατος αὐτῶν καὶ ἔκτρωμα, ἀλλ' ἠλέημαι τις εἶναι, ἢν Θεοῦ ἐπιτύχω.

1 Cor. 15⁸⁻¹⁰.

ἔσχατον δὲ πάντων, ὡσπερεὶ τῷ ἐκτρώματι, ὤφθη κἀμοί. ἐγὼ γάρ ... οὐκ εἰμὶ ἱκανὸς καλεῖσθαι ἀπόστολος ... χάριτι δὲ Θεοῦ εἰμι ὅ εἰμι.

c

(6)   Eph. xv. 3.

πάντα οὖν ποιῶμεν, ὡς αὐτοῦ ἐν ἡμῖν κατοικοῦντος, ἵνα ὦμεν αὐτοῦ ναοὶ καὶ αὐτὸς ἐν ἡμῖν Θεός.

1 Cor. 3¹⁶.

ναὸς Θεοῦ ἐστε, καὶ τὸ Πνεῦμα τοῦ Θεοῦ οἰκεῖ ἐν ὑμῖν.

Cf. also 1 Cor. 6¹⁹ and 2 Cor. 6¹⁶. See (39). Zahn without reason compares Apoc. 21³.

(7)   Trall. ii. 3.

δεῖ δὲ καὶ τοὺς διακόνους ὄντας μυστηρίων Ἰησοῦ Χριστοῦ κατὰ πάντα τρόπον πᾶσιν ἀρέσκειν.

1 Cor. 4¹.

οὕτως ἡμᾶς λογιζέσθω ἄνθρωπος, ὡς ὑπηρέτας Χριστοῦ καὶ οἰκονόμους μυστηρίων Θεοῦ.

Cf. also 1 Cor. 10³³ ἐγὼ πάντα πᾶσιν ἀρέσκω.

(8)   Trall. v. 1.

φοβοῦμαι μὴ νηπίοις οὖσιν ὑμῖν βλάβην παραθῶ.

1 Cor. 3¹, ².

ὡς νηπίοις ἐν Χριστῷ . . . οὔπω γὰρ ἠδύνασθε.

In the next sentence οὐ δυνηθέντες χωρῆσαι is suggested by the same passage.

(9)   Trall. xii. 3.

ἵνα μὴ ἀδόκιμος εὑρεθῶ.

1 Cor. 9²⁷.

μήπως . . . αὐτὸς ἀδόκιμος γένωμαι.

The idea of a race seems to be present in Ignatius as well as in St. Paul.

(10)   Rom. iv. 3.

ἀπελεύθερος Ἰησοῦ Χριστοῦ.

1 Cor. 7²².

ἀπελεύθερος Κυρίου.

Cf. also 1 Cor. 9¹.

(11)   Rom. vi. 1.

καλόν μοι ἀποθανεῖν διὰ 'Ιησοῦν
Χριστόν (v. l. εἰς Χριστὸν 'Ιησοῦν), ἢ
βασιλεύειν τῶν περάτων τῆς γῆς.

1 Cor. 9¹⁵.

καλὸν γάρ μοι μᾶλλον ἀποθανεῖν
ἢ τὸ καύχημά μου οὐδεὶς κενώσει.

(12)   Philad. iv. 1.

μία γὰρ σὰρξ τοῦ Κυρίου ἡμῶν
'Ιησοῦ Χριστοῦ, καὶ ἓν ποτήριον εἰς
ἕνωσιν τοῦ αἵματος αὐτοῦ.

1 Cor. 10¹⁶, ¹⁷.

τὸ ποτήριον ... οὐχὶ κοινωνία ἐστιν
τοῦ αἵματος τοῦ Χριστοῦ; τὸν ἄρτον
ὃν κλῶμεν, οὐχὶ κοινωνία τοῦ σώματος
τοῦ Χριστοῦ ἐστιν; ὅτι εἷς ἄρτος, ἓν
σῶμα οἱ πολλοί ἐσμεν.

(13)   Philad. vii. 1.

τὸ πνεῦμα ... τὰ κρυπτὰ ἐλέγχει.

1 Cor. 2¹⁰.

τὸ γὰρ πνεῦμα πάντα ἐρευνᾷ.

Cf. also 1 Cor. 14²⁵ and Eph. 5¹², ¹³.

(14)   Smyrn. Inscrip.

ἀνυστερήτῳ οὔσῃ πάντος χαρί-
σματος.

1 Cor. 1⁷.

ὥστε ὑμᾶς μὴ ὑστερεῖσθαι ἐν
μηδενὶ χαρίσματι.

d

(15)   Eph. ii. 2.   1 Cor. 16¹⁸.
κατὰ πάντα με ἀνέπαυσεν.

(16)   Eph. ii. 3.   1 Cor. 1¹⁰.
κατηρτισμένοι.
In both passages the idea of *unity* is prominent.

(17)   Eph. iv. 2.   1 Cor. 6¹⁵.
μέλη ὄντας, &c.
Cf. also Trall. xi. 2 ὄντας μέλη αὐτοῦ, and with these compare
Rom. 12⁴, ⁵ and Eph. 5³⁰.

(18)   Eph. viii. 2.   1 Cor. 2¹⁴.
οἱ σαρκικοί, &c.
The resemblance is closer to Rom. 8⁵, ⁸. See below (35).

(19)   Eph. ix. 1.   1 Cor. 3¹⁰⁻¹⁷.
ὡς ὄντες λίθοι ναοῦ, &c.
Cf. also Eph. 2²⁰ ᶠ·, and possibly 1 Pet. 2⁵.

(20) Eph. x. 2 and xx. 1.   1 Cor. 15⁵⁸.
ἑδραῖοι τῇ πίστει.
Cf. also Col. 1²³, (64) a possible allusion.

(21)   Eph. xi. 1.   1 Cor. 7²⁹.
ἔσχατοι καιροί, &c.
There is probably no reference to 1 John 1¹⁸.

(22) Eph. xvii. 2. I Cor. 1²⁴, ³⁰.

διὰ τί ... ὁ Κύριος.

(23) Eph. xx. 1. I Cor. 15⁴⁵, ⁴⁷.

τὸν καινὸν ἄνθρωπον.

See below on Eph. 2¹⁵, 4²⁴ (28).

(24) Trall. vi. 1. I Cor. 7¹⁰.

οὐκ ἐγὼ ἀλλ᾽ ἡ ἀγάπη, &c.

(25) Trall. xi. 2. I Cor. 12¹².

ὄντας μέλη αὐτοῦ.

See above (17).

Ignatius must have known this Epistle almost by heart. Although there are no *quotations* (in the strictest sense, with mention of the source), echoes of its language and thought pervade the whole of his writings in such a manner as to leave no doubt whatever that he was acquainted with the First Epistle to the Corinthians.

B

Ephesians b

(26) Eph. Inscript. Eph. 1³ ff.

τῇ εὐλογημένῃ ἐν μεγέθει, Θεοῦ
πατρὸς πληρώματι, τῇ προωρισμένῃ
πρὸ αἰώνων εἶναι διὰ παντὸς εἰς δόξαν
παράμονον ἄτρεπτον, ἡνωμένῃ καὶ
ἐκλελεγμένῃ ἐν πάθει ἀληθινῷ ἐν θελήματι τοῦ πατρὸς καὶ Ἰησοῦ Χριστοῦ
τοῦ Θεοῦ ἡμῶν, τῇ ἐκκλησίᾳ τῇ
ἀξιομακαρίστῳ τῇ οὔσῃ ἐν Ἐφέσῳ,
πλεῖστα ἐν Ἰησοῦ Χριστῷ καὶ ἐν
ἀμώμῳ χαρᾷ χαίρειν.

εὐλογητὸς ὁ Θεὸς καὶ πατὴρ ... ὁ
εὐλογήσας ἡμᾶς ἐν πάσῃ εὐλογίᾳ ...
καθὼς ἐξελέξατο ἡμᾶς ... πρὸ καταβολῆς κόσμου, εἶναι ἡμᾶς ... ἀμώμους
... προορίσας κατὰ τὴν εὐδοκίαν τοῦ
θελήματος ... διὰ τοῦ αἵματος αὐτοῦ
... τοῦ πληρώματος τῶν καιρῶν ...
προορισθέντες ... κατὰ τὴν βουλὴν
τοῦ θελήματος αὐτοῦ ... εἰς τὸ εἶναι
ἡμᾶς εἰς ἔπαινον δόξης αὐτοῦ.

A comparison of these two passages will show a very large number of correspondences, which Zahn undervalues when he calls them 'not very certain echoes.' The evidence is cumulative, and is not impaired by the fact that Ignatius applies to the Church collectively expressions which St. Paul applies to individual Christians, such adaptations being common to our author.

(27) Polyc. v. 1. Eph. 5²⁵

παράγγελλε ... ἀγαπᾶν τὰς συμ-
βίους, ὡς ὁ Κύριος τὴν ἐκκλησίαν.

ἀγαπᾶτε τὰς γυναῖκας, καθὼς καὶ
ὁ Χριστὸς ἠγάπησε τὴν ἐκκλησίαν.

Cf. also (29).

F 2

c

(28)   Eph. xx. 1.   Eph. 2¹⁵ and 4²⁴.
τὸν καινὸν ἄνθρωπον Ἰησοῦν   καινὸν ἄνθρωπον.
Χριστόν.

St. Paul uses the phrase in a slightly different sense; but, as Lightfoot suggests, Ignatius may have taken 'to put on the new man' as meaning 'to put on Christ,' an explanation, we may add, which St. Paul would not have repudiated. Cf. also 1 Cor. 15⁴⁵ ὁ δεύτερος ἄνθρωπος.

(29)   Smyrn. i. 1.   Eph. 2¹⁶.
ἐν ἑνὶ σώματι τῆς ἐκκλησίας αὐτοῦ.   ἐν ἑνὶ σώματι

The context in both passages contains a reference to Isaiah, as well as the common idea of Jew and Gentile as one body. Cf. also Eph. 1²³ and Col. 1¹⁸.

(30)   Polyc. i. 2.   Eph. 4².
πάντων ἀνέχου ἐν ἀγάπῃ.   ἀνεχόμενοι ἀλλήλων ἐν ἀγάπῃ.

This correspondence is strengthened by the preceding words in Ignatius, τῆς ἑνώσεως φρόντιζε, ἧς οὐδὲν ἄμεινον, which should be compared with the following verse in Ephesians, σπουδάζοντες τηρεῖν τὴν ἑνότητα τοῦ πνεύματος.

d

(31)   Eph. i. 1.   Eph. 5¹.
μιμηταὶ ὄντες Θεοῦ.

Cf. also Eph. x. 3, μιμηταὶ τοῦ Κυρίου, where the context is the same (forgiveness of injuries, &c.).

(32)   Eph. ix. 1.   Eph. 2²⁰⁻²².
λίθοι ναοῦ.

This may well be accounted for by 1 Cor. 3¹⁰⁻¹⁷; see (19). Compare also Col. 2⁷ and 1 Pet. 2⁵.

(33)   Eph. xix.   Eph. 3⁹.
πῶς οὖν ἐφανερώθη τοῖς αἰῶσιν.   τίς ἡ οἰκονομία τοῦ μυστηρίου τοῦ ἀποκεκρυμμένου ἀπὸ τῶν αἰώνων ...
                                        ἵνα γνωρισθῇ.

Cf. also Col. 1²⁶ (66).

(34)   Polyc. vi. 2.   Eph. 6¹³⁻¹⁷.
ὡς ὅπλα, &c.

The parts in the armour are differently assigned, and the metaphor was doubtless a favourite one in Christian preaching. Cf. too 1 Thess. 5⁸, where the resemblance is still slighter.

Though the correspondences between Ignatius and this Epistle are not nearly so numerous as in the case of 1 Corinthians, it may be considered almost certain that they are not accidental. Ignatius mentions St. Paul by name in Eph. xii, calling the Ephesians συμμύσται Παύλου τοῦ ἡγιασμένου, a phrase which reminds us of St. Paul's frequent use of μυστήριον for the Gospel dispensation in this Epistle (Eph. 1⁹, 3³, ⁴, ⁹, 5³², 6¹⁹). The words of Ignatius (Eph. xii) ἐν πάσῃ ἐπιστόλῃ doubtless mean 'in every letter,' and are a pardonable exaggeration of the fact that the Apostle makes mention of the Ephesians in *five* of his Epistles besides that which bears their name.

Von der Goltz considers the literary dependence doubtful, in view of the difference in form of most of the supposed echoes, and of the fact that several of them have parallels also in Colossians, the Pastoral Epistles, or 1 Peter. The strength of the argument must rest mainly on the first passage quoted (26), in which the resemblances are numerous and striking; but even without it a strong case might be made out for the use of the Epistle by Ignatius.

C

Romans c

(35)   Eph. viii. 2.   Rom. 8⁵, ⁸.

οἱ σαρκικοὶ τὰ πνευματικὰ πράσ-   οἱ γὰρ κατὰ σάρκα ὄντες τὰ τῆς
σειν οὐ δύνανται οὐδὲ οἱ πνευματικοὶ   σαρκὸς φρονοῦσιν, οἱ δὲ κατὰ πνεῦμα
τὰ σαρκικά.   τὰ πνεύματος ... οἱ δὲ ἐν σαρκὶ ὄντες
                                    Θεῷ ἀρέσαι οὐ δύνανται.

This passage may be from 1 Cor. 2¹⁴ (18), but the resemblance to Rom. 8⁵, ⁸ is rather closer: cf. also Gal. 5¹⁶, ¹⁷. The use of the word σάρξ in an ethical sense is Pauline; in Ignatius it generally has an anti-docetic force.

(36)   Eph. xix. 3.   Rom. 6⁴.

καθηρεῖτο παλαιὰ βασιλεία, Θεοῦ   ἵνα ἡμεῖς ἐν καινότητι ζωῆς περι-
ἀνθρωπίνως φανερουμένου εἰς καινό-   πατήσωμεν.
τητα ἀιδίου ζωῆς.

The phrase καινότης ζωῆς (='the new state which is life') is probably from St. Paul.

(37)   Smyrn. i. 1.   Rom. 1³, ⁴.

ἐκ γένους Δαυεὶδ κατὰ σάρκα,   περὶ τοῦ υἱοῦ αὐτοῦ, τοῦ γενομένου
υἱὸν Θεοῦ κατὰ θέλημα καὶ δύναμιν.   ἐκ σπέρματος Δαβὶδ κατὰ σάρκα, τοῦ
    ὁρισθέντος υἱοῦ Θεοῦ ἐν δυνάμει κατὰ
    πνεῦμα ἁγιωσύνης.

Cf. also Eph. xviii. 2 ἐκ σπέρματος μὲν Δαυεὶδ πνεύματος
δὲ ἁγίου.

d

(38)   Eph. Inscript.   Rom. 15²⁹.

τῇ εὐλογημένῃ . . . πληρώματι.   ἐν πληρώματι εὐλογίας.

2 Corinthians   d

(39)   Eph. xv. 3.   2 Cor. 6¹⁶.

αὐτοῦ ἐν ἡμῖν κατοικοῦντος, ἵνα   ἡμεῖς γὰρ ναὸς Θεοῦ ἔσμεν ζῶντος.
ὦμεν ναοὶ καὶ αὐτὸς ἐν ἡμῖν θεός.

The resemblance here is close, but may be sufficiently
accounted for by 1 Cor. 3¹⁶, ²⁷ and 6¹⁹ : see (6).

(40)   Trall. ix. 2.   2 Cor. 4¹⁴.

ἐγείραντος, &c

' Apparently a reminiscence' (Lightfoot).

(41)   Philad. vi. 3.   2 Cor. 1¹², 11⁹, 12¹⁶.   Cf. 2⁵.

εὐχαριστῶ τῷ Θεῷ μου ὅτι εὐσυν-
είδητός εἰμι ἐν ὑμῖν, καὶ οὐκ ἔχει τις
καυχήσασθαι . . . ὅτι ἐβάρησά τινα,
&c.

A cumulative case, which is slightly strengthened by καυχήσασθαι; cf. καύχησις 2 Cor. 11¹⁰. Cf. also 1 Thess. 2⁹. None
of the above, taken singly, is more than a possible allusion ;
but taken together they make the use of the Epistle by
Ignatius fairly probable.

Galatians   c

(42)   Philad. i. 1.   Gal. 1¹.

ὃν ἐπίσκοπον ἔγνων οὐκ ἀφ' ἑαυτοῦ   οὐκ ἀπ' ἀνθρώπων οὐδὲ δι' ἀνθρώ-
οὐδὲ δι' ἀνθρώπων.   που.

d

(43)   Eph. xvi. 1.   Gal. 5²¹.

βασιλείαν . . . κληρονομήσουσιν.   οἱ τὰ τοιαῦτα πράσσοντες βασιλείαν
    Θεοῦ οὐ κληρονομήσουσιν.

See above (1) on 1 Cor. 6⁹, ¹⁰.

(44)   Eph. xviii. 1.
σταυροῦ ὅ ἐστι σκάνδαλον.

Gal. 5¹¹.
σκάνδαλον τοῦ σταυροῦ.

(45)   Trall. x. 1.
δωρεὰν ἀποθνήσκω.

Gal. 2²¹.
ἄρα Χριστὸς δωρεὰν ἀπέθανεν.

(46)   Rom. vii. 2.
ὁ ἐμὸς ἔρως ἐσταύρωται.

Gal. 6¹⁴.
ἐμοὶ κόσμος ἐσταύρωται κἀγὼ τῷ κόσμῳ.

The passage in Philad. is the only one which strongly indicates knowledge of this Epistle by Ignatius; and as it stands almost alone, we cannot claim a very high degree of probability for the reference.

Philippians   c

(47)   Smyrn. iv. 2.
πάντα ὑπομένω αὐτοῦ με ἐνδυναμοῦντος.

Phil. 4¹³.
πάντα ἰσχύω ἐν τῷ ἐνδυναμοῦντί με.

Cf. Eph. 6¹³; 1 Tim. 1¹² (54).

(48)   Smyrn. xi. 3.
τέλειοι ὄντες τέλεια καὶ φρονεῖτε.

Phil. 3¹⁵.
ὅσοι οὖν τέλειοι, τοῦτο φρονῶμεν.

d

(49)   Rom. ii and iv.
σπονδισθῆναι and θυσία.

Phil. 2¹⁷.

Cf. also 2 Tim. 4⁶ (59).

(50)   Philad. i. 1.
οὐδὲ κατὰ κενοδοξίαν.

Philad. viii. 2.
μηδὲν κατ' ἐρίθειαν ... ἀλλὰ κατὰ χριστομαθίαν.

Phil. 2³, ⁵.
μηδὲν κατ' ἐριθίαν μηδὲ κατὰ κενοδοξίαν ... ἐν Χριστῷ Ἰησοῦ.

1 *Timothy*   c

(51)   Eph. xiv. 1.
ἀρχὴ μὲν πίστις, τέλος δὲ ἀγάπη.

Eph. xx. 1.
προσδηλώσω ὑμῖν ἧς ἠρξάμην οἰκονομίας.

Magn. viii. 1.
μὴ πλανᾶσθε ταῖς ἑτεροδοξίαις μηδὲ μυθεύμασιν τοῖς παλαιοῖς ἀνωφελέσιν οὖσιν· εἰ γὰρ μέχρι νῦν κατὰ Ἰουδαϊσμὸν ζῶμεν, ὁμολογοῦμεν χάριν μὴ εἰληφέναι.

1 Tim. 1³⁻⁵.
ἵνα παραγγείλῃς τισὶ μὴ ἑτεροδιδασκαλεῖν, μηδὲ προσέχειν μύθοις καὶ γενεαλογίαις ἀπεράντοις αἵτινες ἐκζητήσεις παρέχουσι μᾶλλον ἢ οἰκονομίαν Θεοῦ τὴν ἐν πίστει. τὸ δὲ τέλος τῆς παραγγελίας ἐστὶν ἀγάπη ἐκ καθαρᾶς καρδίας καὶ συνειδήσεως ἀγαθῆς καὶ πίστεως ἀνυποκρίτου.

If these three passages from Ignatius are compared with the opening sentences of 1 Timothy, it will be seen that the resemblance is very close, and that it lies in words and expressions which are not commonplaces. (See, however, Hermas, *Vis.* iii. 8. 3–5, for a list of virtues beginning with πίστις and ending with ἀγάπη.) It is also clear that, if literary dependence be admitted, it is on the side of Ignatius. See also (60).

(52)   Polyc. iv. 3.

δούλους καὶ δούλας μὴ ὑπερηφάνει· ἀλλὰ μηδὲ αὐτοὶ φυσιούσθωσαν, ἀλλ' εἰς δόξαν Θεοῦ πλέον δουλευέτωσαν.

1 Tim. 6².

μὴ καταφρονείτωσαν, ὅτι ἀδελφοί εἰσιν· ἀλλὰ μᾶλλον δουλευέτωσαν.

d

(53)   Rom. ix. 2.

ἀλλ' ἠλέημαί τις εἶναι ἐὰν Θεοῦ ἐπιτύχω.

1 Tim. 1¹³.

ἀλλὰ ἠλεήθην, ὅτι ἀγνοῶν ἐποίησα.

Cf. above, on 1 Cor. 7²⁵, 15⁹,¹⁰ (5).

(54)   Smyrn. iv. 2.

αὐτοῦ με ἐνδυναμοῦντος τοῦ τελείου ἀνθρώπου γενομένου.

1 Tim. 1¹².

Cf. also 2 Tim. 2¹ and 4¹⁷.

2 Timothy   **c**

(55)   Eph. ii. 1.

κατὰ πάντα με ἀνέπαυσεν, ὡς καὶ αὐτὸν ὁ πατὴρ Ἰησοῦ Χριστοῦ ἀναψύξαι.

Smyrn. x. 2.

ἀντίψυχον ὑμῶν τὸ πνεῦμά μου, καὶ τὰ δεσμά μου ἃ οὐκ . . . ἐπησχύνθητε.

2 Tim. 1¹⁶.

δῴη ἔλεος ὁ Κύριος τῷ Ὀνησιφόρου οἴκῳ· ὅτι πολλάκις με ἀνέψυξε, καὶ τὴν ἅλυσίν μου οὐκ ἐπησχύνθη.

These two passages seem to be reminiscences of the same context in 2 Timothy. The following words in Smyrn. x resemble Mark 8³⁸ and Luke 9²⁶ : see (90).

(56)   Polyc. vi. 2.

ἀρέσκετε ᾧ στρατεύεσθε.

2 Tim. 2³.

ἵνα τῷ στρατολογήσαντι ἀρέσῃ.

d

(57)   Eph. xvii. 1.

μὴ αἰχμαλωτίσῃ ὑμᾶς.

Cf. also Rom. 7²³.

2 Tim. 3⁶.

(58)   Trall. vii. 2.   2 Tim 1³.

καθαρός ἐστιν τῇ συνειδήσει.   ἐν καθαρᾷ συνειδήσει.

(59)   Rom. ii. 2.   2 Tim. 4⁶.

μὴ πλέον παράσχησθε τοῦ σπονδι-   ἤδη σπένδομαι.
σθῆναι Θεῷ.

Cf. Phil. 2¹⁷.

The reminiscences of 2 Timothy, as of 1 Timothy, are tolerably clear. Both Epistles are nearly in Class B.

Titus   c
(60)   Magn. viii. 1.   Titus 1¹⁴.

μὴ πλανᾶσθε ταῖς ἑτεροδοξίαις μηδὲ   μὴ προσέχοντες Ἰουδαϊκοῖς μύθοις
μυθεύμασιν τοῖς παλαιοῖς ἀνωφελέσιν   καὶ ἐντολαῖς ἀνθρώπων.
οὖσιν· εἰ γὰρ μέχρι νῦν κατὰ Ἰουδαϊ-   Titus 3⁹.
σμὸν ζῶμεν, ὁμολογοῦμεν χάριν μὴ
εἰληφέναι.   μωρὰς δὲ ζητήσεις καὶ γενεαλογίας
                                    . . . περιΐστασο· εἰσὶ γὰρ ἀνωφελεῖς
                                    καὶ μάταιοι.

See (51) on 1 Tim. 1⁴. The word ἀνωφελής and the reference to 'Judaism' occur in Titus and not in 1 Timothy.

d
(61)   Polyc. vi. 1.   Titus 1⁷.

Θεοῦ οἰκονόμοι.   ὡς Θεοῦ οἰκονόμον.

See (7) for 1 Cor. 4¹; cf. 1 Pet. 4¹⁰.

The evidence in the case of Titus is weaker than in that of 1 Timothy or 2 Timothy.

D
Acts   d
(62)   Magn. v. 1.   Acts 1²⁵.

ἕκαστος εἰς τὸν ἴδιον τόπον μέλλει   ἀφ' ἧς παρέβη Ἰούδας πορευθῆναι
χωρεῖν.   εἰς τὸν τόπον τὸν ἴδιον.

These phenomena must be taken along with those in relation to Luke's Gospel.

(63)   Symrn. iii. 3.   Acts 10⁴¹.

μετὰ δὲ τὴν ἀνάστασιν συνέφαγεν   συνεφάγομεν καὶ συνεπίομεν αὐτῷ
αὐτοῖς καὶ συνέπιεν.   μετὰ τὸ ἀναστῆναι αὐτὸν ἐκ νεκρῶν.

These look like allusions; but the words are common and obvious ones, and may be only the result of coincidence.

Colossians   **d**
(63*)   Eph. ii. 1.   Col. 1⁷, 4⁷.
τοῦ συνδούλου.

Cf. Magn. 2 ; Philad. 4 ; and see Lightfoot's note on Col. 4⁷.

(64)   Eph. x. 2.   Col. 1²³.
ἑδραῖοι τῇ πίστει.
See on 1 Cor. 15⁵⁸ (20).

(65)   Eph. xvii. 2.   Col. 2².
Θεοῦ γνῶσιν.

In the passage of Colossians, St. Paul, according to the best reading, identifies ' the knowledge of God ' with ' Christ.'

(66)   Eph. xix. 2.   Col. 1²⁶.
πῶς οὖν ἐφανερώθη τοῖς αἰῶσιν ;
Cf. also Eph. 3⁹ (33).

(67)   Trall. v. 2.   Col. 1¹⁶.
ὁρατὰ καὶ ἀόρατα.   τὰ ὁρατὰ καὶ τὰ ἀόρατα.

(68)   Smyrn. i. 2.   Col. 2¹⁴.
καθηλωμένους ἐν τῷ σταυρῷ.   προσηλώσας αὐτὸ τῷ σταυρῷ.
The metaphor is the same, but the application is different.

(69)   Smyrn. i. 2.   Col. 1¹⁸.
ἐν ἑνὶ σώματι.

Cf. on Eph. 2¹⁶ (29).
There is thus a considerable number of possible allusions to Colossians in Ignatius, but none of them is at all certain.

1 *Thessalonians*   **d**
(70)   Eph. x. 1.   1 Thess. 5¹⁷.
ἀδιαλείπτως προσεύχεσθε.   The same.

The reading in Ignatius is doubtful (see Lightfoot); the adverb may have been inserted from the passage in 1 Thessalonians. The adjective ἀδιάλειπτος occurs in Polyc. i, but there also it is suspect.

(71)   Rom. ii. 1.   1 Thess. 2⁴.
οὐ θέλω ὑμᾶς ἀνθρωπαρεσκῆσαι,   οὐχ ὡς ἀνθρώποις ἀρέσκοντες, ἀλλὰ
ἀλλὰ Θεῷ.   Θεῷ.
The evidence that Ignatius knew 1 Thessalonians is almost *nil*.

2 *Thessalonians* **d**

(72) Rom. x. 3.   2 Thess. 3⁵.

ἐν ὑπομονῇ 'Ιησοῦ Χριστοῦ. εἰς τὴν ὑπομονὴν τοῦ Χριστοῦ.

Philemon **d**

(73) Eph. ii. 2.   Philem. ²⁰.

ὀναίμην ὑμῶν. ναί, ἀδελφέ, ἐγώ σου ὀναίμην ἐν

        Κυρίῳ.

In spite of the fact that the name Onesimus occurs in this sentence of Ignatius, the allusion is very doubtful. The Pauline phrase ὀναίμην occurs in this sense several times in Ignatius.

Hebrews **d**

(74) Magn. iii. 2.   Heb. 4¹³.

τὸ δὲ τοιοῦτον οὐ πρὸς σάρκα ὁ πάντα δὲ γυμνὰ καὶ τετραχηλισμένα
λόγος, ἀλλὰ πρὸς Θεὸν τὸν τὰ κρύφια τοῖς ὀφθαλμοῖς αὐτοῦ πρὸς ὃν ἡμῖν ὁ
εἰδότα.   λόγος.

We have here a double resemblance, in the *idea* of nothing being hidden from the knowledge of God, and in the *expression* ὁ λόγος [ἡμῖν ἐστι] πρός [τινα].

(75) Philad. ix. 1.   Heb. 7⁷, ¹⁹, ²², ²³, ²⁶.

καλοὶ καὶ οἱ ἱερεῖς· κρεῖσσον δὲ ὁ
ἀρχιερεὺς ὁ πεπιστευμένος τὰ ἅγια τῶν
ἁγίων, ὃς μόνος πεπίστευται τὰ κρυπτὰ
τοῦ Θεοῦ.

Lightfoot also compares Heb. 2¹⁷, 3¹, 4¹⁴, 5⁵, ¹⁰, 6²⁰, 7²⁶, 8¹, 9¹¹. He adds: 'The reference (in ὁ πεπιστευμένος, &c.) is to the special privilege of the High Priest (Heb. 9⁷⁻¹², 10¹⁹ ˢq.) of entering into the Holy Place. This coincidence, combined with those noticed above, shows, I think, that Ignatius must have had the Epistle to the Hebrews in his mind.' It is no doubt true that no other book in N. T. develops the idea of Christ as High Priest, and that Clement of Rome, who also uses it, e. g. (21), shows knowledge of Hebrews; but the comparison may well have been suggested to Ignatius from other sources, and the resemblance does not seem close enough to justify the degree of confidence which Lightfoot expresses. Cf. also Polycarp (65).

1 *Peter*   **d**
(76)   Eph. v. 3.   1 Pet. 5⁵.
γέγραπται γάρ· Ὑπερηφάνοις ὁ Θεὸς   ὁ Θεὸς ὑπερηφάνοις ἀντιτάσσεται.
ἀντιτάσσεται.

The quotation is from Prov. 3³⁴. The words are quoted not only in 1 Peter, but in James 4⁶ and in Clement of Rome (47). In all alike Θεὸς or ὁ Θεός takes the place of the Κύριος of the LXX; but Ignatius alone puts ὑπερηφάνοις first in the sentence.

(77)   Rom. v. 1.   1 Pet. 2²⁵, 5².

The connexion of ποιμήν with ἐπίσκοπος is considered by Lightfoot to present 'a close parallel' with 1 Peter; but the resemblance must not be pressed. See also (19).

GOSPELS.

(I) The Synoptic Gospels.

The much closer parallels with Matthew than with Mark or Luke are a remarkable phenomenon, but one which frequently meets us in the earliest sub-Apostolic literature.

B
Matthew   **b**
(78)   Trall. xi. 1.   Matt. 15¹³.
οὗτοι γὰρ οὔκ εἰσιν φυτεία πατρός.   πᾶσα φυτεία ἣν οὐκ ἐφύτευσεν ὁ
        Philad. iii. 1.   πατήρ μου ὁ οὐράνιος, ἐκριζωθήσεται.
ἀπέχεσθε τῶν κακῶν βοτανῶν,
ἅστινας οὐ γεωργεῖ Ἰησοῦς Χριστός,
διὰ τὸ μὴ εἶναι αὐτοὺς φυτείαν πατρός.

(79)   Smyrn. i. 1.   Matt. 3¹⁵.
βεβαπτισμένον ὑπὸ Ἰωάννου ἵνα   οὕτω γὰρ πρέπον ἐστὶν ἡμῖν πλη-
πληρωθῇ πᾶσα δικαιοσύνη ὑπ' αὐτοῦ.   ρῶσαι πᾶσαν δικαιοσύνην.

Matthew alone of the Evangelists gives this *motive* for our Lord's Baptism. 'The use of the phrase πληρ. πᾶσ. δ. is so peculiar, and falls in so entirely with the characteristic Christian Judaizing of our first Evangelist, that it seems unreasonable to refer it to any one else' (Sanday). The fact that Ignatius elsewhere (Eph. xviii. 2) ascribes a different motive for the Baptism, viz. ἵνα τῷ πάθει τὸ ὕδωρ καθαρίσῃ, perhaps strengthens the case.

(80)　　Smyrn. vi. 1.　　　　　　　　Matt. 19¹².

ὁ χωρῶν χωρείτω.　　　　　　　ὁ δυνάμενος χωρεῖν χωρείτω.

The meaning of the phrase is the same in the two passages; it stamps the doctrine just stated as a difficult and mysterious one.

(81)　　Polyc. ii. 2.　　　　　　　　Matt. 10¹⁶.

φρόνιμος γίνου ὡς ὁ ὄφις ἐν πᾶσιν,　γίνεσθε οὖν φρόνιμοι ὡς οἱ ὄφεις
καὶ ἀκέραιος εἰσαεὶ ὡς ἡ περιστερά.　καὶ ἀκέραιοι ὡς αἱ περιστεραί.

This sentence is wanting in the parallel passage of Luke (10³).

C

(82)　　Eph. v. 2.　　　　　　　　　Matt. 18¹⁹, ²⁰.

εἰ γὰρ ἑνὸς καὶ δευτέρου προσευχὴ　ἐὰν δύο ὑμῶν συμφωνήσωσιν ἐπὶ
τοσαύτην ἰσχὺν ἔχει.　　　　　τῆς γῆς ... γενήσεται αὐτοῖς. οὐ γάρ
　　　　　　　　　　　　　εἰσι δύο ἢ τρεῖς συνηγμένοι εἰς τὸ
　　　　　　　　　　　　　ἐμὸν ὄνομα, ἐκεῖ εἰμὶ ἐν μέσῳ αὐτῶν.

Here Ignatius's ἑνὸς καὶ δευτέρου = δυοῖν. The reference is clearly to the *saying* recorded in Matthew—'probably a well-known saying' of Christ (Zahn). Cf. also James 5¹⁶.

(83)　　Eph. vi. 1.　　　　　　　　　Matt. 10⁴⁰.

πάντα γὰρ ὃν πέμπει ὁ οἰκοδεσπότης　ὁ δεχόμενος ὑμᾶς ἐμὲ δέχεται, καὶ
εἰς ἰδίαν οἰκονομίαν, οὕτως δεῖ ἡμᾶς　ὁ ἐμὲ δεχόμενος δέχεται τὸν ἀποστεί-
αὐτὸν δέχεσθαι, ὡς αὐτὸν τὸν πέμψαντα.　λαντά με.

It is possible that Ignatius may also be alluding to the parable narrated in Matt. 21³³ ˢq· (where οἰκοδεσπότης occurs, not in Mark or Luke). There is also a resemblance to John 13²⁰ (see below (102)), which is perhaps as close as the resemblance to Matthew (John uses πέμπειν). Luke 10¹⁶ is much less similar in language than either.

(84)　　Polyc. i. 2, 3.　　　　　　　Matt. 8¹⁷.

πάντας βάσταζε ὡς καί σε ὁ Κύριος　αὐτὸς τὰς ἀσθενείας ἡμῶν ἔλαβε,
... πάντων τὰς νόσους βάσταζε, ὡς　καὶ τὰς νόσους ἐβάστασεν.
τέλειος ἀθλητής.

The idea is found in Isa. 53⁴; but it is probable that Ignatius borrows from Matthew and not direct from O. T.; for the LXX reading is different, viz. οὗτος τὰς ἁμαρτίας ἡμῶν φέρει καὶ περὶ ἡμῶν ὀδυνᾶται. Ignatius, however, translates the Hebrew correctly, and the possibility that he is using a translation other than the LXX cannot be excluded.

d

(85) Eph. xvii. 1.	Matt. 26[7].
διὰ τοῦτο μύρον ἔλαβεν ἐπὶ τῆς κεφαλῆς ὁ Κύριος, ἵνα πνέῃ τῇ ἐκκλησίᾳ ἀφθαρσίαν.	προσῆλθεν αὐτῷ γυνὴ . . . καὶ κατέχεεν ἐπὶ τῆς κεφαλῆς αὐτοῦ ἀνακειμένου.

Cf. also Mark 14[3 ff.]; John 12[3 ff.]. If there is literary dependence on any of our Gospels, the preference must be given to Matthew rather than Mark, who has κατέχεεν αὐτοῦ τῆς κεφαλῆς, while the reference to the *head* as anointed, and (seemingly) as the quarter from which the fragrance of incorruptibility is shed upon the Church, favours Matthew rather than John.

(86) Magn. v. 2.	Matt. 22[19].
ὥσπερ γάρ ἐστι νομίσματα δύο, &c.	

(87) Magn. ix. 3.	Matt. 27[52].
παρὼν ἤγειρεν αὐτούς.	

Lightfoot shows that the belief in a *descensus ad inferos* was prominent in the early Church. Here Christ is supposed to have *visited* the souls of patriarchs and prophets, and to have *raised* (ἤγειρεν) them either to paradise or heaven. Cf. also Philad. ix; and 1 Pet. 3[19], 4[6] for parallel views of the descent into Hades. The belief appears also in Justin, who quotes Jeremiah in confirmation, and asserts that the passage in question, which does not appear in the Hebrew Bible, had been wilfully excised by the Jews. Irenaeus also quotes it more than once, ascribing it both to Jeremiah and to Isaiah.

(88) Rom. ix. 3.	Matt. 10[40, 41].
τῶν ἐκκλησιῶν τῶν δεξαμένων με εἰς ὄνομα Ἰησοῦ Χριστοῦ.	

The phrase εἰς ὄνομα, as well as the similarity of thought, should be noticed, especially as there may be another echo of this passage in Eph. vi: see (83).

IGNATIUS 79

Ignatius was certainly acquainted either with our Matthew, or with the source of our Matthew, or with a Gospel very closely akin to it. In the present uncertain state of the Synoptic Problem, it would be rash to express any confident opinion; but the indications on the whole favour the hypothesis that he used our Greek Matthew in something like its present shape.

D

Mark	**d**	
(89) Eph. xvi. 1.		Mark 9⁴³.

εἰς τὸ πῦρ τὸ ἄσβεστον.

The phrase, though in quite a different context, occurs in Matt. 3¹² and Luke 3¹⁷.

(90) Smyrn. x. 2.   Mark 8³⁸.

οὐδὲ ὑμᾶς ἐπαισχυνθήσεται ἡ τελεία
πίστις, Ἰησοῦς Χριστός.

Cf. also Luke 9²⁶ (93), and see (55).

Scarcely anything can be built on these very doubtful allusions.

Luke   **d**

(91) Smyrn. i. 2.   Luke 23⁷⁻¹².

ἀληθῶς ἐπὶ Ποντίου Πιλάτου καὶ
Ἡρώδου τετράρχου καθηλωμένον ὑπὲρ
ἡμῶν ἐν σαρκί.

'The part taken by Herod is mentioned by Luke alone in the Canonical writings' (Lightfoot).

(92) Smyrn. iii. 2.   Luke 24³⁹.

καὶ ὅτε πρὸς τοὺς περὶ Πέτρον   ψηλαφήσατέ με καὶ ἴδετε, ὅτι πνεῦ-
ἦλθεν, ἔφη αὐτοῖς· Λάβετε, ψηλαφήσα-   μα σάρκα καὶ ὀστέα οὐκ ἔχει, καθὼς
τέ με, καὶ ἴδετε ὅτι οὐκ εἰμι δαιμόνιον   ἐμὲ θεωρεῖτε ἔχοντα.
ἀσώματον.

Eusebius (*H. E.* iii. 36) says of this passage of Ignatius, οὐκ οἶδ' ὁπόθεν ῥητοῖς συγκέχρηται. Jerome (*Vir. Ill.* 2) says that it is taken from the 'evangelium quod appellatur secundum Hebraeos,' which he had lately translated into Greek and

Latin, and which at the time he was disposed to regard as the original Matthew, though afterwards he spoke less confidently on this point. In another place (*Comm. in Isai.* xviii. *praef.*) he repeats his statement that 'incorporale daemonium' comes from this source. On the other hand, Eusebius, who was well acquainted with this Gospel, cannot verify the quotation; and Origen, who also knew it well, ascribes the words to another apocryphal writing, viz. the *Petri Doctrina* (*de Princ. praef.* 8), which he pronounces to be the work neither of Peter nor of any other inspired writer. The contradiction cannot be explained. Lightfoot suggests that either Jerome's memory failed him, or that his copy of the Gospel according to the Hebrews contained a different recension from that which was known to Origen and Eusebius. As regards Ignatius, he thinks it impossible to say whether he got the story from oral tradition or from some written source. Considering the carelessness of Ignatius in quotation, it is strange that Eusebius should not have suggested that he took the story from Luke; and but for these Patristic comments, we should probably have formed that opinion. Ignatius mentions the incident as if it were already well-known to his readers.

(93)   Smyrn. x. 2.   Luke 9²⁶.

Οὐδὲ ὑμᾶς ἐπαισχυνθήσεται ... Ἰησοῦς Χριστός. Cf. Luke 9²⁶ ; as also Mark 8³⁸, see on (90).

The balance of probability seems to be slightly in favour of a knowledge of the Third Gospel by Ignatius : cf. Acts (62).

(II) The Synoptic Tradition.

(94)   Eph. xiv. 2.   Matt. 12³³.

φανερὸν τὸ δένδρον ἀπὸ τοῦ καρποῦ   ἐκ γὰρ τοῦ καρποῦ τὸ δένδρον
αὐτοῦ.   γινώσκεται.

                                         Luke 6⁴⁴.

                                         ἕκαστον γὰρ δένδρον ἐκ τοῦ ἰδίου
                                         καρποῦ γινώσκεται.

The words have the look of a current saying of Christ.

(95)   Eph. xi. 1.

ἦν γὰρ τὴν μέλλουσαν ὀργὴν φοβηθῶμεν, ἢ τὴν ἐνεστῶσαν χάριν ἀγαπή-
σωμεν.

(96)   Magn. x. 2.

ἁλισθῆτε ἐν αὐτῷ.

Matt. 3⁷.

γεννήματα ἐχιδνῶν, τίς ὑπέδειξεν
ὑμῖν φυγεῖν ἀπὸ τῆς μελλούσης ὀργῆς,
Luke 3⁷ (the same words).

Matt. 5¹³; Mark 9⁵⁰; Luke
14³⁴.

The mention of the 'kingdoms of the world' may be a
reminiscence of the narrative of the Temptation in Matt. 4⁸;
Luke 4⁵.

(97)   Rom. vi. 1.

οὐδέν με ὠφελήσει . . . τούτου.

Matt. 16²⁶.

Also in Mark and Luke.

This is at best a very doubtful allusion.

(III) The Fourth Gospel.

B

John

(98)   Rom. vii. 2.

b

οὐκ ἔστιν ἐν ἐμοὶ πῦρ φιλόϋλον,
ὕδωρ δὲ ζῶν καὶ λαλοῦν ἐν ἐμοί,
ἔσωθέν μοι λέγον· Δεῦρο πρὸς τὸν
πατέρα.

John 4¹⁰, ¹⁴.

σὺ ἂν ᾔτησας αὐτόν, καὶ ἔδωκεν ἄν
σοι ὕδωρ ζῶν . . . τὸ ὕδωρ ὃ ἐγὼ δώσω
αὐτῷ γενήσεται ἐν αὐτῷ πηγὴ ὕδατος
ἁλλομένου εἰς ζωὴν αἰώνιον.

Lightfoot's assertion that 'the whole passage is inspired by
the Fourth Gospel' seems to be justified, especially in view of
John 4²³ καὶ γὰρ ὁ πατὴρ τοιούτους ζητεῖ τοὺς προσκυνοῦντας αὐτόν.
Besides the close parallel quoted above, τροφῇ φθορᾶς just below
is probably suggested by John 6²⁷ τὴν βρῶσιν τὴν ἀπολλυμένην,
and ἄρτον Θεοῦ by John 6³³; cf. also 7³⁸. If we adopt the reading ζῶν ἁλλόμενον from the interpolator's text, we have another
striking parallel with John 4¹⁴: πηγὴ ὕδατος ζῶντος occurs in
Justin, *Dial.* 69. On the other side (against the Johannine
reference) it might be urged that the words about the 'living
water' may have been a well-known saying of Christ, with
which Ignatius may have been acquainted from other sources.
The words of Ignatius about the 'pleasures of this life' have
a Synoptic ring, and there is nothing corresponding to them,
nor to the remarkable phrase about ἀγάπη ἄφθαρτος as 'the
blood of Christ,' in John. Moreover, the passage in John
speaks of present advantage, Ignatius of future reward. This

CARLYLE   G

last objection is not serious; and on the whole direct literary dependence seems much the most probable hypothesis.

(99)   Philad. vii. 1.

τὸ πνεῦμα οὐ πλανᾶται, ἀπὸ Θεοῦ
ὅν' οἶδεν γὰρ πόθεν ἔρχεται καὶ ποῦ
ὑπάγει, καὶ τὰ κρυπτὰ ἐλέγχει.

John 3⁸.

τὸ πνεῦμα ὅπου θέλει πνεῖ, καὶ τὴν
φωνὴν αὐτοῦ ἀκούεις, ἀλλ' οὐκ οἶδας
πόθεν ἔρχεται καὶ ποῦ ὑπάγει.

The passage reads like an echo of the words in the Gospel, though the thought is quite different. This, however, is in Ignatius's manner. The idea in τὰ κρυπτὰ ἐλέγχει has nothing corresponding to it in the discourse to Nicodemus. The phrase πόθεν ἔρχεται recurs John 8¹⁴ and 1 John 2¹¹, in a different connexion. John 8¹⁴ (οἶδα πόθεν ἦλθον καὶ ποῦ ὑπάγω) is in some ways nearer to Ignatius than 3⁸. Both passages may have been floating in his mind.

c

(100)   Magn. vii. 1.

ὥσπερ οὖν ὁ Κύριος ἄνευ τοῦ πατρὸς οὐδὲν ἐποίησεν, . . . οὕτως μηδὲ
ὑμεῖς, &c.

Magn. viii. 2.

[Ἰησοῦς Χριστὸς] κατὰ πάντα εὐηρέ-
στησεν τῷ πέμψαντι αὐτόν.

John 8²⁸, ²⁹.

ἀπ' ἐμαυτοῦ ποιῶ οὐδέν, ἀλλὰ
καθὼς ἐδίδαξέ με ὁ πατήρ, ταῦτα
λαλῶ. καὶ ὁ πέμψας με μετ' ἐμοῦ
ἐστιν· οὐκ ἀφῆκέ με μόνον, ὅτι τὰ
ἀρεστὰ αὐτῷ ποιῶ πάντοτε.

This parallel is much strengthened by the *double* reminiscence.

d

(101) Eph. v. 2 and Rom. 7³.
ἄρτος τοῦ Θεοῦ.

John 6³³.
ἄρτος τοῦ Θεοῦ.

(102)   Eph. vi. 1.
πάντα γὰρ ὃν πέμπει, &c.
See above on Matt. 10⁴⁰ (83).

John 13²⁰.

(103)   Eph. xvii. 1.
μύρον ἔλαβεν, &c.

John 12 ff.

Some commentators (e. g. Zahn and Lightfoot) have argued that this passage shows knowledge of John's Gospel as well as of Matthew's, because of the mention of the *fragrance* of the ointment (ἡ δὲ οἰκία ἐπληρώθη, &c.); but this can hardly be pressed: see (85). Similarly, τοῦ ἄρχοντος τοῦ αἰῶνος τούτου need not imply knowledge of John 16¹¹, for St. Paul (1 Cor. 2⁶, ⁸) has the same phrase. The dominant thought in Ignatius is that the Church, as the Body of Christ, has a share in the anointing of the Head. Cf. Origen, c. Celsum, vi. 79, for the same idea.

(104)   Philad. ix. 1.   John 10⁹.

αὐτὸς ὢν θύρα τοῦ πατρός.

Cf. also John 14⁶ and Apoc. 3⁸. The Johannine doctrine of the pre-incarnate activity of the Logos is emphasized by Ignatius in this sentence. Compare his words about Abraham, &c., with John 8⁵⁶. Besides the word θύρα, compare Ignatius's εἰσέρχονται and σωτῆρος with John's εἰσέλθῃ and σωθήσεται. But the metaphor of the Door occurs also in Hermas; and in John 10⁹ there is no reference to 'drawing' to the Father, nor to the Old Testament saints (as in Ignatius's next line). John 14⁶ would have been more to the purpose, if Ignatius had wished to quote the Fourth Gospel here.

Ignatius's use of the Fourth Gospel is highly probable, but falls some way short of certainty. The objections to accepting it are mainly (1) our ignorance how far some of the Logia of Christ recorded by John may have been current in Asia Minor before the publication of the Gospel. If they formed part of the Apostle's oral teaching, they must have been familiar to his disciples, and may have been collected and written down long before our Gospel was composed. (2) The paucity of phrases which recall the language of the Gospel, and the absence of direct appeals to it; phenomena which are certainly remarkable when we consider the close resemblance between the theology of Ignatius and that of the Fourth Gospel. It is difficult, for example, to think of any reason why Ignatius did not quote John 20 in Smyrn. iii. 2 (93).

(IV) Apocryphal Gospels.

See under (92), for possible use of Gospel according to the Hebrews.

THE EPISTLE OF POLYCARP

INTRODUCTION.

Standard of Accuracy in Quotation. Very little help can be gained from Polycarp's use of O. T., as the number of cases in which he can be proved to have made use of O. T. is small. The clearest case of a quotation is from Tobit 12⁹ ἐλεημοσύνη ἐκ θανάτου ῥύεται (Polycarp. x. 2 'eleemosyna de morte liberat'). In Polycarp xi. 2 ('qui ignorant iudicium domini') there seems undoubtedly to be a reference to Jer. 5⁴ (οὐκ ἔγνωσαν ὁδὸν Κυρίου καὶ κρίσιν Θεοῦ), and the freedom of the quotation deserves notice. There are many places where the language of O. T. may have influenced Polycarp, but the quotations, if they are such, are generally allusive and worked into the structure of the writer's sentences. Polycarp's use of O. T. is in fact very similar in its general phenomena to his use of those parts of N. T. on which he relies most frequently.

In his undoubted quotations from N. T. we find that, while short collections of words are sometimes repeated exactly, in longer passages the order is treated very freely, omissions occur for which no reason can be assigned, and the spirit rather than the actual words is sometimes reproduced. The quotations have the appearance of having been made from memory; rarely, if ever, from a book.

The following *formulae of citation* may be mentioned:—

(i) εἰδότες ὅτι: see Galatians (31), Ephesians (36), 1 Timothy (48), Gospels (82).

(ii) καθὼς εἶπεν ὁ Κύριος: see Gospels (77).

(iii) μνημονεύοντες ὧν εἶπεν ὁ Κύριος διδάσκων: see Gospels (75).

(iv) 'sicut Paulus docet': see 1 Corinthians (2).

(v) 'ut his scripturis dictum est': see Ephesians (37).

A

1 *Corinthians*

a

(1)   Pol. v. 3.   1 Cor. 6⁹.

οὔτε πόρνοι οὔτε μαλακοὶ οὔτε ἀρσε-   οὔτε πόρνοι, οὔτε εἰδωλολάτραι,
νοκοῖται βασιλείαν Θεοῦ κληρονομή-   οὔτε μοιχοί, οὔτε μαλακοί, οὔτε ἀρσενο-
σουσιν, οὔτε οἱ ποιοῦντες τὰ ἄτοπα.   κοῖται, οὔτε κλέπται, οὔτε πλεονέκται,
                            οὐ μέθυσοι, οὐ λοίδοροι, οὐχ ἅρπαγες,
                            βασιλείαν Θεοῦ κληρονομήσουσιν.

These passages agree verbally, except for omissions in Polycarp. The last words cited from Polycarp suggest that he may have been conscious of making omissions in his quotation, but these omissions do not appear to proceed on any fixed principle, and the quotation was probably therefore made from memory. On the other hand, it seems impossible to doubt that the passage in 1 Corinthians is the source of Polycarp's words.

(2)   Pol. xi. 2.   1 Cor. 6².

'aut nescimus quia sancti   ἢ οὐκ οἴδατε ὅτι οἱ ἅγιοι τὸν κόσμον
mundum iudicabunt?   sicut   κρινοῦσιν,
Paulus docet.'

The reference to St. Paul by name makes Polycarp's use of 1 Corinthians practically certain, though it occurs in a part of the letter for which the Latin version alone is extant.

                               c

(3)   Pol. iii. 2, 3.   1 Cor. 13¹³.

τὴν δοθεῖσαν ὑμῖν πίστιν ... ἐπα-   νυνὶ δὲ μένει πίστις, ἐλπίς, ἀγάπη,
κολουθούσης τῆς ἐλπίδος, προαγούσης   τὰ τρία ταῦτα· μείζων δὲ τούτων ἡ
τῆς ἀγάπης.   ἀγάπη.

The collocation of 'faith, hope, love,' occurs elsewhere in St. Paul (1 Thess. 1³; Col. 1⁴,⁵), but 1 Cor. 13 is the chief passage, and the order there is the same as in Polycarp.

                            d

(4)   Pol. iii. 2.   1 Cor. 8¹⁰.

οἰκοδομεῖσθαι εἰς τὴν δοθεῖσαν ὑμῖν   οἰκοδομηθήσεται εἰς τὸ τὰ εἰδωλό-
πίστιν.   θυτα ἐσθίειν.

    Pol. xi. 4.

'hoc enim agentes, vos ipsos   1 Cor. 14¹⁰.
aedificatis.'   ὁ λαλῶν γλώσσῃ ἑαυτὸν οἰκοδομεῖ.

    Pol. xii. 2.

'aedificet vos in fide et veritate.'

οἰκοδομεῖν is a commoner word in 1 Corinthians than elsewhere in N. T.; outside Polycarp, on the other hand, it does not occur in the Apostolic Fathers.

(5)   Pol. iv. 3.   1 Cor. 14²⁵.

οὔτε τι τῶν κρυπτῶν τῆς καρδίας.   τὰ κρυπτὰ τῆς καρδίας cf. 4⁵.

See also Rom. 2¹⁵, ¹⁶.

(6)   Pol. x. 1.   1 Cor. 15⁵⁸.   Col. 1²³.

'firmi in fide et   ἑδραῖοι γίνεσθε, ἀμε-   εἴ γε ἐπιμένετε τῇ
immutabiles.'   τακίνητοι.   πίστει τεθεμελιωμένοι
                                                καὶ ἑδραῖοι καὶ μὴ μετα-
                                                κινούμενοι.

The parallel with Colossians is verbally stronger, as τῇ
πίστει does not occur in 1 Corinthians; but the order is that
of 1 Corinthians, and the evidence for Polycarp's use of
Colossians is weak (see under Colossians).

(7)   Pol. xi. 4.   1 Cor. 12²⁶.

'sicut passibilia membra et   εἴτε πάσχει ἐν μέλος, συμπάσχει
errantia eos revocate.'   πάντα τὰ μέλη.

It is possible that *passibilia* contains an allusion to the
metaphor of 1 Corinthians. See also 1 Peter (17).

(8)   Pol. ii. 1.   1 Cor. 15²⁸.

ᾧ ὑπετάγη τὰ πάντα ἐπουράνια   ὅταν δὲ ὑποταγῇ αὐτῷ τὰ πάντα.
καὶ ἐπίγεια.

This parallelism is too weak to be classed. See also
Philippians (42).

In view of the fact that Polycarp's use of 1 Corinthians
may be regarded as certain, the small amount of verifiable
influence from 1 Corinthians is worthy of notice.

1 *Peter*   a
(9)   Pol. i. 3.   1 Pet. 1⁸.

εἰς ὃν οὐκ ἰδόντες πιστεύετε χαρᾷ   ὃν οὐκ ἰδόντες ἀγαπᾶτε, εἰς ὃν ἄρτι
ἀνεκλαλήτῳ καὶ δεδοξασμένῃ.   μὴ ὁρῶντες πιστεύοντες δὲ ἀγαλλιᾶσθε
                                    χαρᾷ ἀνεκλαλήτῳ καὶ δεδοξασμένῃ.

1 Peter is almost certainly presupposed by Polycarp here,
but the points of difference between the passages are instruc-
tive for Polycarp's method of quotation.

(10) Pol. viii. 1, 2.   1 Pet. 2²¹.   Isa. 53⁹.

ὃς ἀπήνεγκεν ἡμῶν τὰς   ἔπαθεν ὑπὲρ ὑμῶν,   ὅτι ἀνομίαν οὐκ ἐποίη-
ἀμαρτίας τῷ ἰδίῳ σώματι   ὑμῖν ὑπολιμπάνων ὑπο-   σεν οὐδὲ δόλον [v. l.
ἐπὶ τὸ ξύλον, ὃς ἁμαρ-   γραμμὸν ... ὃς ἁμαρτίαν   εὑρέθη δόλος] ἐν τῷ
τίαν οὐκ ἐποίησεν, οὔτε   οὐκ ἐποίησεν, οὐδὲ εὑρέθη   στόματι αὐτοῦ.
εὑρέθη δόλος ἐν τῷ   δόλος ἐν τῷ στόματι
στόματι αὐτοῦ· ἀλλὰ δι'   αὐτοῦ ... ὃς τὰς
ἡμᾶς, ἵνα ζήσωμεν ἐν   ἁμαρτίας ἡμῶν αὐτὸς

αὐτῷ, πάντα ὑπέμεινεν.
... καὶ ἐὰν πάσχωμεν
διὰ τὸ ὄνομα αὐτοῦ, δοξ-
άζωμεν αὐτόν. τοῦτον
γὰρ ἡμῖν τὸν ὑπογραμμὸν
ἔθηκε.

ἀνήνεγκεν ἐν τῷ σώματι
αὐτοῦ ἐπὶ τὸ ξύλον, ἵνα
ταῖς ἁμαρτίαις ἀπογενό-
μενοι τῇ δικαιοσύνῃ ζή-
σωμεν.
4¹⁶ εἰ δὲ ὡς Χριστι-
ανός, μὴ αἰσχυνέσθω,
δοξαζέτω δὲ τὸν Θεὸν ἐν
τῷ ὀνόματι τούτῳ.

The whole of this passage is very strongly Petrine, and it will be noticed that all the parallel passages in 1 Peter (except one) come from the same context. In the place where 1 Peter is dependent on Isaiah (as quoted above), Polycarp seems clearly to be dependent on 1 Peter. At the same time, the variations of order and the occasional verbal differences should be noticed; but there is a striking identity of thought, even where the form is different.

(11)   Pol. x. 2.

'omnes vobis invicem subiecti estote, conversationem vestram irreprehensibilem habentes in gentibus, ut ex bonis operibus vestris et vos laudem accipiatis et Dominus in vobis non blasphemetur.'

1 Pet. 2¹².

τὴν ἀναστροφὴν ὑμῶν ἐν τοῖς ἔθνεσιν ἔχοντες καλήν, ἵνα ἐν ᾧ καταλαλοῦσιν ὑμῶν ὡς κακοποιῶν, ἐκ τῶν καλῶν ἔργων ἐποπτεύοντες δοξάσωσιν τῷ Θεῷ ἐν ἡμέρᾳ ἐπισκοπῆς. ὑποτάγητε πάσῃ ἀνθρωπίνῃ κτίσει διὰ τὸν Κύριον.
5⁵ πάντες δὲ ἀλλήλοις [ὑποτάγητε].

The second clause in the passage quoted from Polycarp seems to be a certain quotation from 1 Peter, and the unconscious change implied by the word *irreprehensibilem* is therefore to be noticed.

These three passages (9) (10) (11), taken together, strengthen each other, and justify the inclusion of all three in the first class.

b

(12)   Pol. ii. 1.

διὸ ἀναζωσάμενοι τὰς ὀσφύας δουλεύσατε τῷ Θεῷ ἐν φόβῳ καὶ ἀληθείᾳ,
... πιστεύσαντες εἰς τὸν ἐγείραντα τὸν Κύριον ἡμῶν Ἰησοῦν Χριστὸν ἐκ νεκρῶν καὶ δόντα αὐτῷ δόξαν.

1 Pet. 1¹³.

διὸ ἀναζωσάμενοι τὰς ὀσφύας τῆς διανοίας ὑμῶν, νήφοντες, τελείως ἐλπίσατε κτλ.

1 Pet. 1²¹.

τοὺς δι' αὐτοῦ πιστοὺς εἰς Θεὸν τὸν ἐγείραντα αὐτὸν ἐκ νεκρῶν καὶ δόξαν αὐτῷ δόντα.

It may be noticed that these two pairs of passages, which agree closely, follow each other in the same order in Polycarp and 1 Peter. In the first passage, Polycarp appears to conflate a passage from 1 Peter with Ps. 2¹¹ : see Lightfoot, ad loc.

(13)   Pol. ii. 2.

μὴ ἀποδιδόντες κακὸν ἀντὶ κακοῦ ἢ λοιδορίαν ἀντὶ λοιδορίας ἢ γρόνθον ἀντὶ γρόνθου ἢ κατάραν ἀντὶ κατάρας.

1 Pet. 3⁹.

μὴ ἀποδιδόντες κακὸν ἀντὶ κακοῦ ἢ λοιδορίαν ἀντὶ λοιδορίας.

This is almost certainly a quotation from 1 Peter, but the possibility cannot be excluded that both Polycarp and 1 Peter are quoting a proverb in the part common to them. Polycarp's method of continuing the quotation by additions of his own is worth notice.

(14)   Pol v. 3.

καλὸν γὰρ τὸ ἀνακόπτεσθαι ἀπὸ τῶν ἐπιθυμιῶν ἐν τῷ κόσμῳ, ὅτι πᾶσα ἐπιθυμία κατὰ τοῦ πνεύματος στρατεύεται.

1 Pet. 2¹¹.

ἀπέχεσθαι τῶν σαρκικῶν ἐπιθυμιῶν, αἵτινες στρατεύονται κατὰ τῆς ψυχῆς.

Gal. 5¹⁷.

ἡ γὰρ σὰρξ ἐπιθυμεῖ κατὰ τοῦ πνεύματος.

It is highly probable that this is a quotation from 1 Peter, in view of the use of στρατεύεται, a word of strong colouring. A fusion with Gal. 5¹⁷ (34) may be responsible for κατὰ τοῦ πνεύματος.

(15)   Pol. vii. 2.

νήφοντες πρὸς τὰς εὐχάς.

Pol. xi. 4.

'sobrii ergo estote.'

1 Pet. 4⁷.

νήψατε εἰς προσευχάς.

The expression in vii. 2 is so striking, that it is very probably a quotation.

d

(16)   Pol. i. 3.

εἰς ἣν πολλοὶ ἐπιθυμοῦσιν εἰσελθεῖν.

1 Pet. 1¹².

εἰς ἃ ἐπιθυμοῦσιν ἄγγελοι παρακύψαι.

Polycarp may possibly be influenced by 1 Peter here, as his words follow immediately the certain quotation (9), while the words in 1 Peter follow the words cited from that Epistle under (9) after a short interval.

(17)   Pol. vi. 1.

ἐπιστρέφοντες τὰ ἀποπεπλανημένα.

Pol. xi. 4.

'sicut passibilia membra et errantia eos revocate.'

1 Pet. 2²⁵.

ἦτε γὰρ ὡς πρόβατα πλανώμενοι, ἀλλ' ἐπεστράφητε νῦν.

Ezek. 34⁴.

τὸ πλανώμενον οὐκ ἐπεστρέψατε (v. l. ἀπεστρέψατε).

As Polycarp cannot be proved to have made much use of O. T., it is possible that 1 Peter has influenced these passages. The word *passibilia* may be due to 1 Cor. 12²⁶ ; see 1 Corinthians (7).

(18) Pol. vi. 3.	1 Pet. 3¹³.	Titus 2¹⁴.
ζηλωταὶ περὶ τὸ καλόν.	τοῦ ἀγαθοῦ ζηλωταί.	ζηλωτὴν καλῶν ἔργων.

This is a possible case of influence, but the expression is not striking or distinctive enough to make the inference necessary.

(19) Pol. xii. 2.	1 Pet. 1²¹.	Rom. 4²⁴, 10⁹ ;
'qui credituri sunt in Dominum nostrum et Deum Iesum Christum et in ipsius patrem qui resuscitavit eum a mortuis.'	quoted under (12).	Gal. 1¹ ; Col. 2¹², &c.

The idea is too common in early Christian liteɪature to be assigned to any one source; but as this passage of 1 Peter has almost certainly influenced Polycarp in another place (12), it may also have influenced him here.

(20) Pol. v. 2, vi. 1.	1 Pet. 3⁸.	Eph. 4³².
εὔσπλαγχνοι.	εὔσπλαγχνοι.	

In these passages the word means 'tender-hearted,' whereas its classical sense is 'brave'; but no inference can be drawn from this, as the meaning 'tender-hearted' seems to be fairly common in later Greek (cf., e.g., Test. xii Patr. *Zeb.* 5, 8, 9).

B

Romans	b	
(21) Pol. vi. 2.	Rom. 14¹⁰, ¹².	2 Cor. 5¹⁰.
πάντας δεῖ παραστῆναι τῷ βήματι τοῦ Χριστοῦ, καὶ ἕκαστον ὑπὲρ ἑαυτοῦ λόγον δοῦναι.	πάντες γὰρ παραστησόμεθα τῷ βήματι τοῦ Θεοῦ (v. l. Χριστοῦ) . . . ἄρα οὖν ἕκαστος ἡμῶν περὶ ἑαυτοῦ λόγον δώσει τῷ Θεῷ.	τοὺς γὰρ πάντας ἡμᾶς φανερωθῆναι δεῖ ἔμπροσθεν τοῦ βήματος τοῦ Χριστοῦ ἵνα κομίσηται ἕκαστος τὰ διὰ τοῦ σώματος πρὸς ἃ ἔπραξεν, εἴτε ἀγαθὸν εἴτε φαῦλον.

This passage is very probably influenced by Romans, but there may be unconscious conflation with 2 Corinthians. The chief points of connexion between Polycarp and 2 Corinthians are in the word δεῖ and in τοῦ Χριστοῦ (which is not found in any early text of this passage in Romans). But the latter alteration might have been introduced by Polycarp himself, and the case for Romans is decidedly stronger than that for 2 Corinthians.

d

(22)   Pol. iv. 1.   Rom. 13¹².   2 Cor. 6⁷.

ὁπλισώμεθα τοῖς ὅ-   ἐνδυσώμεθα δὲ τὰ ὅπλα   διὰ τῶν ὅπλων τῆς δι-
πλοις τῆς δικαιοσύνης.   τοῦ φωτός.   καιοσύνης. Cf. also
                        6¹³ ὅπλα δικαιοσύνης.   Eph. 6¹³.

This passage is certainly influenced by Pauline metaphors. It suggests the reference to Romans, but not much stress can be laid upon this.

(23)   Pol. iii. 3.   Rom. 13⁸.

προαγούσης τῆς ἀγάπης τῆς εἰς Θεὸν   μηδενὶ μηδὲν ὀφείλετε, εἰ μὴ τὸ
καὶ Χριστὸν καὶ εἰς τὸν πλησίον. ἐὰν   ἀγαπᾶν ἀλλήλους. ὁ γὰρ ἀγαπῶν
γάρ τις τούτων ἐντὸς ᾖ, πεπλήρωκεν   τὸν ἕτερον νόμον πεπλήρωκε. τὸ
ἐντολὴν δικαιοσύνης.   γὰρ . . . ἐν τούτῳ τῷ λόγῳ ἀνακε-
                                        φαλαιοῦται, ἐν τῷ ἀγαπήσεις τὸν
                                        πλησίον σου ὡς ἑαυτόν. ἡ ἀγάπη
                                        τῷ πλησίον κακὸν οὐκ ἐργάζεται·
                                        πλήρωμα οὖν νόμου ἡ ἀγάπη.

Gal. 5¹⁴ ὁ γὰρ πᾶς νόμος ἐν ἑνὶ λόγῳ πεπλήρωται, ἐν τῷ ἀγαπήσεις τὸν πλησίον σου ὡς σεαυτόν.

Possibly a reminiscence of Rom. 13⁸, which, as being a more fully developed passage than Gal. 5¹⁴, is more probably the source of Polycarp's words than the latter.

(24)   Pol. ix. 2.   Rom. 8¹⁷.

εἰς τὸν ὀφειλόμενον αὐτοῖς τόπον   εἴπερ συμπάσχομεν, ἵνα καὶ συν-
εἰσὶ παρὰ τῷ Κυρίῳ, ᾧ καὶ συνέπαθον.   δοξασθῶμεν.

In view of the context, this should rather be treated as dependent on 2 Tim. 2¹¹, see (56).

(25)   Pol. x. 1.   Rom. 12¹⁰.

'fraternitatis amatores, dili-   τῇ φιλαδελφίᾳ εἰς ἀλλήλους φιλό-
gentes invicem . . . mansuetu-   στοργοι, τῇ τιμῇ ἀλλήλους προηγού-
dine Domini alterutri praesto-   μενοι.
lantes.'

Lightfoot's reconstruction of the Greek (see his note) gives the best explanation of the passage in Polycarp yet brought forward; this reconstruction involves a reference to Romans, but too much stress ought not to be laid on what after all remains a conjecture.

2 *Corinthians*　　　　**b**
(26)　　Pol. ii. 2.　　　　　2 Cor. 4¹⁴.

ὁ δὲ ἐγείρας αὐτὸν ἐκ νεκρῶν καὶ　εἰδότες ὅτι ὁ ἐγείρας τὸν Κύριον
ἡμᾶς ἐγερεῖ.　　　　　'Ιησοῦν καὶ ἡμᾶς σὺν 'Ιησοῦ ἐγερεῖ.

The resemblance between these two passages is not verbally exact, and the idea contained in them may have become a Christian commonplace. The fact that God is described as ὁ ἐγείρας might be accounted for by the previous section in Polycarp, but the most noticeable connexion is contained in καὶ ἡμᾶς ἐγερεῖ. On the whole, it is difficult to resist the conclusion that we have here a reminiscence of 2 Corinthians.

c
(27)　　Pol. vi. 2.　　　　　2 Cor. 5¹⁰.

See Romans (21) where the passages are quoted. Probably Polycarp is thinking primarily of Rom. 14¹⁰, but has unconsciously been influenced by 2 Cor. 5¹⁰ also.

d
(28) Pol. v. 1.　　2 Cor. 8²¹.　　Prov. 3⁴.　　Rom. 12¹⁷.

προνοοῦντες ἀεὶ　προνοοῦμεν γὰρ　καὶ προνοοῦ καλὰ　προνοούμενοι καλὰ
τοῦ καλοῦ ἐνώπιον　καλὰ οὐ μόνον ἐνώ-　ἐνώπιον Κυρίου καὶ　ἐνώπιον πάντων ἀν-
Θεοῦ καὶ ἀνθρώπων.　πιον Κυρίου, ἀλλὰ καὶ　ἀνθρώπων.　θρώπων.
　　　　ἐνώπιον ἀνθρώπων.

The parallel to 2 Corinthians is closer than that to Romans, as the latter omits the characteristic words Θεοῦ (Κυρίου) καί. But as the passage in St. Paul is dependent on Proverbs, no stress can be laid on the resemblance, for Polycarp may be also thinking of Proverbs, though the number of passages in which he can be proved to have made use of O. T. is small.

(29)　　Pol. xi. 3.　　　　　2 Cor. 3².

'qui estis in principio epi-　ἡ ἐπιστολὴ ἡμῶν ὑμεῖς ἐστε.
stulae eius.'

If Lightfoot's interpretation of the Latin version is correct (see his note), the reference to 2 Corinthians seems certain; but the interpretation cannot be regarded as probable (see Harnack in *T. u. U.* xx. 2. 91).

(30) Pol. iii. 2 Παύλου, ὃς γενόμενος ἐν ὑμῖν κατὰ πρόσωπον τῶν τότε ἀνθρώπων ἐδίδαξεν, . . . ὃς καὶ ἀπὼν ὑμῖν ἔγραψεν ἐπιστολάς.

No stress can be laid on the very slight resemblance of this passage to 2 Cor. 10¹.

Galatians   **b**

(31)   Pol. v. 1.   Gal. 6⁷.

εἰδότες οὖν ὅτι Θεὸς οὐ μυκτηρίζεται.   μὴ πλανᾶσθε.   Θεὸς οὐ μυκτη-
                                                          ρίζεται.

There is no doubt that the words in Polycarp are a quotation, especially in view of the formula εἰδότες ὅτι which
introduces them. They also occur in a very Pauline context.
No real parallel for Θεὸς οὐ μυκτηρίζεται appears to be known,
and it is therefore highly probable that Polycarp is dependent
on Galatians. But the possibility cannot be excluded that
the words may be a quotation in Galatians also (μὴ πλανᾶσθε
perhaps suggests this inference), and that Polycarp may be
dependent on the lost source.

(32)   Pol. iii. 3.   Gal. 4²⁶.

πίστιν· ἥτις ἐστὶν μήτηρ πάντων   ἡ δὲ ἄνω Ἰερουσαλὴμ ἐλευθέρα ἐστίν,
ἡμῶν.   ἥτις ἐστὶν μήτηρ [πάντων] ἡμῶν.

It is highly probable that this is a quotation, though the
word πάντων appears to have been inserted in the later texts
of Galatians through the influence of the passage in Polycarp.
The application in Polycarp may well have been suggested by
the thought that the Jerusalem that is above corresponds in
Galatians to the dispensation of faith.

d

(33)   Pol. iii. 3.   Gal. 5¹⁴.

See under Romans (23), which is more likely to be the
source of the common matter.

(34)   Pol. v. 3.   Gal. 5¹⁷.

πᾶσα ἐπιθυμία κατὰ τοῦ πνεύματος   ἡ γὰρ σὰρξ ἐπιθυμεῖ κατὰ τοῦ πνεύ-
στρατεύεται.   ματος.

See under 1 Peter (14). The passage in Galatians may have
influenced the quotation.

(35)   Pol. ix. 2.   Gal. 2².

οὗτοι πάντες οὐκ εἰς κενὸν ἔδραμον.   μή πως εἰς κενὸν τρέχω ἢ ἔδραμον.

See under Philippians (41).

Ephesians   **b**

(36)   Pol. i. 3.   Eph. 2⁸.

εἰδότες ὅτι χάριτί ἐστε σεσωσμένοι,   τῇ γὰρ χάριτί ἐστε σεσωσμένοι διὰ
οὐκ ἐξ ἔργων, ἀλλὰ θελήματι Θεοῦ διὰ   πίστεως· καὶ τοῦτο οὐκ ἐξ ὑμῶν, Θεοῦ
Ἰησοῦ Χριστοῦ.   τὸ δῶρον· οὐκ ἐξ ἔργων, ἵνα μή τις
                                                   καυχήσηται.

The words εἰδότες ὅτι seem to imply a consciousness in Polycarp that he is making a quotation, the two passages agree verbally, except for the absence in Polycarp of some unessential words ; and it is to be noted that the sharp Pauline antithesis of faith and works is not characteristic of the Apostolic Fathers generally.

(37) Pol. xii. 1.	Eph. 4²⁶.	Ps. 4⁵.
'modo, ut his scripturis dictum est, Irascimini et nolite peccare, et Sol non occidat super iracundiam vestram.'	ὀργίζεσθε καὶ μὴ ἁμαρτάνετε· ὁ ἥλιος μὴ ἐπιδυέτω ἐπὶ παροργισμῷ ὑμῶν.	ὀργίζεσθε καὶ μὴ ἁμαρτάνετε.

Except for the insertion of *et* between the two clauses, Polycarp agrees verbally (if the Latin version can be trusted) with Ephesians. The passage in Ephesians consists in a quotation from Ps. 4⁵ and a comment on it by St. Paul (cf. Deut. 24¹³ ἀποδώσεις τὸ ἐνέχυρον αὐτοῦ πρὸς δυσμὰς ἡλίου, 24¹⁵ οὐκ ἐπιδύσεται ὁ ἥλιος ἐπ' αὐτῷ, Jer. 15⁹). Even if St. Paul's comment is influenced by these passages in Deuteronomy, the collocation of the two passages in Polycarp is almost certainly due to Ephesians. The words *his scripturis* and *et* may imply that Polycarp regards himself as making two separate quotations, but the second of the two can hardly be other than from Ephesians. The supposition that St. Paul and Polycarp are quoting a common proverb (e. g. Plut. *Mor.* 488 b, as quoted by Lightfoot) seems to be excluded by *his scripturis*.

c

(38) Pol. xi. 2.	Eph. 5⁵.	Col. 3⁵.
'si quis non se abstinuerit ab avaritia, ab idololatria coinquinabitur.'	πλεονέκτης, ὅ ἐστιν εἰδωλολάτρης.	τὴν πλεονεξίαν, ἥτις ἐστὶν εἰδωλολατρεία.

There certainly seems to be a reference in Polycarp to one of these two passages, although ideas of this kind may have been Christian commonplaces. The words in Colossians are nearer to those in Polycarp, but as the evidence is inadequate for Polycarp's use of Colossians elsewhere, the passage in Ephesians ought probably to be preferred here.

(39)   Pol. xii. 3.   d   Eph. 6¹⁸.

' pro omnibus sanctis orate.'   προσευχόμενοι ὑπὲρ πάντων τῶν
                                   ἁγίων.

The idea here is very obvious, but there may be a reminiscence of language.

Philippians

(40) Pol. iii. 2 ὃς καὶ ἀπὼν ὑμῖν ἔγραψεν ἐπιστολάς.

This passage shows that Polycarp knew that St. Paul had
written letters to the Philippians (or possibly, a letter : see
Lightfoot, *Philippians*, p. 138).   It is highly probable that he
knew the extant letter ; but the amount of evidence of his use
of it is not large, though it must be added that the general
impression in favour of his acquaintance with it is stronger
than can be fairly estimated from the isolated examination of
single passages.

b

(41)   Pol. ix 2.   Phil. 2¹⁶.   Gal. 2².

ὅτι οὗτοι πάντες οὐκ εἰς   ὅτι οὐκ εἰς κενὸν   μή πως εἰς κενὸν τρέχω
κενὸν ἔδραμον.   ἔδραμον.   ἢ ἔδραμον.

Besides the verbal parallel, the context in Polycarp, referring
to life in the prospect of death, suggests the context in Philippians, while the general meaning of Galatians is different.

c

(42)   Pol. ii. 1.   Phil. 2¹⁰.

ᾧ ὑπετάγη τὰ πάντα ἐπουράνια καὶ   ἵνα ἐν τῷ ὀνόματι Ἰησοῦ πᾶν γόνυ
ἐπίγεια, . . . οὗ τὸ αἷμα ἐκζητήσει ἀπὸ   κάμψῃ ἐπουρανίων καὶ ἐπιγείων καὶ
τῶν ἀπειθούντων αὐτῷ.   καταχθονίων.

                                     3²¹ ὑποτάξαι αὐτῷ τὰ πάντα.

As the context in Polycarp shows clearly that the passage
refers to Christ, it is likely that he is dependent on Philippians.

(43)   Pol. xii. 3.   Phil. 3¹⁸.

' et pro inimicis crucis.'   τοὺς ἐχθροὺς τοῦ σταυροῦ τοῦ
                                   Χριστοῦ.

The expression is sufficiently striking to make it probable
that Polycarp is thinking of the passage in Philippians.

d

(44)   Pol. i. 1. ˙   Phil. 2¹⁷.

συνεχάρην ὑμῖν μεγάλως ἐν Κυρίῳ   χαίρω καὶ συγχαίρω πᾶσιν ὑμῖν.
ἡμῶν Ἰησοῦ Χριστῷ.   4¹⁰ ἐχάρην δὲ ἐν Κυρίῳ μεγάλως ὅτι . . .

Compare 2 Thessalonians (46).

(45) Pol. v. 2.

ἐὰν πολιτευσώμεθα
ἀξίως αὐτοῦ.

Phil. 1²⁷.

μόνον ἀξίως τοῦ
εὐαγγελίου τοῦ Χριστοῦ
πολιτεύεσθε.

1 Clem. xxi. 1.

ἐὰν μὴ ἀξίως αὐτοῦ
πολιτευόμενοι τὰ καλὰ
καὶ εὐάρεστα ἐνώπιον
αὐτοῦ ποιῶμεν.

Polycarp may here be thinking of the passage in Clement.
Cf. Clement (40).

2 *Thessalonians*.   b

(46)   Pol. xi. 3.

'ego autem nihil tale sensi
in vobis vel audivi, in quibus
laboravit beatus Paulus, qui
estis in principio epistulae eius :
de vobis etenim gloriatur in
omnibus ecclesiis.'

2 Thess. 1⁴.

ὥστε αὐτοὺς ἡμᾶς ἐν ὑμῖν ἐγκαυ-
χᾶσθαι ἐν ταῖς ἐκκλησίαις τοῦ Θεοῦ.

The context shows that Polycarp supposes himself to be
quoting words addressed to the Philippians (cf. *etenim*).
Similar words actually occur only in 2 Thessalonians, an
Epistle addressed to another Macedonian Church, which Polycarp might easily have thought of, by a lapse of memory, as
sent to the Philippians. The present tense of *gloriatur* also
suggests that he is quoting.

c

(47)   Pol. xi. 4.

'et non sicut inimicos tales
existimetis.'

2 Thess. 3¹⁵.

καὶ μὴ ὡς ἐχθρὸν ἡγεῖσθε, ἀλλὰ
νουθετεῖτε ὡς ἀδελφόν.

Polycarp's words sound as though he had purposely adapted
the expression of 2 Thessalonians for his own object.

In spite of the fact that both these passages occur in the
part of Polycarp for which the Latin version alone is extant,
his use of 2 Thessalonians appears to be very probable.

1 *Timothy*   b

(48)   Pol. iv. 1.

ἀρχὴ δὲ πάντων χαλεπῶν φιλαργυρία. εἰδότες οὖν ὅτι οὐδὲν εἰσηνέγκαμεν εἰς τὸν κόσμον, ἀλλ' οὐδὲ
ἐξενεγκεῖν τι ἔχομεν.

1 Tim. 6⁷.

οὐδὲν γὰρ εἰσηνέγκαμεν εἰς τὸν
κόσμον, ὅτι οὐδὲ ἐξενεγκεῖν τι δυνάμεθα.

1 Tim. 6¹⁰.

ῥίζα γὰρ πάντων τῶν κακῶν ἐστιν ἡ
φιλαργυρία.

It is almost impossible to believe that these passages are
independent. The formula (εἰδότες ὅτι) with which Polycarp
introduces the second of the two sentences, indicates that he

is conscious of quoting and points to the priority of 1 Timothy. The word οὖν may perhaps show that reference is being made to a well-known source, and that the one quotation has suggested the other. It may further be noted that ἀρχή is less vivid than ῥίζα; this also points to the priority of 1 Timothy.

c

(49) Pol. iv. 3.	1 Tim. 5⁵.

(49)   Pol. iv. 3.

τὰς χήρας σωφρονούσας περὶ τὴν τοῦ Κυρίου πίστιν, ἐντυγχανούσας ἀδιαλείπτως περὶ πάντων, μακρὰν οὔσας πάσης διαβολῆς.

ἡ δὲ ὄντως χήρα καὶ μεμονωμένη ἤλπικεν ἐπὶ θεὸν καὶ προσμένει ταῖς δεήσεσιν καὶ ταῖς προσευχαῖς νυκτὸς καὶ ἡμέρας.

(50)   Pol. v. 2.

1 Tim. 3⁸.

ὁμοίως διάκονοι ἄμεμπτοι κατενώπιον αὐτοῦ τῆς δικαιοσύνης. ... μὴ διάβολοι, μὴ δίλογοι, ἀφιλάργυροι, ἐγκρατεῖς περὶ πάντα, εὐσπλαγχνοι, ἐπιμελεῖς, πορευόμενοι κατὰ τὴν ἀλήθειαν τοῦ Κυρίου.

διακόνους ὡσαύτως σεμνούς, μὴ διλόγους, μὴ οἴνῳ πολλῷ προσέχοντας, μὴ αἰσχροκερδεῖς, ἔχοντας τὸ μυστήριον τῆς πίστεως ἐν καθαρᾷ συνειδήσει ... εἶτα διακονείτωσαν ἀνέγκλητοι ὄντες. γυναῖκας ὡσαύτως σεμνάς, μὴ διαβόλους, νηφαλίους, πιστὰς ἐν πᾶσιν.

In these passages the general character of thought and treatment is very similar, and there are a considerable number of verbal parallels.

(51)   Pol. viii. 1.

1 Tim. 1¹.

προσκαρτερῶμεν τῇ ἐλπίδι ἡμῶν καὶ τῷ ἀρραβῶνι τῆς δικαιοσύνης ἡμῶν, ὅς ἐστι Χριστὸς Ἰησοῦς.

Χριστοῦ Ἰησοῦ τῆς ἐλπίδος ἡμῶν.

The unusual order Χριστὸς Ἰησοῦς is to be noted: it does not seem to occur elsewhere in Polycarp, and is not found in the passages of Ignatius which are general parallels (*Magn.* 11; *Trall.* Inscr., 2).

(52)   Pol. xii. 3.

1 Tim. 2¹.

'orate pro regibus.'

ποιεῖσθαι δεήσεις ... ὑπὲρ βασιλέων.

That kings and rulers were mentioned in the praises of the Church is clear from 1 Clem. lxi. The plural *regibus* is strange as applied to the Emperor, and has even suggested to some critics an argument in favour of the spuriousness of Polycarp's Epistle (Lightfoot, *Ignatius and Polycarp*, i. 592). But the later date suggested is impossible on other grounds, and the plural is most easily explained by a reference to 1 Timothy.

d

(53)   Pol. xi. 2.

1 Tim. 3⁵.

'qui autem non potest se in his gubernare, quomodo alii pronuntiat hoc?'

εἰ δέ τις τοῦ ἰδίου οἴκου προστῆναι οὐκ οἶδεν, πῶς ἐκκλησίας Θεοῦ ἐπιμελήσεται;

The language in Polycarp may be suggested by a rather weakened reminiscence of 1 Timothy.

(54)   Pol. xii. 3.

1 Tim. 4¹⁵.

'ut fructus vester manifestus sit in omnibus.'

ἵνα σου ἡ προκοπὴ φανερὰ ᾖ πᾶσιν.

Possibly a reminiscence.

2 *Timothy*

b

(55)   Pol. ix. 2.

2 Tim. 4¹⁰.

οὐ γὰρ τὸν νῦν ἠγάπησαν αἰῶνα.

ἀγαπήσας τὸν νῦν αἰῶνα.

The dependence on 2 Timothy seems almost certain, especially as ὁ νῦν αἰών occurs only in the Pastoral Epistles among the books of N. T. (cf. 1 Tim. 6¹⁷; Titus 2¹²). Besides the similarity of language, the reference in both cases is to loyalty in face of danger.

c

(56)   Pol. v. 2.

2 Tim. 2¹¹.

καθὼς ὑπέσχετο ἡμῖν ἐγεῖραι ἡμᾶς ἐκ νεκρῶν καὶ ὅτι, ἐὰν πολιτευσώμεθα ἀξίως αὐτοῦ, καὶ συμβασιλεύσομεν, εἴγε πιστεύομεν.

πιστὸς ὁ λόγος, εἰ γὰρ συναπεθάνομεν καὶ συζήσομεν, εἰ ὑπομένομεν καὶ συμβασιλεύσομεν.

Whatever may be the case with the first part of the promise referred to, the latter seems to be connected with some current λόγος (cf. ὅτι in Polycarp) like that quoted in 2 Timothy, whether directly or indirectly through that passage. The word συμβασιλεύειν is unique in the Apostolic Fathers, nor does the simple βασιλεύειν occur with the meaning here implied. The notion of continuance in the present πιστεύομεν brings it nearer in meaning to ὑπομένομεν than might at first appear, especially when taken in connexion with πολιτευσώμεθα that has preceded.

(57)   Pol. xi. 4.

2 Tim. 2²⁵.

'quibus det Dominus poenitentiam veram.'

μήποτε δῴη αὐτοῖς ὁ Θεὸς μετάνοιαν εἰς ἐπίγνωσιν ἀληθείας.

The words of Polycarp certainly recall 2 Timothy: in view

of the other evidence this should probably be regarded as
a reminiscence.

d

(58)   Pol. xii. 1.   2 Tim. 1⁵.

'quod ego credo esse in vobis.'   πέπεισμαι δὲ ὅτι καὶ ἐν σοί.

Possibly a reminiscence of language.

C

Acts   c

(59)   Pol. i. 2.   Acts 2²⁴.

ὃν ἤγειρεν ὁ Θεὸς λύσας τὰς ὠδῖνας   ὃν ὁ Θεὸς ἀνέστησεν, λύσας τὰς
τοῦ ᾅδου.   ὠδῖνας τοῦ θανάτου (ᾅδου is an early
Western variant).

ὠδῖνες θανάτου occurs in 2 Kings 22⁶ (Ps. 17⁵), Ps. 114³, and
ὠδῖνες ᾅδου in Ps. 17⁶; but the expression λύσας τὰς ὠδῖνας
depends upon a mistranslation of חבלי (='pains' or 'fetters').
It is difficult to account for the same mistake being made
wholly independently, and so it seems probable that Polycarp
is dependent on Acts. But the mistake may also be due to
an earlier writer followed both by the author of Acts and by
Polycarp, especially as we have no particular reason for
supposing the author of Acts to have been acquainted with
Hebrew.

d

(60)   Pol. ii. 1.   Acts 10⁴².

κριτὴς ζώντων καὶ νεκρῶν.   κριτὴς ζώντων καὶ νεκρῶν.

Acts 10⁴² is the only passage in N.T. where these exact
words occur, but 2 Tim. 4¹, 1 Pet. 4⁵ are closely parallel;
cf. also 2 Clem. i. 1.

(61)   Pol. ii. 3.   Acts 20³⁵.

μνημονεύοντες ὧν εἶπεν ὁ Κύριος   μνημονεύειν τε τῶν λόγων τοῦ Κυ-
διδάσκων.   ρίου Ἰησοῦ, ὅτι αὐτὸς εἶπε . . .

No stress can be laid on the use of this formula of introduction, as the words are in themselves very natural, and
1 Clem. xiii. 1 has a very similar expression (see below, under
(75)).

(62)   Pol. vi. 3.   Acts 7⁵².

οἱ προφῆται οἱ προκηρύξαντες τὴν   τίνα τῶν προφητῶν οὐκ ἐδίωξαν
ἔλευσιν τοῦ Κυρίου.   οἱ πατέρες ὑμῶν; καὶ ἀπέκτειναν τοὺς
προκαταγγείλαντας περὶ τῆς ἐλεύσεως
τοῦ δικαίου.

Possibly a reminiscence of the language of Acts.

(63)   Pol. xii. 2.

'det vobis sortem et partem
inter sanctos suos, et nobis vo-
biscum, et omnibus qui sunt
sub caelo.'

Acts 26¹⁸.

κλῆρον ἐν τοῖς ἡγιασμένοις.
8²¹ οὐκ ἐστίν σοι μερὶς οὐδὲ κλῆρος.
2⁵ ἀπὸ παντὸς ἔθνους τῶν ὑπὸ τὸν
οὐρανόν.

There seems some possibility that Polycarp is here unconsciously influenced by various expressions in Acts, though no
certainty can be felt in regard to the matter. μερὶς οὐδὲ κλῆρος
occurs in Deut. 12¹², 14²⁶, ²⁸ ; while the order of these words
in Acts and Deuteronomy is the same, Polycarp, if the Latin
version can be trusted, adopted the opposite order. For the
first clause quoted from Polycarp there is a further parallel
in Col. 1¹² (εἰς τὴν μερίδα τοῦ κλήρου τῶν ἁγίων ἐν τῷ φωτί), which
is, however, less close than the parallel in Acts : in connexion
with the last clause, Col. 1²³ (ἐν πάσῃ κτίσει τῇ ὑπὸ τὸν οὐρανόν)
may also be noted, but the phrase 'omnibus qui sunt sub
caelo' is a very obvious one.

Hebrews   **c**
(64) Pol. vi. 3.   Heb. 12²⁸.   Ps. 2¹¹.

δουλεύσωμεν   αὐτῷ   ἔχωμεν χάριν, δι' ἧς   δουλεύσατε τῷ Θεῷ ἐν
μετὰ φόβου καὶ πάσης   λατρεύωμεν εὐαρέστωςτῷ   φόβῳ.
εὐλαβείας.   καθὼς αὐτὸς   Θεῷ μετὰ εὐλαβείας καὶ
ἐνετείλατο καὶ οἱ εὐαγ-   δέους.
γελισάμενοι ἡμᾶς ἀπό-
στολοι καὶ οἱ προφῆται
οἱ προκηρύξαντες τὴν
ἔλευσιν τοῦ Κυρίου ἡμῶν.

Though the reference seems to be a general one to the
tenour of O. T. as well as the Gospel, yet the phrase may very
possibly be coloured by Hebrews ; for εὐλαβεία, which is not
found in the parallel passage of Psalms, occurs in N. T. only
in Hebrews, and Polycarp refers to οἱ εὐαγγελισάμενοι ἡμᾶς
ἀπόστολοι.

(65)   Pol. xii. 2.   Heb. 6²⁰.

'et ipse sempiternus pontifex,   ἀρχιερεὺς γενόμενος εἰς τὸν αἰῶνα.
Dei filius.'   Heb. 7³.

ἀφωμοιωμένος δὲ τῷ υἱῷ τοῦ Θεοῦ.

The occurrence of *sempiternus pontifex* and *Dei filius* in
the same context, both in Polycarp and Hebrews, render it
not improbable that Polycarp is directly dependent on Hebrews

here. If we may trust the prayer in *Mart. Polyc.* xiv as giving his actual words (διὰ τοῦ αἰωνίου καὶ ἐπουρανίου ἀρχιερέως Ἰησοῦ Χριστοῦ ἀγαπητοῦ σου παιδός), we may suppose that the idea was one which had a strong hold on his mind. The conception of Christ as ἀρχιερεύς occurs prominently in 1 Clement (see 1 Clement (21)) which, however, may also be dependent on Hebrews; cf. Ignatius (75); but in none of these passages is there anything corresponding to *sempiternus* or to *Dei filius*.

d

(66)　Pol. ix. 1.

παρακαλῶ οὖν πάντας ὑμᾶς πει-
θαρχεῖν τῷ λόγῳ τῆς δικαιοσύνης.

Heb. 5¹³.

πᾶς γὰρ ὁ μετέχων γάλακτος ἄπειρος
λόγου δικαιοσύνης.

The phrase λόγος δικαιοσύνης occurs only here in N. T.; but the context is widely different from that of Polycarp.

1 *John*　　　　**c**

(67)　Pol. vii. 1.

πᾶς γάρ, ὃς ἂν μὴ ὁμολογῇ Ἰησοῦν
Χριστὸν ἐν σαρκὶ ἐληλυθέναι, ἀντί-
χριστός ἐστιν   καὶ ὃς ἂν μὴ ὁμολογῇ
τὸ μαρτύριον τοῦ σταυροῦ, ἐκ τοῦ
διαβόλου ἐστίν.

1 John 4².

πᾶν πνεῦμα ὃ ὁμολογεῖ Ἰησοῦν
Χριστὸν ἐν σαρκὶ ἐληλυθότα ἐκ τοῦ
Θεοῦ ἐστίν· καὶ πᾶν πνεῦμα ὃ μὴ
ὁμολογεῖ (v. l. λύει) τὸν Ἰησοῦν ἐκ
τοῦ Θεοῦ οὐκ ἔστιν.

3⁸ ὁ ποιῶν τὴν ἁμαρτίαν ἐκ τοῦ
διαβόλου ἐστίν.

Cf. 2 John ⁷ ὅτι πολλοὶ πλάνοι
ἐξῆλθον εἰς τὸν κόσμον, οἱ μὴ ὁμολο-
γοῦντες Ἰησοῦν Χριστὸν ἐρχόμενον
ἐν σαρκί. οὗτός ἐστιν ὁ πλάνος καὶ ὁ
ἀντίχριστος.

Notice especially ὁμολογεῖν, ἐν σαρκὶ ἐληλυθέναι, ἀντίχριστος, ἐκ τοῦ διαβόλου, which are all characteristic of 1 John throughout. The numerous coincidences of language render it probable that Polycarp either used 1 John or was personally acquainted with its author. [See also Stanton, *The Gospels as Historical Documents*, i. 20, notes 3 and 4; and in *Hibbert Journal*, ii. 805.]

d

(68)　Pol. i. 1.

τὰ μιμήματα τῆς ἀληθοῦς ἀγάπης.

1 John 4⁸, ¹⁶.

ὁ Θεὸς ἀγάπη ἐστίν.

The expression of Polycarp has an Ignatian rather than a Johannine sound; cf. for instance Ign. *Magn.* vii. 1.

D

Colossians   **d**

(69)   Pol. i. 2.   Col. 1⁵, ⁶.

These passages are parallel in thought, but except for the one word καρποφορεῖ there is no verbal connexion between them.

(70)   Pol. x. 1.   Col. 1²³.
See under 1 Corinthians (6).

(71)   Pol. xi. 2.   Col. 3⁵.
See under Ephesians (38).

(72)   Pol. xii. 2.   Col. 1¹².
See under Acts (63).

GOSPELS.

(I) The Synoptic Gospels.

UNCLASSED

(73) Pol. v. 2.   Mark 9³⁵.   Matt. 20²⁸.

κατὰ τὴν ἀλήθειαν τοῦ | εἴ τις θέλει πρῶτος | ὁ υἱὸς τοῦ ἀνθρώπου
Κυρίου, ὃς ἐγένετο διά- | εἶναι, ἔσται πάντων ἔ- | οὐκ ἦλθεν διακονηθῆναι
κονος πάντων. | σχατος, καὶ πάντων διά- | ἀλλὰ διακονῆσαι.
 | κονος. |

The sentence in Polycarp reads like a homiletic application of the saying in Mark, suggested by the mention of διάκονοι on the one hand, and by the example of Christ, as the great fulfiller of His own precept, on the other. The actual words πάντων διάκονος are only found in Mark, but the conception is applied to Christ in Matthew, and the application is so natural as to make it impossible to treat the passage as serious evidence for Polycarp's use of Mark.

(74)   Pol. xi. 2.   Matt. 18¹⁷.
'tanquam inter gentes.'   ὥσπερ ὁ ἐθνικός.

(II) The Synoptic Tradition.

(75) Pol. ii. 3.   Matt. 7¹.   Luke 6³⁵.   1 Clem. xiii. 1 f.

μνημονεύοντες δὲ | μὴ κρίνετε, ἵνα μὴ | καὶ μὴ κρίνετε, καὶ | μάλιστα μεμνημένοι
ὧν εἶπεν ὁ Κύριος | κριθῆτε· ἐν ᾧ γὰρ μέ- | οὐ μὴ κριθῆτε . . . ᾧ | τῶν λόγων τοῦ Κυρίου
διδάσκων· μὴ κρίνετε, | τρῳ μετρεῖτε, μετρη- | γὰρ μέτρῳ μετρεῖ- | Ἰησοῦ, οὓς ἐλάλησεν
ἵνα μὴ κριθῆτε· ἀφί- | θήσεται ὑμῖν. | τε, ἀντιμετρηθήσεται | διδάσκων ἐπιείκειαν
ετε, καὶ ἀφεθήσεται | 5³ μακάριοι οἱ | ὑμῖν. | καὶ μακροθυμίαν· οὕ-

ὑμῖν· ἐλεᾶτε, ἵνα ἐλεηθῆτε· ᾧ μέτρῳ μετρεῖτε, ἀντιμετρηθήσεται ὑμῖν· καὶ ὅτι μακάριοι οἱ πτωχοὶ καὶ οἱ διωκόμενοι ἕνεκεν δικαιοσύνης, ὅτι αὐτῶν ἐστιν ἡ βασιλεία τοῦ Θεοῦ.

πτωχοὶ τῷ πνεύματι, ὅτι αὐτῶν ἐστιν ἡ βασιλεία τῶν οὐρανῶν.

5¹⁰ μακάριοι οἱ δεδιωγμένοι ἕνεκεν δικαιοσύνης, ὅτι αὐτῶν ἐστιν ἡ βασιλεία τῶν οὐρανῶν.

6²⁰ μακάριοι οἱ πτωχοί, ὅτι ὑμετέρα ἐστὶν ἡ βασιλεία τοῦ Θεοῦ.

τως γὰρ εἶπεν· ἐλεᾶτε ἵνα ἐλεηθῆτε, ἀφίετε ἵνα ἀφεθῇ ὑμῖν· ὡς ποιεῖτε, οὕτω ποιηθήσεται ὑμῖν· ὡς δίδοτε, οὕτως δοθήσεται ὑμῖν. ὡς κρίνετε, οὕτως κριθήσεσθε· ὡς χρηστεύεσθε, οὕτως χρηστευθήσεται ὑμῖν· ᾧ μέτρῳ μετρεῖτε, ἐν αὐτῷ μετρηθήσεται ὑμῖν.

Polycarp assumes that a body of teaching, oral or written, similar to the Sermon on the Mount, was familiar to the Philippian Church. It is possible that his language, including the form of citation [cf. Acts (61)], may have been influenced by Clement. Polycarp does not, however, quote Clement directly, as he omits some of Clement's most characteristic phrases. In detail he agrees almost equally with Matthew and Luke, but not completely with either. Compare the discussion on 1 Clem. (55).

(76) Pol. vi. 1, 2.	Matt. 6¹².	Luke 11⁴.
μὴ ταχέως πιστεύοντες κατά τινος, μὴ ἀπότομοι ἐν κρίσει, εἰδότες ὅτι πάντες ὀφειλέται ἐσμὲν ἁμαρτίας. εἰ οὖν δεόμεθα τοῦ Κυρίου ἵνα ἡμῖν ἀφῇ, ὀφείλομεν καὶ ἡμεῖς ἀφιέναι.	καὶ ἄφες ἡμῖν τὰ ὀφειλήματα ἡμῶν, ὡς καὶ ἡμεῖς ἀφήκαμεν τοῖς ὀφειλέταις ἡμῶν. Cf. 6¹⁴, ¹⁵, 18³⁵.	καὶ ἄφες ἡμῖν τὰς ἁμαρτίας ἡμῶν, καὶ γὰρ αὐτοὶ ἀφίεμεν παντὶ ὀφείλοντι ἡμῖν.

The words δεόμεθα τοῦ Κυρίου evidently introduce a reference to the Lord's Prayer. But no quotation from the Lord's Prayer can be used as evidence for acquaintance with our Gospels, as there are clear signs of its early ecclesiastical use as current elsewhere (see e. g. Didache (11)). Possibly, the context here, emphasizing a large charity in judgement, points to the context of the Sermon on the Mount as colouring Polycarp's thoughts (see Matt. 6¹⁴, 7¹⁻⁵). But even if Polycarp were inclined to treat the Lord's Prayer as belonging to the Sermon on the Mount, this would not necessarily imply a knowledge of our Matthew.

(77) Pol. vii. 2.

δεήσεσιν αἰτούμενοι
τὸν παντεπόπτην Θεὸν
μὴ εἰσενεγκεῖν ἡμᾶς εἰς
πειρασμόν, καθὼς εἶπεν
ὁ Κύριος· τὸ μὲν πνεῦμα
πρόθυμον, ἡ δὲ σὰρξ
ἀσθενής.

Matt. 6¹³(=Luke 11⁴).

καὶ μὴ εἰσενέγκῃς
ἡμᾶς εἰς πειρασμόν.
26⁴¹ γρηγορεῖτε καὶ
προσεύχεσθε, ἵνα μὴ
εἰσέλθητε εἰς πειρασμόν.
τὸ μὲν πνεῦμα πρόθυμον,
ἡ δὲ σὰρξ ἀσθενής.

Mark 14³⁸.

γρηγορεῖτε καὶ προσ-
εύχεσθε, ἵνα μὴ ἔλθητε
εἰς πειρασμόν· τὸ μὲν
πνεῦμα πρόθυμον, ἡ δὲ
σὰρξ ἀσθενής.

For the quotation from the Lord's Prayer (Polycarp's words are identical with those of Matthew and Luke), see the note to the preceding passage. The quotation introduced by καθὼς εἶπεν ὁ Κύριος agrees *verbatim* with Matthew and Mark, and appears in a very similar context to that in the Gospels. But this quotation might well be due to oral tradition; or it might be from a document akin to our Gospels, though not necessarily those Gospels themselves.

(78) Pol. xii. 3.

'orate etiam . . .
pro persequentibus
et odientibus vos.'

Matt. 5⁴⁴.

ἀγαπᾶτε τοὺς ἐχθροὺς
ὑμῶν, καὶ προσεύχεσθε
ὑπὲρ τῶν διωκόντων
ὑμᾶς.

Luke 6²⁷.

ἀγαπᾶτε τοὺς ἐχθροὺς
ὑμῶν, καλῶς ποιεῖτε τοῖς
μισοῦσιν ὑμᾶς, εὐλο-
γεῖτε τοὺς καταρωμένους
ὑμᾶς, προσεύχεσθε περὶ
τῶν ἐπηρεαζόντων ὑμᾶς.

Here again the language of Polycarp seems to be influenced by teaching like that of the Sermon on the Mount, but the passage affords no evidence for the use of either of our Gospels in its present form.

(79) Pol. i. 3.

εἰς ἣν πολλοὶ ἐπιθυμοῦσιν εἰσελθεῖν.

Matt. 13¹⁷.
Luke 10²⁴.

There is no reason to suppose that the parallel here is more than accidental.

(III) The Fourth Gospel.
C

(80) Pol. v. 2.

καθὼς ὑπέσχετο ἡμῖν ἐγεῖραι ἡμᾶς
ἐκ νεκρῶν.

c John 5²¹.

ὥσπερ γὰρ ὁ πατὴρ ἐγείρει τοὺς
νεκροὺς καὶ ζωοποιεῖ, οὕτω καὶ ὁ υἱὸς
οὓς θέλει ζωοποιεῖ.

5²⁵ οἱ νεκροὶ ἀκούσονται τῆς φωνῆς
τοῦ υἱοῦ τοῦ Θεοῦ, καὶ οἱ ἀκούσαντες
ζήσονται.

6⁴⁴ καὶ ἐγὼ ἀναστήσω αὐτὸν ἐν τῇ
ἐσχάτῃ ἡμέρᾳ.

No such promise is given in the Synoptic Gospels, whereas it is put plainly in John. The reference seems certainly to be to a Johannine tradition, though it need not necessarily be to our Fourth Gospel.

UNCLASSED

(81)   Pol. xii. 3   John 15[16].

'ut fructus vester manifestus   ἵνα ὑμεῖς ὑπάγητε καὶ καρπὸν
sit in omnibus.'   φέρητε, καὶ ὁ καρπὸς ὑμῶν μένῃ.

The sentence in Polycarp sounds like a reminiscence of I Tim. 4[15], see (54); the only point of contact with John is in the word *fructus*, and this might be accounted for, e. g. by Gal. 5[22], if so natural an expression requires any assignable source.

(IV) Apocryphal Gospels.

The passages resembling the Sermon on the Mount, (75)–(78), have appeared to some to suggest a use by Polycarp of some non-canonical source; but, in view of the inexactness of some of his other quotations, this inference does not seem to be justified.

UNCLASSED

(82) In vi. 1 the formula εἰδότες ὅτι introduces the words πάντες ὀφειλέται ἐσμὲν ἁμαρτίας, which, in view of their style, are probably a quotation; there is, however, nothing to indicate the source from which the quotation (if such it be) is derived.

SHEPHERD OF HERMAS

INTRODUCTION.

THE author of the Shepherd of Hermas nowhere supplies us with a direct quotation from the Old or New Testament, and we are therefore obliged to fall back upon allusions which always admit of some degree of doubt. He may sometimes be consciously borrowing ideas from N. T. writers when the reference is veiled by an intentional change of words; and sometimes he may use identical words, and yet have derived them from some other source, oral or written. In these circumstances it is clear that references which might reasonably be assumed if we knew that the author was familiar with our canonical books, cannot be used to establish his familiarity with them in opposition to critics who dispute it. The following arrangement of passages, therefore, does not represent what the editors may consider historically probable, but what they think may be reasonably deduced from a mere comparison of texts.

EPISTLES, ACTS.

B

1 *Corinthians*   **b**

(1)   Mand. IV. iv. 1, 2.

1 Cor. 7$^{39, 40}$.

'Εὰν γυνή, . . . ἢ πάλιν ἀνήρ τις κοιμηθῇ, καὶ γαμήσῃ τις ἐξ αὐτῶν, μήτι ἁμαρτάνει ὁ γαμῶν, Οὐχ ἁμαρτάνει, φησίν· ἐὰν δὲ ἐφ' ἑαυτῷ μείνῃ τις, περισσοτέραν ἑαυτῷ τιμὴν . . . περιποιεῖται πρὸς τὸν Κύριον· ἐὰν δὲ καὶ γαμήσῃ, οὐχ ἁμαρτάνει.

ἐὰν δὲ κοιμηθῇ ὁ ἀνήρ, ἐλευθέρα ἐστὶν ᾧ θέλει γαμηθῆναι . . . μακαριωτέρα δέ ἐστιν ἐὰν οὕτω μείνῃ, . . . δοκῶ δὲ κἀγὼ Πνεῦμα Θεοῦ ἔχειν. vs. ^{28} ἐὰν δὲ καὶ γήμῃς*, οὐχ ἥμαρτες.

* γαμήσῃς, Tisch., W. H.

d

(2)   Sim. IX. xii. 1.

1 Cor. 10^4.

Ἡ πέτρα . . . αὕτη καὶ ἡ πύλη ὁ υἱὸς τοῦ Θεοῦ ἐστί.

ἡ δὲ πέτρα ἦν ὁ Χριστός.

The resemblance here seems purely accidental, the rock being quite different in the two cases.

Ephesians **b**

(3) Mand. X. ii. 1, 2, 4, 5.

ἡ λύπη ἐκτρίβει τὸ πνεῦμα τὸ ἅγιον
καὶ πάλιν σώζει . . . ἡ λύπη αὕτη
εἰσπορεύεται εἰς τὸν ἄνθρωπον, καὶ
λυπεῖ τὸ πνεῦμα τὸ ἅγιον καὶ ἐκτρίβει
αὐτό . . . ἡ μὲν διψυχία . . . ἡ δὲ
ὀξυχολία λυπεῖ τὸ πνεῦμα . . . μὴ
θλῖβε τὸ πνεῦμα τὸ ἅγιον.
See also iii. 2, and Mand.
III. 4.

Eph. 4³⁰.

μὴ λυπεῖτε τὸ Πνεῦμα τὸ Ἅγιον
τοῦ Θεοῦ.
5¹⁸, ¹⁹ πληροῦσθε ἐν Πνεύματι, . . .
ψάλλοντες.

In view of the originality and boldness of the phrase in
Ephesians, it seems likely that Hermas is developing in his
own way a phrase that has lodged in his mind. On the other
hand, it is to be noticed that his conception of the Holy
Spirit as essentially joyous might have led him up to the
idea in a way suggested by the expression, 'grief enters and
grieves.' Nevertheless, this does not seem to explain fully so
remarkable a phrase.

(4) Sim. IX. xiii. 5.

οἱ πιστεύσαντες . . . ἔσονται εἰς ἓν
πνεῦμα, καὶ ἓν σῶμα, μιᾷ χρόᾳ τῶν
ἱματίων αὐτῶν. 7 ἓν πνεῦμα καὶ ἓν
σῶμα. xvii. 4 λαβόντες οὖν τὴν
σφραγῖδα [= baptism] μίαν φρόνησιν
ἔσχον καὶ ἕνα νοῦν, καὶ μία πίστις αὐτῶν
ἐγένετο καὶ [μία] ἀγάπη. xviii. 4
ἔσται ἡ ἐκκλησία τοῦ Θεοῦ ἐν σῶμα,
μία φρόνησις, εἷς νοῦς, μία πίστις, μία
ἀγάπη. καὶ τότε ὁ υἱὸς τοῦ Θεοῦ
ἀγαλλιάσεται . . . ἀπειληφὼς τὸν λαὸν
αὐτοῦ καθαρόν.

Eph. 4³⁻⁶.

ἐν ἀγάπῃ . . . ἓν σῶμα καὶ ἓν Πνεῦμα,
. . . ἐν μιᾷ ἐλπίδι . . . εἷς Κύριος, μία
πίστις, ἓν βάπτισμα, εἷς Θεός.
5²⁵, ²⁶ ὁ Χριστὸς ἠγάπησε τὴν ἐκκλησίαν . . . ἵνα αὐτὴν ἁγιάσῃ καθα-
ρίσας.
1¹³, 4³⁰ ἐσφραγίσθητε.

These passages have all the appearance of being imitated
from Ephesians. It is the way of Hermas not to quote, but to
take suggestions, and alter to suit his own purposes.

d

(5) Mand. III. i.

Ἀλήθειαν ἀγάπα, καὶ πᾶσα ἀλήθεια
ἐκ τοῦ στόματός σου ἐκπορευέσθω.

Eph. 4²⁵.

λαλεῖτε ἀλήθειαν. ²⁹ πᾶς λόγος
σαπρὸς ἐκ τοῦ στόματος ὑμῶν μὴ
ἐκπορευέσθω.

Both the language and the sentiment are too common to

SHEPHERD OF HERMAS

SHEPHERD OF HERMAS 107

afford evidence of borrowing. Cf. Matt. 4⁴ ἐπὶ παντὶ ῥήματι
ἐκπορευομένῳ διὰ στόματος Θεοῦ.

(6)   Sim. IX. iv. 3.   Eph. 2²⁰.

οὗτοι πάντες ἐβλήθησαν εἰς τὴν   ἐποικοδομηθέντες ἐπὶ τῷ θεμελίῳ
οἰκοδομὴν τοῦ πύργου· ἐγένοντο οὖν   τῶν ἀποστόλων καὶ προφητῶν.
στοῖχοι τέσσαρες ἐν τοῖς θεμελίοις τοῦ   4¹¹,¹² ἀποστόλους ... διδασκάλους
πύργου. XV. 4 οἱ δὲ τριάκοντα πέντε   ... εἰς οἰκοδομήν.
προφῆται ... οἱ δὲ τεσσαράκοντα
ἀπόστολοι καὶ διδάσκαλοι.

There may be here a reminiscence of Ephesians, and indeed
the whole figure of the tower may have been suggested by
Eph. 2¹⁰⁻²².

(7)   Sim. IX. xvi. 2, 3.   Eph. 2¹.

ἵνα ζωοποιηθῶσιν ... πρὶν γάρ, φησί,   ὑμᾶς ὄντας νεκροὺς τοῖς παραπτώ-
φορέσαι τὸν ἄνθρωπον τὸ ὄνομα [τοῦ   μασι.
υἱοῦ] τοῦ Θεοῦ, νεκρός ἐστιν.   vs. ⁵ συνεζωοποίησε.

C
c

Hebrews

(8)   Vis. II. iii. 2.   Heb. 3¹².

σώζει σε τὸ μὴ ἀποστῆναί σε ἀπὸ   καρδία πονηρὰ ἀπιστίας ἐν τῷ
Θεοῦ ζῶντος.   ἀποστῆναι ἀπὸ Θεοῦ ζῶντος.

Vis. III. vii. 2.

οἱ εἰς τέλος ἀποστάντες τοῦ Θεοῦ
τοῦ ζῶντος.

(9)   Sim. I. i, ii.   Heb. 11¹³.

οἴδατε, φησίν, ὅτι ἐπὶ ξένης κατοι-   πόρρωθεν ... ἰδόντες ... ξένοι ...
κεῖτε ὑμεῖς ... ἡ γὰρ πόλις ὑμῶν   ¹⁵ εἶχον ἂν καιρὸν ἀνακάμψαι ...
μακράν ἐστιν ἀπὸ τῆς πόλεως ταύτης·   ¹⁶ ἡτοίμασεν γὰρ αὐτοῖς πόλιν.
... τί ὦδε ὑμεῖς ἑτοιμάζετε ἀγροὺς   13¹⁴ οὐ γὰρ ἔχομεν ὧδε μένουσαν
... ., ταῦτα οὖν ὁ ἑτοιμάζων εἰς   πόλιν.
ταύτην τὴν πόλιν οὐ προσδοκᾷ ἐπανα-
κάμψαι εἰς τὴν ἰδίαν πόλιν.

Both the ideas and the words in these passages seem to
indicate dependence.

d

(10) Mand. IV. iii. 1, 2.   Heb. 6⁴⁻⁶.

ἤκουσα ... παρά τινων διδασκάλων,   ἀδύνατον γὰρ τοὺς ἅπαξ φωτισθέντας
ὅτι ἑτέρα μετάνοια οὐκ ἔστιν εἰ μὴ   ... πάλιν ἀνακαινίζειν εἰς μετάνοιαν.
ἐκείνη, ὅτε εἰς ὕδωρ κατέβημεν ...
καλῶς ἤκουσας· οὕτω γὰρ ἔχει.

Sim. IX. xxvi. 6.

ἀδύνατον γάρ ἐστι σωθῆναι τὸν μέλ-
λοντα νῦν ἀρνεῖσθαι τὸν Κύριον.

The allusion to teachers, showing that the question was a subject of discussion, and the want of verbal correspondence, make the reference to Hebrews doubtful.

James

(11) Mand. IX. i.

ἆρον ἀπὸ σεαυτοῦ τὴν διψυχίαν καὶ μηδὲν ὅλως διψυχήσῃς αἰτήσασθαι παρὰ τοῦ Θεοῦ. 2 μὴ διαλογίζου ταῦτα, ἀλλ᾽ ... αἰτοῦ παρ᾽ αὐτοῦ ἀδιστάκτως. 4 ἐὰν ἀδιστάκτως αἰτήσῃς. 5 ἐὰν δὲ διστάσῃς ... οἱ γὰρ διστάζοντες εἰς τὸν Θεόν, οὗτοί εἰσιν οἱ δίψυχοι, καὶ οὐδὲν ὅλως ἐπιτυγχάνουσι τῶν αἰτημάτων αὐτῶν. There are several other references to διψυχία in the same passage: see also Herm. (39).

Sim. I. iii.

ἄφρον καὶ δίψυχε καὶ ταλαίπωρε ἄνθρωπε.

c

Jas. 1⁶⁻⁸.

αἰτείτω δὲ ἐν πίστει μηδὲν διακρινόμενος· ... μὴ γὰρ οἰέσθω ὁ ἄνθρωπος ἐκεῖνος ὅτι λήψεταί τι παρὰ τοῦ Κυρίου, ἀνὴρ δίψυχος, ἀκατάστατος ἐν πάσαις ταῖς ὁδοῖς αὐτοῦ.

Clem. Rom. I. xxiii. 3.

ἡ γραφὴ αὕτη, ὅπου λέγει· Ταλαίπωροί εἰσιν οἱ δίψυχοι, οἱ διστάζοντες τὴν ψυχήν [τῇ καρδίᾳ in Clem. II. xi. 2, where it is quoted as ὁ προφητικὸς λόγος].

Did. iv. 4.

οὐ διψυχήσεις, πότερον ἔσται ἢ οὔ.

Barn. xix. 5.

οὐ μὴ διψυχήσῃς.

Mand. IX. vi.

οἱ δὲ ὁλοτελεῖς ὄντες ἐν τῇ πίστει πάντα αἰτοῦνται.

Jas. 1⁴.

τὸ δοκίμιον ὑμῶν τῆς πίστεως κατεργάζεται ὑπομονήν. ἡ δὲ ὑπομονὴ ἔργον τέλειον ἐχέτω, ἵνα ἦτε τέλειοι καὶ ὁλόκληροι.

Mand. IX. i.

μηδὲν ὅλως διψυχήσῃς αἰτήσασθαι παρὰ τοῦ Θεοῦ. 2 αἰτοῦ παρ᾽ αὐτοῦ [4 and 7, παρὰ τοῦ Κυρίου]. 3 οὐκ ἔστι γὰρ ὁ Θεὸς ὡς οἱ ἄνθρωποι οἱ μνησικακοῦντες.

Jas. 1⁵.

αἰτείτω παρὰ τοῦ διδόντος Θεοῦ πᾶσιν ἁπλῶς καὶ μὴ ὀνειδίζοντος.

Sim. IX. xxiv. 1, 2.

οἱ πιστεύσαντες ... πάντοτε ἁπλοῖ καὶ ἄκακοι, ... καὶ ἐκ τῶν κόπων αὐτῶν παντὶ ἀνθρώπῳ ἐχορήγησαν ἀνονειδίστως καὶ ἀδιστάκτως.

Mand. IX. ii.

αἰτοῦ . . . καὶ γνώσῃ τὴν πολυευσπλαγχνίαν αὐτοῦ.

Mand. IX. xi.

ἡ πίστις ἄνωθέν ἐστι παρὰ τοῦ Κυρίου.

Mand. XI. v.

πᾶν γὰρ πνεῦμα ἀπὸ Θεοῦ δοθὲν . . . ἄνωθέν ἐστιν. 8 πρῶτον μὲν ὁ ἔχων τὸ πνεῦμα τὸ ἄνωθεν πραΰς ἐστι καὶ ἡσύχιος.

Mand. IX. xi.

ἡ δὲ διψυχία ἐπίγειον πνεῦμά ἐστι παρὰ τοῦ διαβόλου.

Mand. XI. vi.

τὸ δὲ πνεῦμα . . . κατὰ τὰς ἐπιθυμίας . . . ἐπίγειόν ἐστι. xi περὶ τοῦ πνεύματος τοῦ ἐπιγείου.

Jas. 5¹¹.

πολύσπλαγχνός ἐστιν ὁ Κύριος καὶ οἰκτίρμων.

Jas. 1¹⁷.

πᾶσα δόσις ἀγαθὴ καὶ πᾶν δώρημα τέλειον ἄνωθέν ἐστι, καταβαῖνον ἀπὸ τοῦ πατρὸς τῶν φώτων. 3¹⁷ ἡ δὲ ἄνωθεν σοφία πρῶτον μὲν ἁγνή ἐστιν, ἔπειτα εἰρηνική.

Jas. 3¹⁵.

οὐκ ἔστιν αὕτη ἡ σοφία ἄνωθεν κατερχομένη, ἀλλ᾽ ἐπίγειος, ψυχική, δαιμονιώδης.

In the foregoing passages there is sufficient similarity of thought and language to suggest a literary connexion with James; but some of the most striking expressions in James are absent from Hermas, and where the language is similar, the connexion of thought is sometimes quite different. The resemblance, therefore, is not sufficient to prove direct dependence, and may perhaps be explained by the use of a common source, such as is actually quoted by Clement in regard to the δίψυχοι. A προφητικὸς λόγος was likely to be used by Hermas, e. g. *Eldad and Modat,* cited below (16).

⟨12⟩   Sim. IX. xxiii. 2–4.

ἀπὸ τῶν καταλαλιῶν ἑαυτῶν μεμαρασμένοι εἰσὶν ἐν τῇ πίστει . . . αἱ καταλαλιαί . . . ταῖς καταλαλιαῖς αὐτῶν . . . εἰ ὁ Θεὸς . . . ἵλεως γίνεται, ἄνθρωπος . . . ἀνθρώπῳ μνησικακεῖ ὡς δυνάμενος ἀπολέσαι ἢ σῶσαι αὐτόν,

Mand. XII. vi. 3.

φοβήθητε τὸν πάντα δυνάμενον σῶσαι καὶ ἀπολέσαι.

Jas. 4¹¹, ¹².

μὴ καταλαλεῖτε ἀλλήλων, ἀδελφοί. ὁ καταλαλῶν ἀδελφοῦ . . . καταλαλεῖ νόμου . . . εἷς ἐστιν ὁ νομοθέτης καὶ κριτής, ὁ δυνάμενος σῶσαι καὶ ἀπολέσαι· σὺ δὲ τίς εἶ ὁ κρίνων τὸν πλησίον,

Cf. Matt. 10²⁸ φοβήθητε . . . τὸν δυνάμενον καὶ ψυχὴν καὶ σῶμα ἀπολέσαι.

Here both the identity of expression and the resemblance in the context are strongly suggestive of literary dependence. It is possible that both writers used a common document; but there is no evidence of this in the present case.

d

(13) Vis. II. ii. 7.

μακάριοι ὑμεῖς ὅσοι
ὑπομένετε τὴν θλῖψιν τὴν
ἐρχομένην τὴν μεγάλην,
καὶ ὅσοι οὐκ ἀρνήσονται
τὴν ζωὴν αὐτῶν.

Jas. 1¹².

Μακάριος ἀνὴρ ὃς
ὑπομένει πειρασμόν· ...
λήψεται τὸν στέφανον
τῆς ζωῆς.

Rev. 7¹⁴.

οἱ ἐρχόμενοι ἐκ τῆς
θλίψεως τῆς μεγάλης.

Matt. 10²² and 24¹³.

ὁ δὲ ὑπομείνας εἰς
τέλος, οὗτος σωθήσεται.

There is some verbal resemblance; but the words are very common, the deviations are strongly marked, and the sentiment is quite different.

(14) Vis. III. ix. 4–6.

αὕτη οὖν ἡ ἀσυν
κρασία βλαβερὰ ὑμῖν
τοῖς ἔχουσιν καὶ μὴ
μεταδιδοῦσιν τοῖς ὑστε
ρουμένοις. βλέπετε τὴν
κρίσιν τὴν ἐπερχομένην
... μήποτε στενάξουσιν
οἱ ὑστερούμενοι, καὶ ὁ
στεναγμὸς αὐτῶν ἀνα
βήσεται πρὸς τὸν Κύ
ριον.

Jas. 5¹,⁴.

οἱ πλούσιοι, ... κλαύ
σατε ὀλολύζοντες ἐπὶ ταῖς
ταλαιπωρίαις ὑμῶν ταῖς
ἐπερχομέναις ... ὁ
μισθὸς τῶν ἐργατῶν ...
ὁ ἀπεστερημένος ἀφ'
ὑμῶν κράζει· καὶ αἱ βοαὶ
τῶν θερισάντων εἰς τὰ
ὦτα Κυρίου Σαβαὼθ
εἰσεληλύθασιν.

Lev. 19¹³.

οὐ μὴ κοιμηθήσεται ὁ
μισθὸς τοῦ μισθωτοῦ
παρὰ σοὶ ἕως πρωί.

Deut. 24¹⁵.

πένης ... καταβοή
σεται κατὰ σοῦ πρὸς
Κύριον.

Ps. 11⁶.

τοῦ στεναγμοῦ τῶν
πενήτων.

Ps. 17⁷.

ἡ κραυγή μου ...
εἰσελεύσεται εἰς τὰ ὦτα
αὐτοῦ.

Cf. Enoch xciv.
7–10.

With a resemblance of sentiment and expression, the differences are considerable, and both may be explained from the O. T.

(15) Mand. II. ii, iii.

μηδενὸς καταλάλει ...
πονηρὰ ἡ καταλαλιά,
ἀκατάστατον δαιμόνιον.

V. ii. 7 ἀκαταστατεῖ
ἐν πάσῃ πράξει αὐτοῦ.

Sim. VI. iii. 4, 5.

τιμωροῦνται ... ἀκα
ταστασίᾳ ... ἀκαταστα
τοῦντες ταῖς βουλαῖς
αὐτῶν.

Jas. 4¹¹.

μὴ καταλαλεῖτε ἀλ
λήλων.

3⁸ τὴν δὲ γλῶσσαν
... ἀκατάστατον κακόν.

1⁸ ἀκατάστατος ἐν
πάσαις ταῖς ὁδοῖς αὐτοῦ.

Prov. 26²⁸.

στόμα δὲ ἄστεγον
ποιεῖ ἀκαταστασίας.

20¹⁶ μὴ ἀγάπα κατα
λαλεῖν.

Wisd. 1¹¹.

ἀπὸ καταλαλιᾶς φεί
σασθε γλώσσης.

See also Ps. 49²⁰,
100⁵.

Isa. 54¹¹.

ἀκατάστατος οὐ παρε
κλήθης.

See also Tobit 4¹³.

The sentiment and the words are sufficiently common. Ἀκατάστατον δαιμόνιον reminds one of James ; but with the change from κακόν, the connexion is too slight to be relied on.

(16) Mand. III. i.	Jas. 4⁵.	Test. of Twelve

(16) Mand. III. i.

τὸ πνεῦμα ὃ ὁ Θεὸς κατῴκισεν ἐν τῇ σαρκὶ ταύτῃ ... ὁ Κύριος ὁ ἐν σοὶ κατοικῶν.

Mand. V. ii. 5–7.

οὗ καὶ τὸ πνεῦμα τὸ ἅγιον κατοικεῖ ... κατοικεῖν ... ζητεῖ κατοικεῖν ... οὗ κατοικεῖ.

Sim. V. vi. 5, 7.

τὸ πνεῦμα τὸ ἅγιον ... κατῴκισεν ὁ Θεὸς εἰς σάρκα ... ἐν ᾗ κατῴκησε τὸ πνεῦμα τὸ ἅγιον ... ἐν ᾗ τὸ πνεῦμα τὸ ἅγιον κατῴκησεν.

Jas. 4⁵.

ἢ δοκεῖτε ὅτι κενῶς ἡ γραφὴ λέγει; πρὸς φθόνον ἐπιποθεῖ τὸ πνεῦμα ὃ κατῴκισεν ἐν ἡμῖν ;

Test. of Twelve Patriarchs, Simeon 4

ἔχων πνεῦμα Θεοῦ ἐν αὐτῷ. Joseph 10 Κύριος κατοικήσει ἐν ὑμῖν ... κατοικεῖ ... ὁ ἐν αὐτῷ κατοικῶν. Benj. 6 Κύριος γὰρ ἐν αὐτῷ κατοικεῖ.

Though the parallels in the *Testaments of the Twelve Patriarchs* show that the idea of a Divine indwelling, expressed by the word κατοικεῖν is not unusual, nevertheless the words of Hermas are sufficiently close to those of James to indicate some kind of literary connexion ; but as the latter is avowedly quoting an unknown scripture, Hermas and he may be dependent on a common source, possibly *Eldad and Modat*, which is quoted in Vision II. iii. 4 Ἐγγὺς Κύριος τοῖς ἐπιστρεφομένοις, ὡς γέγραπται ἐν τῷ Ἐλδὰδ καὶ Μωδάτ. We should note that the striking expression in James, πρὸς φθόνον ἐπιποθεῖ, is wanting in Hermas.

(17) Mand. XII. i. 1.

μισήσεις τὴν πονηρὰν ἐπιθυμίαν καὶ χαλιναγωγήσεις αὐτὴν καθὼς βούλει. 2 δυσκόλως ἡμεροῦται.

Jas. 1²⁶.

μὴ χαλιναγωγῶν γλῶσσαν αὐτοῦ. 3² δυνατὸς χαλιναγωγῆσαι καὶ ὅλον τὸ σῶμα. vs. ⁴ ὅπου ... βούλεται. vs. ⁸ τὴν δὲ γλῶσσαν οὐδεὶς δύναται ... δαμάσαι.

Polycarp v. 3.

χαλιναγωγοῦντες ἑαυτοὺς ἀπὸ παντὸς κακοῦ.

The metaphorical use of 'bridling' is not uncommon, but the word is of rare occurrence. It is found, however, in

Lucian, applied to τὰς τῶν ἡδονῶν ὀρέξεις, which shows how unsafe it is to infer literary connexion from a mere resemblance of words and thought. Here, however, we must notice the presence of the ideas of willing and taming, which occur also in the context of James.

(18) Mand. XII. ii. 4.

ἡ ἐπιθυμία . . . φεύ-
ξεται ἀπὸ σοῦ.
iv. 7 ὁ διάβολος μόνον
φόβον ἔχει . . . μὴ φοβή-
θητε οὖν αὐτόν, καὶ φεύ-
ξεται ἀφ' ὑμῶν.
v. 2 ἐὰν οὖν ἀντι-
σταθῆτε αὐτῷ, νικηθεὶς
φεύξεται ἀφ' ὑμῶν.
4 ἀνθεστήκασιν αὐτῷ . . .
κἀκεῖνος ἀποχωρεῖ ἀπ'
αὐτῶν.

Jas. 4⁷.

ἀντίστητε δὲ τῷ δια-
βόλῳ, καὶ φεύξεται ἀφ'
ὑμῶν.

Tobit 6¹⁸.

ὀσφρανθήσεται τὸ δαι-
μόνιον καὶ φεύξεται.

Test. of Twelve
Patr., Simeon 3.

ἀποτρέχει τὸ πονηρὸν
πνεῦμα ἀπ' αὐτοῦ.

Isachar 7.

πᾶν πνεῦμα τοῦ Βε-
λιὰρ φεύξεται ἀφ' ὑμῶν.

Napht. 8.

ὁ διάβολος φεύξεται
ἀφ' ὑμῶν.

1 Pet. 5⁹.

ᾧ ἀντίστητε στερεοὶ τῇ
πίστει.

The words and the thought in the above passages are sufficiently close to James to justify the conclusion that they are probably based on the Epistle. But a doubt is permissible because the words are few and in regular use, and the sentiment may have been common in Christian circles.

(19)   Sim. I. viii.

χήρας καὶ ὀρφανοὺς ἐπισκέπτεσθε.

Mand. VIII. x.

χήραις ὑπηρετεῖν, ὀρφανοὺς καὶ
ὑστερουμένους ἐπισκέπτεσθαι.

Vis. III. ix. 2.

ἐπισκέπτεσθε ἀλλήλους.

Jas. 1²⁷.

ἐπισκέπτεσθαι ὀρφανοὺς καὶ χήρας
ἐν τῇ θλίψει αὐτῶν.

The verbal resemblance in the first passage is striking; but ἐπισκέπτεσθαι is a common word in this kind of connexion, being very frequent in the LXX, and the union of orphans and widows as specially entitled to kindness is met with several times in the O. T. (see in the LXX Exod. 22²²; Deut. 10¹⁸; Job 22⁹, Ps. 93⁶, 145⁹; Isa. 1¹⁷, 9¹⁷; Jer. 7⁶, 22³; Ezek. 22⁷; Zech. 7¹⁰). Moreover, the parallel passages in

Hermas deviate much more widely from James. It is therefore impossible to feel confident that there is dependence.

(20)   Sim. II. v.

ὁ μὲν πλούσιος ἔχει χρήματα πολλά, τὰ δὲ πρὸς τὸν Κύριον πτωχεύει ... ὁ πένης πλούσιός ἐστιν ἐν τῇ ἐντεύξει, καὶ δύναμιν μεγάλην ἔχει ἡ ἔντευξις αὐτοῦ παρὰ τῷ Θεῷ.

Jas. 2⁵.

ὁ Θεὸς ἐξελέξατο τοὺς πτωχοὺς ... πλουσίους ἐν πίστει. 5¹⁶ πολὺ ἰσχύει δέησις δικαίου ἐνεργουμένη.

The idea of the poor man as richer in spiritual life is common to the two works; but this is suggested also by Luke 6²⁰, 12²¹, 16¹⁹⁻³¹; 2 Cor. 6¹⁰, 8⁹. The idea of the power of prayer is differently connected and applied; and there is no verbal resemblance that can suggest literary dependence.

(21)   Sim. VIII. vi. 4.

ὧν αἱ ῥάβδοι ξηραὶ καὶ βεβρωμέναι ὑπὸ σητὸς εὑρέθησαν, οὗτοί εἰσιν οἱ ἀπο-στάται ... καὶ βλασφημήσαντες ἐν ταῖς ἁμαρτίαις αὐτῶν τὸν Κύριον, ἔτι δὲ καὶ ἐπαισχυνθέντες τὸ ὄνομα Κυρίου τὸ ἐπικληθὲν ἐπ' αὐτούς.

Jas. 5².

ὁ πλοῦτος ὑμῶν σέσηπε, καὶ τὰ ἱμάτια ὑμῶν σητόβρωτα γέγονεν. 2⁷ οὐκ αὐτοὶ (sc. οἱ πλούσιοι) βλασφημοῦσι τὸ καλὸν ὄνομα τὸ ἐπι-κληθὲν ἐφ' ὑμᾶς; See also 1 Pet. 4¹⁶ (31).

(22)   The following passages may also be compared; but it is not necessary to present them, as the language which is used in common by the two writers is not sufficiently characteristic to require remark. The context is quite different, and the use of the same words or figures may be explained from the O. T., or from general literary usage.

Vis. I. i. 8, ii. 1.   Cf. Mand. IV. i. 2.   Jas. 1¹⁴, ¹⁵.
Mand. II. iv.   Sim. II. vii.   1⁵, ¹⁷.
Mand. XII. vi. 5   1²⁷, 4⁸.
Sim. VI. i. 1.   1²¹.
Sim. VI. i. 2.   Vis. IV. i. 8.   2¹, ⁴.
Sim. VI. i. 6, ii. 4.   5⁵.
Sim. VIII. ix. 1.   2¹⁴.
Sim. IX. xix. 2.   3¹, ¹⁴, ¹⁸, 2¹⁴, ¹⁷, ²⁰.
Sim. IX. xxi (especially 3).   1¹¹, ¹⁸, 2⁷.
Sim. IX. xxvi. 7.   3⁸.

Although the passages which point to dependence on James fail to reach, when taken one by one, a high degree of proba-bility, yet collectively they present a fairly strong case, but we should be hardly justified in placing the Epistle higher than Class C.

D

Acts	d	
(23) Vis. IV. ii. 4.	Acts 4¹².	Isa. 24¹⁵.

Acts

(23) Vis. IV. ii. 4.

ἐπὶ τὸν Θεὸν ... πρὸς
τὸν Κύριον, πιστεύσας
ὅτι δι᾽ οὐδενὸς δύνῃ σω-
θῆναι εἰ μὴ διὰ τοῦ
μεγάλου καὶ ἐνδόξου
ὀνόματος.

d

Acts 4¹².

οὐδὲ γὰρ ὄνομά ἐστιν
ἕτερον ὑπὸ τὸν οὐρανὸν
τὸ δεδομένον ἐν ἀνθρώ-
ποις, ἐν ᾧ δεῖ σωθῆναι
ἡμᾶς.

Isa. 24¹⁵.

τὸ ὄνομα Κυρίου ἔνδο-
ξον.

43¹¹ οὐκ ἔστιν παρὲξ
ἐμοῦ σώζων.

Ps. 53³.

Ὁ Θεός, ἐν τῷ ὀνόματί
σου σῶσόν με.

11² Σῶσόν με, Κύριε.
19² ὑπερασπίσαι σου
τὸ ὄνομα τοῦ Θεοῦ.

See also Ps. 32²¹,
78⁹, 105⁸, 123⁸, &c.

It seems doubtful whether 'the Lord' and 'the name' refer
to God or to Christ. In III. i. 9 and ii. 1, where suffering
for the sake of the name (in v. 2 'the name of the Lord') is
alluded to, the name is most naturally understood as that of
Christ. But in III. iv. 3 'the name of God' is expressly
mentioned; and in IV. i. 3 'his great and glorious name'
seems most probably to refer to God. The same may be said
of 'the almighty and glorious name' in III. iii. 5.   In
III. vii. 3 Κύριος seems to be used of Christ. This ambiguity
qualifies the first impression of resemblance. In any case the
usage of the O. T. may furnish a sufficient basis for the
passage ; and even the negative form of the sentence, which
particularly reminds us of Acts, has a parallel in Isa. 43¹¹.
The context is totally different from that in Acts.

(24)   Mand. IV. iii. 4.   Acts 1²⁴.

καρδιογνώστης γὰρ ὢν ὁ Κύριος.   Κύριε, καρδιογνῶστα πάντων.
                                         15⁸ ὁ καρδιογνώστης Θεός.

The only appearance of dependence here is in the use of an
uncommon word. But even if that word originated with the
author of Acts, it may have passed into Christian use, so as
to be familiar to many who had not read Acts. If we suppose
a direct connexion, there is nothing to show on which side
the priority lies.

Romans **d**

(25) Mand. X. ii. 5.

μὴ θλῖβε τὸ πνεῦμα τὸ ἅγιον τὸ ἐν σοὶ κατοικοῦν, μήποτε ἐντεύξηται [κατὰ σοῦ] τῷ Θεῷ.

Rom. 8²⁶, ²⁷.

αὐτὸ τὸ πνεῦμα ὑπερεντυγχάνει ... ἐντυγχάνει ὑπὲρ ἁγίων.

1 *Thessalonians*

(26) Vis. III. ix. 10.

παιδεύετε οὖν ἀλλήλους καὶ εἰρηνεύετε ἐν αὐτοῖς.

1 Thess. 5¹³ f.

εἰρηνεύετε ἐν ἑαυτοῖς· παρακαλοῦμεν δὲ ὑμᾶς, ἀδελφοί, νουθετεῖτε τοὺς ἀτάκτους ...

These passages use the same phrase in rather similar contexts dealing with mutual exhortation.

1 *Peter* **d**

(27) Vis. III. iii. 5.

ἡ ζωὴ ὑμῶν διὰ ὕδατος ἐσώθη καὶ σωθήσεται.

1 Pet. 3²⁰, ²¹.

ἐν ἡμέραις Νῶε, κατασκευαζομένης κιβωτοῦ, εἰς ἣν ὀλίγοι ... διεσώθησαν δι᾽ ὕδατος ... σώζει βάπτισμα.

The context is quite different, the reference to Noah and the ark being absent from Hermas. The idea of salvation through water springs directly from the practice of baptism, and would readily suggest the figure of founding the tower ἐπὶ ὑδάτων.

(28) Vis. III. xi. 3.

οὐκ ἐπερίψατε ἑαυτῶν τὰς μερίμνας ἐπὶ τὸν Κύριον.
IV. ii. 4 ἐξέφυγες ... ὅτι τὴν μέριμνάν σου ἐπὶ τὸν Θεὸν ἐπέριψας. ... 5 ἐπιρίψατε τὰς μερίμνας ὑμῶν ἐπὶ τὸν Κύριον, καὶ αὐτὸς κατορθώσει αὐτάς.

1 Pet. 5⁷.

πᾶσαν τὴν μέριμναν ὑμῶν ἐπιρίψαντες ἐπ᾽ αὐτόν [τὸν Θεόν], ὅτι αὐτῷ μέλει περὶ ὑμῶν.

Ps. 54²³.

ἐπίριψον ἐπὶ Κύριον τὴν μέριμνάν σου, καὶ αὐτός σε διαθρέψει.

The quotation seems taken independently from the Psalm; for, though the latter part differs from the LXX, it differs more widely from Peter. The huge beast, introduced as a type of the great tribulation, might be suggested by the 'roaring lion' of Peter; but the figure, as used by Hermas, is too obvious to require such an explanation.

(29)   Vis. IV. iii. 4.

ὥσπερ γὰρ τὸ χρυσίον δοκιμάζεται
διὰ τοῦ πυρός, ... οὕτως καὶ ὑμεῖς
δοκιμάζεσθε.

1 Pet. 1[7].

τὸ δοκίμιον ὑμῶν τῆς πίστεως πολυ-
τιμότερον χρυσίου τοῦ ἀπολλυμένου
διὰ πυρὸς δὲ δοκιμαζομένου.

The words are not sufficiently close, and the comparison is
far too obvious and common, to prove literary dependence.

(30) Sim. IX. xii. 2, 3.

ὁ μὲν υἱὸς τοῦ Θεοῦ
πάσης τῆς κτίσεως αὐτοῦ
προγενέστερός *   ἐστιν
... ἐπ᾽ ἐσχάτων τῶν
ἡμερῶν τῆς συντελείας
φανερὸς ἐγένετο.

* Not used in N T.

1 Pet. 1[20].

Χριστοῦ προεγνωσμέ-
νου μὲν πρὸ καταβολῆς
κόσμου φανερωθέντος δὲ
ἐπ᾽ ἐσχάτου τῶν χρόνων.

Heb. 1[2].

ἐπ᾽ ἐσχάτου [al. ἐσχά-
των] τῶν ἡμερῶν.

1 John 3[5].

ἐκεῖνος   ἐφανερώθη.
Also 3[8].
1[2] ἡ ζωὴ ἐφανερώθη.

Col. 1[15].

πρωτότοκος πάσης κτί-
σεως.

The antithesis which is here expressed reminds one of the
Epistle; but the thought is somewhat different, and the
phraseology, as the parallels show, is not necessarily connected with Peter. If we suppose that there is a literary
connexion, we may observe that the doctrine is rather more
developed in Hermas, and so may indicate that the dependence is on that side.

(31) Sim. IX. xiv. 6.

οὐκ ἐπαισχύνονται τὸ
ὄνομα αὐτοῦ φορεῖν.
xxi. 3 ὅταν θλῖψιν
ἀκούσωσι, ... τὸ ὄνομα
ἐπαισχύνονται τοῦ Κυρίου
αὐτῶν. xxviii. 5, 6
οἱ πάσχοντες ἕνεκεν τοῦ
ὀνόματος δοξάζειν ὀφεί-
λετε τὸν Θεόν, ὅτι ἀξίους
ὑμᾶς ἡγήσατο ὁ Θεὸς ἵνα
τοῦτο τὸ ὄνομα βαστά-
ζητε ... πεπόνθατε ἕνε-
κεν τοῦ ὀνόματος Κυρίου.
VIII. vi. 4 ἐπαι-
σχυνθέντες   τὸ   ὄνομα
Κυρίου τὸ ἐπικληθὲν ἐπ᾽
αὐτούς. See (21).

1 Pet. 4[14-16].

εἰ ὀνειδίζεσθε ἐν ὀνό-
ματι Χριστοῦ ... πα-
σχέτω· ... εἰ δὲ ὡς
Χριστιανός, μὴ αἰσχυ-
νέσθω, δοξαζέτω δὲ τὸν
Θεὸν ἐν τῷ ὀνόματι τού-
τῳ.

Polycarp viii. 2.

ἐὰν πάσχωμεν διὰ τὸ
ὄνομα αὐτοῦ, δοξάζωμεν
αὐτόν. τοῦτον γὰρ ἡμῖν
τὸν ὑπογραμμὸν ἔθηκε
δι᾽ ἑαυτοῦ.

Mark 8[38]; Luke 9[26].

ὃς γὰρ ἂν ἐπαισχυνθῇ
με.

Cf. Acts 5[41]: see
(46).

The probability that there is here a reminiscence of 1 Peter is confirmed by the parallel from Polycarp; for the latter has just quoted 1 Peter, and that he still has the Epistle in mind is indicated by the last clause: see 1 Pet. 2²¹. But the citation is not sufficiently close to make us feel confident that there is direct literary dependence.

(32) Sim. IX. xxix.	1 Pet. 2¹, ².	Matt. 18³.
1, 3.	ἀποθέμενοι οὖν πᾶσαν	γένησθε ὡς τὰ παιδία.
ὡς νήπια βρέφη εἰσίν,	κακίαν... ὡς ἀρτιγέννητα	1 Cor. 14²⁰.
οἷς οὐδεμία κακία ἀνα-	βρέφη.	τῇ κακίᾳ νηπιάζετε.
βαίνει ἐπὶ τὴν καρδίαν ...		
ὅσοι οὖν, κτλ.		

The comparison is too obvious to require borrowing; and if Hermas uses the βρέφη of 1 Peter, he fails to use the more striking ἀρτιγέννητα.

On the whole, then, the evidence seems to place 1 Peter on the border line between C and D.

GOSPELS.

Dr. C. Taylor has elaborated a striking argument in support of the thesis that Hermas based the Church upon four Gospels[1]. It is impossible to do justice to this in a meagre summary, and the reader ought to consult the work for himself. The important passages are the following:—

Vis. III. xiii. 3 ὅτι ἐπὶ συμψελίου εἶδες καθημένην, ἰσχυρὰ ἡ θέσις· ὅτι τέσσαρας πόδας ἔχει τὸ συμψέλιον καὶ ἰσχυρῶς ἕστηκεν· καὶ γὰρ ὁ κόσμος διὰ τεσσάρων στοιχείων κρατεῖται.

Sim. IX. iv. 3 ἐγένοντο οὖν στοῖχοι τέσσαρες ἐν τοῖς θεμελίοις τοῦ πύργου. xv. 4 οἱ μὲν πρῶτοι [λίθοι], φησίν, οἱ δέκα οἱ εἰς τὰ θεμέλια τεθειμένοι, πρώτη γενεά· οἱ δὲ εἴκοσι πέντε δευτέρα γενεὰ ἀνδρῶν δικαίων· οἱ δὲ τριάκοντα πέντε προφῆται τοῦ Θεοῦ καὶ διάκονοι αὐτοῦ· οἱ δὲ τεσσαράκοντα ἀπόστολοι καὶ διδάσκαλοι τοῦ κηρύγματος τοῦ υἱοῦ τοῦ Θεοῦ.

Dr. Taylor finds the key to this allusion to the four elements in the well-known passage of Irenaeus[2], in which

---

[1] The Witness of Hermas to the Four Gospels, 1892.
[2] III. xi. 8, 9 Stieren; 11, 12 Harvey.

he tries to prove that there must be neither more nor fewer
than four Gospels. He connects the four στοῖχοι in the
foundation of the tower with the στοιχεῖα. The four genera-
tions have their parallel in the four covenants of Irenaeus.
'The numbers of the stones in the four rows are 10, 25, 35,
and 40 respectively, of which the decades are expressed in
Greek by the initials of John, Cephas, Luke, and Matthew.
St. Peter was the traditional authority for St. Mark's Gospel.'
The bench, with its four feet, represents the four Gospels
united in the one Gospel.

The argument is certainly plausible, and if we knew that
Hermas had four and only four Gospels, the explanation of
his imagery would be probable. But on the hypothesis that
the Church had not yet definitely selected the Four Canonical
Gospels, it may be that Hermas had other reasons for his use
of the number four, and that nevertheless his use of that
number may have helped to guide the decision of the Church,
and to furnish Irenaeus with arguments. It is curious that
Irenaeus, though referring to four regions of the world and
four catholic winds, makes no mention of elements even when
he speaks of the world as 'compounded and fitted together.'
Moreover, the mere correspondence of numbers is not to be
depended upon. Thus twelve mountains represent the twelve
tribes or nations of the world. The twelve virgins at the
gates of the tower, of whom four were more glorious than
the rest, do not stand for Apostles and Evangelists, but for
the virtues, of which the first four are faith, temperance,
power, and long-suffering. Dr. Taylor, however, makes them
represent the Holy Spirit as distributed to the twelve
Apostles. While we fully recognize the value of Dr. Taylor's
interpretations, we cannot place much confidence in them as
an independent proof of the use of our four Gospels by
Hermas.

Dr. Taylor supports his principal argument by pointing out
several apparent allusions to special features in our Gospels;
but here again, though the references are probable on the
assumption that Hermas had our Gospels, they are not of
a kind to prove that he had them to any one who is disposed
to deny their currency at that time.

(I) The Synoptic Gospels.

C

Matthew   **c**

(33) Mand. XII. i. 2.

τοὺς μὴ ἔχοντας ἔνδυμα τῆς ἐπιθυμίας τῆς ἀγαθῆς.

Sim. IX. xiii. 2.

ἄνθρωπος οὐ δύναται εὑρεθῆναι εἰς τὴν βασιλείαν τοῦ Θεοῦ, ἐὰν μὴ αὗται [αἱ παρθένοι = ἅγια πνεύματα, or δυνάμεις τοῦ υἱοῦ τοῦ Θεοῦ] αὐτὸν ἐνδύσωσι τὸ ἔνδυμα αὐτῶν.

Matt. 22¹¹.

εἶδεν ἐκεῖ ἄνθρωπον οὐκ ἐνδεδυμένον ἔνδυμα γάμου. ¹² πῶς εἰσῆλθες ὧδε ; ¹³ ἐκβάλετε αὐτόν.

This might have been suggested by the parable of the marriage feast; but the resemblance is not very close.

(34) Sim. III. iii.

ἐν τῷ αἰῶνι τούτῳ οὐ φαίνονται οὔτε οἱ δίκαιοι οὔτε οἱ ἁμαρτωλοί, ἀλλὰ πάντες ὅμοιοί εἰσιν. IV. 2 ὁ γὰρ αἰὼν ὁ ἐρχόμενος θέρος ἐστὶ τοῖς δικαίοις, τοῖς δὲ ἁμαρτωλοῖς χειμών. 4 ὡς ξύλα κατακαυθήσονται. V. v. 2 ὁ ἀγρὸς ὁ κόσμος οὗτός ἐστιν.

Matt. 13³⁰.

ἄφετε συναυξάνεσθαι ἀμφότερα μέχρι τοῦ θερισμοῦ . . . συλλέξατε πρῶτον τὰ ζιζάνια . . . σῖτον συναγάγετε. ⁴⁰ πυρὶ κατακαίεται. ³⁸ ὁ δὲ ἀγρός ἐστιν ὁ κόσμος.

This might certainly have been suggested by the parable of the tares, the general idea being similar, and the last-quoted words being almost identical. It is the custom of Hermas to transform ideas of which he avails himself, and adapt them to his own composition.

(35) Sim. V. vi. 4.

ἐξουσίαν πᾶσαν λαβὼν παρὰ τοῦ πατρὸς αὐτοῦ.

Matt. 28¹⁸

ἐδόθη μοι πᾶσα ἐξουσία. 11²⁷ πάντα μοι παρεδόθη ὑπὸ τοῦ πατρός μου.

The words are sufficiently related to suggest dependence, but are too few to admit of a confident inference.

d

(36) Vis. III. ix. 8.

παρὰ τοῦ βασιλέως τοῦ μεγάλου.

Matt. 5³⁵.

τοῦ μεγάλου βασιλέως.

The expression is a fairly common one (see Ps. 46³, 47³, 94³; also Tobit 13¹⁵), and the context is quite different.

(37)   Mand. XI. xvi.   Matt. 7^{15, 16}.

δοκίμαζε οὖν ἀπὸ τῶν ἔργων καὶ   τῶν ψευδοπροφητῶν . . . ἀπὸ τῶν
τῆς ζωῆς τὸν ἄνθρωπον τὸν λέγοντα   καρπῶν αὐτῶν ἐπιγνώσεσθε αὐτούς.
ἑαυτὸν πνευματοφόρον εἶναι.

The resemblance here is solely in the sentiment, and that
is not sufficiently characteristic to be of weight apart from
verbal coincidence.

Mark   C

(38)   Mand. IV. ii. 1.   Mark 6⁵².

οὐ συνίω οὐδέν, καὶ ἡ καρδία μου   οὐ γὰρ συνῆκαν . . . ἀλλ' ἦν ἡ καρδία
πεπώρωται.   αὐτῶν πεπωρωμένη [see also 8¹⁷].

The combination of words is confined to Mark, where it
occurs twice, and the verbal agreement is sufficient to suggest
dependence.   It is as if Hermas said, ' I am like those men
who are reproached in the Gospel.'   Nevertheless, we cannot,
on the strength of this single passage, assign a very high
degree of probability to the use of Mark by Hermas.   See
also (43) and the references in (46), which exclude Matthew,
as that Gospel does not use ἐπαισχύνεσθαι.

Luke   D

(39)   Mand. IX. viii.   Luke 18¹.

σὺ οὖν μὴ διαλίπῃς αἰτούμενος . . .   πρὸς τὸ δεῖν πάντοτε προσεύχεσθαι
ἐὰν δὲ ἐκκακήσῃς.   αὐτοὺς καὶ μὴ ἐγκακεῖν [al. ἐκ-].

This connexion of ideas is confined to Luke in the N. T.,
and the expression is sufficiently close to suggest dependence.
The last word is used by Paul, 2 Cor. 4^{1, 16}; Gal. 6⁹; Eph. 3¹³;
2 Thess. 3¹³, but not in reference to prayer, as it is in 2 Clem.
ii. 2.   See also (11).

(II) The Synoptic Tradition.

(40)   Vis. III. vi. 5.   Matt. 13^{20, 21}.

ἔχοντες μὲν πίστιν, ἔχοντες δὲ καὶ   ὁ τὸν λόγον ἀκούων καὶ εὐθὺς μετὰ
πλοῦτον τοῦ αἰῶνος τούτου. ὅταν   χαρᾶς λαμβάνων αὐτόν· . . . γενομένης
γένηται θλῖψις, διὰ τὸν πλοῦτον αὐτῶν   δὲ θλίψεως . . . σκανδαλίζεται.
καὶ διὰ τὰς πραγματείας ἀπαρνοῦνται
τὸν Κύριον αὐτῶν.   Mark 4^{18, 19}.

Sim. IX. xx. 1, 2.   οἱ εἰς τὰς ἀκάνθας σπειρόμενοι . . .
                                        αἱ μέριμναι τοῦ αἰῶνος καὶ ἡ ἀπάτη τοῦ
οἱ μὲν τρίβολοί εἰσιν οἱ πλούσιοι,   πλούτου καὶ αἱ περὶ τὰ λοιπὰ ἐπιθυμίαι
αἱ δὲ ἄκανθαι οἱ ἐν ταῖς πραγματείαις   . . . συμπνίγουσιν τὸν λόγον.

ταῖς ποικίλαις ἐμπεφυρμένοι . . . πνιγό-
μενοι ὑπὸ τῶν πράξεων αὐτῶν.

Luke 8¹⁴.
οὗτοι . . . συμπνίγονται.

See also xxi. 3.

The resemblance here may very well indicate acquaintance with the parable of the sower, though it is impossible to connect this acquaintance with a particular Gospel.

(41) Vis. IV. ii. 6.   Matt. 26²⁴; Mark 14²¹.   1 Clem. xlvi. 8.

οὐαὶ τοῖς . . . παρακού-
σασιν· αἱρετώτερον ἦν
αὐτοῖς τὸ μὴ γεννηθῆναι.

καλὸν ἦν αὐτῷ, εἰ οὐκ
ἐγεννήθη ὁ ἄνθρωπος
ἐκεῖνος.

εἶπεν γάρ· Οὐαὶ τῷ
ἀνθρώπῳ ἐκείνῳ· καλὸν
ἦν αὐτῷ εἰ οὐκ ἐγεννήθη.

This might certainly be borrowed from the Synoptic saying, the change being no greater than we may expect when there is no express quotation. The quotation in Clement (56) proves that the saying was known in Rome, but does not attach it to a particular Gospel.

(42)   Mand. IV. i. 1.

μὴ ἀναβαινέτω σου ἐπὶ τὴν καρδίαν
περὶ γυναικὸς ἀλλοτρίας.

Matt. 5²⁸.

πᾶς ὁ βλέπων γυναῖκα πρὸς τὸ ἐπιθυ-
μῆσαι αὐτῆς ἤδη ἐμοίχευσεν αὐτὴν ἐν
τῇ καρδίᾳ αὐτοῦ.

Mand. IV. i. 6.

ἐὰν δὲ ἀπολύσας τὴν γυναῖκα ἑτέραν
γαμήσῃ, καὶ αὐτὸς μοιχᾶται.

Matt. 19⁹; Mark 10¹¹.

ὃς ἂν ἀπολύσῃ τὴν γυναῖκα αὐτοῦ, εἰ
μὴ ἐπὶ πορνείᾳ [Mk. om.], καὶ γαμήσῃ
ἄλλην, μοιχᾶται [Mk. add. ἐπ' αὐτήν].

The first of these passages is similar in sentiment, though not in words, to Matthew. The second resembles the Gospels both in thought and language. It goes beyond 1 Cor. 7¹⁰, ¹¹, and, with Mark, omits the qualification in Matthew. Paul's reference shows there was a Christian doctrine on the subject apart from a written Gospel; but the words here are so much closer to the Gospels than are Paul's that we may reasonably infer some kind of literary dependence. At all events, the passages indicate acquaintance with the Synoptic tradition.

(43)   Sim. IX. xx. 2.

οἱ πλούσιοι . . . δυσκόλως εἰσελεύσονται εἰς τὴν βασιλείαν τοῦ Θεοῦ.

Matt. 19²³.

δυσκόλως πλούσιος [Tisch. πλ.
δυσ.] εἰσελεύσεται εἰς τὴν βασιλείαν
τῶν οὐρανῶν. Mark 10²³ πῶς δυσκόλως οἱ τὰ χρήματα ἔχοντες εἰς τὴν βασιλείαν τοῦ Θεοῦ εἰσελεύσονται. Luke
18²⁴ nearly the same as Mark.

We can hardly doubt that this is a quotation.

(44)   Sim. V. ii. 1.
τὴν παραβολήν. 2 ἐφύτευσεν ἀμπελῶνα . . . δοῦλον . . . παρεκαλέσατο
αὐτόν . . . ἐξῆλθε δὲ ὁ δεσπότης . . .
εἰς τὴν ἀποδημίαν. 5 μετὰ χρόνον ἦλθεν
ὁ δεσπότης τοῦ δούλου. 7 θέλω αὐτὸν
συγκληρονόμον τῷ υἱῷ μου ποιῆσαι.

Matt. 21³³ ; Mark 12¹ ; Luke 20⁹.
παραβολήν [Mk. ἐν παραβολαῖς]
. . . ἐφύτευσεν ἀμπελῶνα [Mk. ἀμπ.
ἐφύτ.] . . . ἀπεδήμησεν.
Matt. 25¹⁴.
ἐκάλεσεν . . . δούλους [Lk. 19¹³].
¹⁹ μετὰ δὲ πολὺν χρόνον ἔρχεται
ὁ κύριος τῶν δούλων.
Mark 12⁷ ; Luke 20¹⁴.
ὁ κληρονόμος [ὁ υἱός].

This may possibly have been suggested by the Gospels;
and the whole parable seems framed on the model of the
evangelical parables.

(45)   Sim. IX. xxix. 1, 2, 3.
ὡς νήπια βρέφη . . . οἱ τοιοῦτοι . . .
κατοικήσουσιν ἐν τῇ βασιλείᾳ τοῦ
Θεοῦ . . . πάντα γὰρ τὰ βρέφη ἔνδοξά
ἐστι παρὰ τῷ Θεῷ καὶ πρῶτα παρ᾽
αὐτῷ.
See also xxxi. 3 'felices vos
iudicio omnes . . . quicumque
estis innocentes sicut infantes,
quoniam pars vestra bona est
et honorata apud Deum.'

Matt. 18³.
ἐὰν μὴ . . . γένησθε ὡς τὰ παιδία,
οὐ μὴ εἰσέλθητε εἰς τὴν βασιλείαν τῶν
οὐρανῶν. ¹⁰ οἱ ἄγγελοι αὐτῶν . . .
βλέπουσι τὸ πρόσωπον τοῦ πατρός
μου. ⁴ ὁ μείζων ἐν τῇ βασιλείᾳ τῶν
οὐρανῶν. 19¹⁴; Mark 10¹⁴ τῶν γὰρ
τοιούτων ἐστὶν ἡ βασιλεία τῶν οὐρανῶν
[Mark τοῦ Θεοῦ]. Cf. Matt. 20²⁷
πρῶτος.

It is not improbable that this is derived from some such
saying as we find in the Gospels.

(46)   Sim. VIII. vi. 4.
ἐπαισχυνθέντες τὸ ὄνομα Κυρίου.
Sim. IX. xiv. 6.
ὅτι οὐκ ἐπαισχύνονται τὸ ὄνομα αὐτοῦ
φορεῖν.
Sim. IX. xxi. 3.
τὸ ὄνομα ἐπαισχύνονται τοῦ Κυρίου.

Mark 8³⁸ ; Luke 9²⁶.
ὃς γὰρ ἂν ἐπαισχυνθῇ με καὶ τοὺς
ἐμοὺς λόγους.
Comp. (31).

(III) The Fourth Gospel.
D

John
(47) Vis. II. ii. 8.
τοὺς ἀρνησαμένους τὸν
Κύριον αὐτῶν ἀπεγνω-
ρίσθαι ἀπὸ τῆς ζωῆς
αὐτῶν.

d
John 11²⁵, 14⁶.
Ἐγώ εἰμι . . . ἡ ζωή.

Col. 3⁴.
ὁ Χριστὸς . . . ἡ ζωὴ
ἡμῶν.
Matt. 10³³.
ὅστις δ᾽ ἂν ἀρνήσηταί
με ἔμπροσθεν τῶν ἀνθρώ-
πων, ἀρνήσομαι αὐτὸν
κἀγώ. Also Luke 12⁹,
somewhat varied.

SHEPHERD OF HERMAS   123

The only connexion is in the word ζωή, and it is by no
means certain that it refers to Christ in Hermas; in any case,
the verse in Colossians is sufficient to show that the expression need not be borrowed from John. The sentiment of the
passage is closer to the Synoptics.

(48)   Sim. V. vi. 3.   John 10¹⁸.
δοὺς αὐτοῖς τὸν νόμον ὃν ἔλαβε παρὰ   ταύτην τὴν ἐντολὴν ἔλαβον παρὰ
τοῦ πατρὸς αὐτοῦ.   τοῦ πατρός μου. Cf. 12⁴⁹, 14³¹, 15¹⁰.

The identity of expression may be accidental, for it is
sufficiently explained by the context.

(49)   Sim. IX. xii. 1.   John 10⁷, ⁹.
ἡ πύλη ὁ υἱὸς τοῦ Θεοῦ ἐστι. 5   ἐγώ εἰμι ἡ θύρα. vs. ¹⁷ διὰ τοῦτό
εἰς τὴν βασιλείαν τοῦ Θεοῦ ἄλλως   με ὁ πατὴρ ἀγαπᾷ.
εἰσελθεῖν οὐ δύναται ἄνθρωπος εἰ μὴ   14⁶ οὐδεὶς ἔρχεται πρὸς τὸν πατέρα,
διὰ τοῦ ὀνόματος τοῦ υἱοῦ αὐτοῦ τοῦ   εἰ μὴ δι' ἐμοῦ.
ἠγαπημένου ὑπ' αὐτοῦ. 6 ἡ δὲ πύλη
ὁ υἱὸς τοῦ Θεοῦ ἐστίν· αὕτη μία εἴσοδός
ἐστι πρὸς τὸν Κύριον. ἄλλως οὖν οὐδεὶς
εἰσελεύσεται πρὸς αὐτὸν εἰ μὴ διὰ τοῦ
υἱοῦ αὐτοῦ.

The figure of a gate admitting to the tower which represents the Church is a natural one, and need not be borrowed.
Nevertheless, the passage has a Johannine colouring; but
whether this is sufficient to prove a literary connexion may
be reasonably questioned. Such sentiments must have spread
among Christians apart from direct literary influence.

(50)   Sim. IX. xv. 3.   John 3³⁻⁵.
ταῦτα τὰ ὀνόματα [of various   οὐ δύναται ἰδεῖν τὴν βασιλείαν τοῦ
vices] ὁ φορῶν τοῦ Θεοῦ δοῦλος τὴν   Θεοῦ . . . οὐ δύναται εἰσελθεῖν εἰς τὴν
βασιλείαν μὲν ὄψεται τοῦ Θεοῦ, εἰς   βασιλείαν τοῦ Θεοῦ.
αὐτὴν δὲ οὐκ εἰσελεύσεται.

The two expressions remind one of the passage in John;
but in the latter they are synonymous, whereas in Hermas
they are contrasted. The idea of *entering* into the kingdom
of God is too common to be an indication of any particular
passage; and the *idea* of seeing it, though not so frequently
expressed, occurs in Mark 9¹, with the parallel in Luke 9²⁷,
and the notion of seeing it without entering it is suggested by
Matthew 26⁶⁴, with the parallel in Mark 14⁶², where the word
ὄψεσθε is used. See also Luke 21²⁷.

II CLEMENT

INTRODUCTION.

PHOTIUS (Biblioth. Cod. 126) says of 2 Clement, ῥητά τινα ὡς ἀπὸ τῆς θείας γραφῆς ξενίζοντα παρεισάγει, ὧν οὐδ' ἡ πρώτη ἀπήλλακτο παντελῶς. A case of such alien 'scripture' quotation common to 1 and 2 Clement is that found most fully in 2 Clem. xi. 2–4 (1 Clem. xxiii. 3 f.) λέγει γὰρ καὶ ὁ προφητικὸς λόγος, Ταλαίπωροί εἰσιν οἱ δίψυχοι, κτλ. 'The prophetic discourse' in question may or may not be 'Eldad and Modat': but at any rate it shows that our homilist's quotations of divinely authoritative words are not controlled by any strict canonical idea, even in relation to O.T. writings. Yet we must beware of mistaking free citations for verbal quotations from unknown Gospels. For what follows the words λέγει ἡ γραφὴ ἐν τῷ Ἰεζεκιήλ, in vi. 8, is in fact a free paraphrase ; and he is apt to use φησίν with words which merely give the effect of a passage (e. g. xii. 6 with allusion to xii. 2 ; cf. vii. 6 where words of Isa. 66²⁴ are adapted). In v. 2, however, he certainly cites a non-canonical Gospel with λέγει ὁ Κύριος, as also in viii. 5, with the addition ἐν τῷ εὐαγγελίῳ.

In xiv. 2 our author appeals, for teaching about the Church, to 'The Books (τὰ βιβλία + prophetarum, Syriac) and the Apostles.' Thus, on the one hand, he co-ordinates the apostolic writings with the O.T. as to authority ; but, on the other, he does not include them under the same term, 'the Books,' i. e. his Bible. Whether, again, he reckons Gospel narratives under 'the Apostles' must be held doubtful, in view of his free use of at least one apocryphal Gospel, possibly that 'According to (the) Egyptians'—which he can hardly have believed Apostolic in origin (assuming that he cites it at all). This suggests that he thought only of the sayings of the Lord in such narratives as the authoritative element ; just as he refers (xiii. 3) to 'the Oracles of God' on the lips of Christians, and cites the substance of words found in Luke 6³², ³⁵, as embodying a divine oracle (λέγει ὁ Θεός). Here God is con-

ceived as speaking in Christ, who elsewhere is Himself cited
as the authority behind the Gospel, e. g. 'For the Lord saith
in the Gospel' (viii. 5), where an Evangelic source distinct
from any of our Gospels seems to be cited. All this prevents
any very strict inference from the fact that words found in
Matt. 9¹³, Mark 2¹⁷ (cf. Luke 5³²) are cited (ii. 4), after an
O. T. passage, with καὶ ἑτέρα δὲ γραφὴ λέγει. Thus the book
in question is 'a scripture' primarily because of what it
embodies, viz. part of the Gospel spoken by the Lord ; and
elsewhere he can quote with equal deference matter certainly
not found in any of our Gospels. Indeed, all the facts would
be fairly satisfied by the hypothesis that our homilist quotes
throughout from a single Evangelic source, if we were at
liberty to imagine it a sort of combined recension of two or
more of our Synoptists, embodying such additions as made it
correspond more completely to the notion of Christ's 'Gospel'
prevalent in the non-Jewish part of the Alexandrine Church.
In that case it would be an earlier local type of harmony [1]
than Tatian's *Diatessaron*, which so largely superseded our
Gospels, even at a later date, among Syriac-speaking Christians.
As regards the N. T. Epistles, the phrase 'The Books and the
Apostles' prepares us to find pretty free use of them, even
though they are not formally quoted.

EPISTLES.

C

Hebrews   c
(1)   2 Clem. xi. 6.   Heb. 10²³.
πιστὸς γάρ ἐστιν ὁ ἐπαγγειλάμενος.   πιστὸς γὰρ ὁ ἐπαγγειλάμενος.

The context of the two passages is similar, referring to the
need of hope in the presence of grounds for doubt.

d

(2)   2 Clem. i. 6.   Heb. 12¹.
ἀποθέμενοι ἐκεῖνο ὃ περικείμεθα   τοσοῦτον ἔχοντες περικείμενον ἡμῖν
νέφος τῇ αὐτοῦ θελήσει.   νέφος μαρτύρων, ὄγκον ἀποθέμενοι
                                     πάντα . . .

[1] On such a view we should of course have to treat the phenomena pointing
to Clement's use of any of our Synoptists as evidence of indirect or second-
hand use—so pushing back the origin of such a Gospel to a period prior
to that of the immediate source.

Although the thought of these two passages is so different, it seems difficult, in view of the verbal coincidences, to resist the conclusion that the language of 2 Clement is unconsciously influenced by that of Hebrews.

The following points of similarity may be added, though they cannot be classed.

(a)   2 Clem. xvi. 4.   Heb. 13[18].

προσευχὴ . . . ἐκ καλῆς συνειδή-   προσεύχεσθε περὶ ἡμῶν· πειθόμεθα
σεως.   γὰρ ὅτι καλὴν συνείδησιν ἔχομεν.

The expression καλὴ συνείδησις does not occur elsewhere in N. T.

(b) xx. 2 has a general similarity with Heb. 10[32-39]; and the expression Θεοῦ ζῶντος occurs in 2 Clem. xx. 2 and Heb. 10[31] (cf. 3[12]).

D

1 *Corinthians*   d

(3)   2 Clem. ix. 3.   1 Cor. 6[19].

δεῖ οὖν ἡμᾶς ὡς ναὸν Θεοῦ φυλάσ-   ἢ οὐκ οἴδατε ὅτι τὸ σῶμα ὑμῶν ναὸς
σειν τὴν σάρκα.   τοῦ ἐν ὑμῖν Ἁγίου Πνεύματός ἐστιν,
                                     οὗ ἔχετε ἀπὸ Θεοῦ;
                                              1 Cor. 3[16].
                                     οὐκ οἴδατε ὅτι ναὸς Θεοῦ ἐστε . . . ;
                                              Cf. Eph. 2[20-22].

The phrase in 2 Clement has the same meaning as that of 1 Cor. 6[19], and it is very possible that it is derived from St. Paul; but the conception had probably become a common-place among Christians, and we cannot assert a necessary dependence upon any particular passage.

UNCLASSED

(4)   2 Clem. vii. 1.   1 Cor. 9[24, 25].

The metaphor of the games is very common in ancient literature. Cf. Lightfoot, ad loc.

(5) 2 Clem. xi. 7, xiv. 5.   1 Cor. 2[9].

See note on the passage in relation to 1 Clem. (14).

Ephesians   d

(6)   2 Clem. xiv. 2.   Eph. 1[22].

οὐκ οἴομαι δὲ ὑμᾶς ἀγνοεῖν ὅτι   καὶ αὐτὸν ἔδωκε κεφαλὴν ὑπὲρ
ἐκκλησία ζῶσα σῶμά ἐστι Χριστοῦ   πάντα τῇ ἐκκλησίᾳ, ἥτις ἐστὶ τὸ σῶμα
(λέγει γὰρ ἡ γραφή· Ἐποίησεν ὁ θεὸς   αὐτοῦ, τὸ πλήρωμα τοῦ τὰ πάντα ἐν
τὸν ἄνθρωπον ἄρσεν καὶ θῆλυ· τὸ   πᾶσι πληρουμένου.

ἄρσεν ἐστὶν ὁ Χριστός, τὸ θῆλυ ἡ
ἐκκλησία), καὶ ὅτι τὰ βιβλία καὶ οἱ
ἀπόστολοι τὴν ἐκκλησίαν οὐ νῦν εἶναι
ἀλλὰ ἄνωθεν [φασίν].

Eph. 5²³.

ὅτι ἀνήρ ἐστι κεφαλὴ τῆς γυναικός,
ὡς καὶ ὁ Χριστὸς κεφαλὴ τῆς ἐκκλησίας, κτλ.·

Eph. 1⁴.

καθὼς ἐξελέξατο ἡμᾶς ἐν αὐτῷ πρὸ
καταβολῆς κόσμου.

We have to notice here :—

1. The treatment of the Church as the body of Christ.

2. The comparison of the union of Christ and the Church to the union of man and woman.

3. The conception of the Church as pre-existing, which possibly corresponds in some degree with St. Paul's conception of the election before the foundation of the world.

UNCLASSED

(7)   2 Clem. xix. 2.   Eph. 4¹⁸.

ἐσκοτίσμεθα τὴν διάνοιαν. Cf. (17).

(8)   2 Clem. xiii. 1.   Eph. 6⁶.

ἀνθρωπάρεσκοι.   Cf. Col. 3²².

James   d

(9)   2 Clem. vi. 3, 5.   Jas. 4⁴.

ἔστιν δὲ οὗτος ὁ αἰὼν καὶ ὁ μέλλων   οὐκ οἴδατε ὅτι ἡ φιλία τοῦ κόσμου
δύο ἐχθροί... οὐ δυνάμεθα οὖν τῶν   ἔχθρα τοῦ Θεοῦ ἐστιν, ὃς ἂν οὖν
δύο φίλοι εἶναι· δεῖ δὲ ἡμᾶς τούτῳ   βουληθῇ φίλος εἶναι τοῦ κόσμου,
ἀποταξαμένους ἐκείνῳ χρᾶσθαι.   ἐχθρὸς τοῦ Θεοῦ καθίσταται.

There is a similarity of feeling between these passages, but no verbal parallel, except in the occurrence of φίλοι and φιλία.

(10)   2 Clem. xv. 1.   Jas. 5¹⁶.

μισθὸς γὰρ οὐκ ἔστιν μικρὸς πλανω-   εὔχεσθε ὑπὲρ ἀλλήλων, ὅπως ἰαθῆτε.
μένην ψυχὴν καὶ ἀπολλυμένην ἀπο-   πολὺ ἰσχύει δέησις δικαίου ἐνεργου-
στρέψαι εἰς τὸ σωθῆναι.   μένη.

(11)   2 Clem. xvi. 4.   Jas. 5²⁰.

κρείσσων νηπτεία προσευχῆς, ἐλεη-   ὁ ἐπιστρέψας ἁμαρτωλὸν ἐκ πλάνης
μοσύνη δὲ ἀμφοτέρων· ἀγάπη δὲ   ὁδοῦ αὐτοῦ σώσει ψυχὴν ἐκ θανάτου,
καλύπτει πλῆθος ἁμαρτιῶν· προσευχὴ   καὶ καλύψει πλῆθος ἁμαρτιῶν.
δὲ ἐκ καλῆς συνειδήσεως ἐκ θανάτου
ῥύεται.

The occurrence in 2 Clement of so many points similar to those in Jas. 5¹⁶, ²⁰ is worthy of notice, although none of the resemblances may be very striking in themselves.

(12)   2 Clem. xx. 2–4.   Jas. 5⁷· ⁸· ¹⁰

πιστεύωμεν οὖν, ἀδελφοὶ καὶ ἀδελ-   μακροθυμήσατε οὖν, ἀδελφοί, ἕως
φαί· Θεοῦ ζῶντος πεῖραν ἀθλοῦμεν,   τῆς παρουσίας τοῦ Κυρίου. ἰδού, ὁ
καὶ γυμναζόμεθα τῷ νῦν βίῳ ἵνα τῷ   γεωργὸς ἐκδέχεται τὸν τίμιον καρπὸν
μέλλοντι στεφανωθῶμεν. οὐδεὶς τῶν   τῆς γῆς, μακροθυμῶν ἐπ' αὐτῷ, ἕως
δικαίων ταχὺν καρπὸν ἔλαβεν, ἀλλ'   λάβῃ ὑετὸν πρώιμον καὶ ὄψιμον.
ἐκδέχεται αὐτόν. εἰ γὰρ τὸν μισθὸν   μακροθυμήσατε καὶ ὑμεῖς . . . ὑπό-
τῶν δικαίων ὁ θεὸς συντόμως ἀπεδίδου,   δειγμα λάβετε, ἀδελφοί, τῆς κακο-
εὐθέως ἐμπορίαν ἠσκοῦμεν καὶ οὐ   παθείας καὶ τῆς μακροθυμίας τοὺς
θεοσέβειαν.   προφήτας.

There is a general similarity between these passages in the
spirit of their teaching, but these parallels, like the others
cited with passages in James, are insufficient to give positive
evidence in favour of literary dependence.

    1 *Peter*   d
(13)   2 Clem. xiv. 2.   1 Pet. 1²⁰.

ἐφανερώθη δὲ ἐπ' ἐσχάτων τῶν   φανερωθέντος δὲ ἐπ' ἐσχάτου τῶν
ἡμερῶν ἵνα ἡμᾶς σώσῃ.   χρόνων δι' ὑμᾶς.

Cf. also ἀπὸ τῆς ἐκκλησίας τῆς ζωῆς and ἐκκλησία ζῶσα (occurring
in the same section of 2 Clement) with λίθοι ζῶντες (1 Pet. 2⁴).

(14)   2 Clem xvi. 4.   1 Pet. 4⁸.

ἀγάπη δὲ καλύπτει πλῆθος ἁμαρτιῶν   ἀγάπη καλύπτει πλῆθος ἁμαρτιῶν.
See note on 1 Clement (48).

UNCLASSED

    Romans
(15)   2 Clem. i. 8.   Rom. 4¹⁷.

ἐκάλεσεν γὰρ ἡμᾶς οὐκ ὄντας καὶ   καλοῦντος τὰ μὴ ὄντα ὡς ὄντα.
ἠθέλησεν ἐκ μὴ ὄντος εἶναι ἡμᾶς.

The correspondence is superficial, and the phrase in some
sense is not uncommon.   Cf. Lightfoot, ad loc.

(16)   2 Clem. viii. 2.   Rom. 9²¹.

The metaphor of the clay and the potter is used by Jeremiah
(18⁴ ff.), and it would therefore be unsafe to assert the dependence of 2 Clement on Romans.

(17)   2 Clem. xix. 2.   Rom. 1²¹.

ἐσκοτίσμεθα τὴν διάνοιαν.   καὶ ἐσκοτίσθη ἡ ἀσύνετος αὐτῶν
                                  καρδία.

                                  Eph. 4¹⁸.

                                  ἐσκοτισμένοι τῇ διανοίᾳ.

The phrase is parallel to that of Romans and Ephesians, but closer to the latter. Cf. (7).

1 *Timothy*

(18) 2 Clem. xx. 5. 1 Tim. 1¹⁷.

There is considerable resemblance between these doxologies, but it seems to us impossible to lay much stress upon this, as it is very possible that they are both based upon liturgical forms.

(19) 2 Clem. xv. 1. 1 Tim. 4¹⁰.
Cf. Jas. 5¹⁹, ²⁰ (11).

2 *Peter*

(20) 2 Clem. xvi. 3.

γινώσκετε δὲ ὅτι ἔρχεται ἤδη ἡ ἡμέρα τῆς κρίσεως ὡς κλίβανος καιό- μενος, καὶ τακήσονταί τινες τῶν οὐρα- νῶν, καὶ πᾶσα ἡ γῆ ὡς μόλιβος ἐπὶ πυρὶ τηκόμενος, καὶ τότε φανήσεται τὰ κρύφια καὶ φανερὰ ἔργα τῶν ἀν- θρώπων.

Mal. 4¹ ἰδοὺ ἡμέρα ἔρχεται καιομένη ὡς κλίβανος.
Isa. 34⁴ τακήσονται πᾶσαι αἱ δυνάμεις τῶν οὐρανῶν.

This affords parallels to 2 Pet. 3⁶⁻⁷, ¹⁰; notice also the variant εὑρεθήσεται in 2 Pet. 3¹⁰, which is near to φανήσεται in 2 Clem. xvi. 3.

[Lightfoot thinks the agreement of 2 Clem. xi. 2 with 2 Pet. 1¹⁹ in ὁ προφητικὸς λόγος, and with 2⁸ in ἡμέραν ἐξ ἡμέρας, worthy of notice.]

Jude

(21) 2 Clem. xx. 4. Jude ⁶.

διὰ τοῦτο θεία κρίσις ἔβλαψεν πνεῦμα μὴ ὂν δίκαιον, καὶ ἐβάρυνεν δεσμοῖς.

ἀγγέλους τε τοὺς μὴ τηρήσαντας τὴν ἑαυτῶν ἀρχήν . . . εἰς κρίσιν μεγάλης ἡμέρας δεσμοῖς ἀϊδίοις ὑπὸ ζόφον τετήρηκεν.

These passages seem parallel, but it is to be remembered that the interpretation of 2 Clem. xx. 4 is very doubtful, that the variant δεσμός (C) is found for δεσμοῖς (S, considerably weakening the parallel), and that changes of the text have also been proposed.

GOSPELS.

(I) The Synoptic Gospels.

C
c

Matthew

(22) 2 Clem. v. 5, vi. 7 (viii. 4).

Matt. 11²⁸ f., 25⁴⁵ f.

ἡ δὲ ἐπαγγελία τοῦ Χριστοῦ μεγάλη καὶ θαυμαστή ἐστιν, καὶ [+ ἡ, C] ἀνάπαυσις τῆς μελλούσης βασιλείας καὶ ζωῆς αἰωνίου.

ποιοῦντες γὰρ τὸ θέλημα τοῦ Χριστοῦ εὑρήσομεν ἀνάπαυσιν· εἰ δὲ μήγε, οὐδὲν ἡμᾶς ῥύσεται ἐκ τῆς αἰωνίου κολάσεως, ἐὰν παρακούσωμεν τῶν ἐντολῶν αὐτοῦ.

τὰς ἐντολὰς τοῦ Κυρίου φυλάξαντες ληψόμεθα ζωὴν αἰώνιον.

δεῦτε πρός με, . . . κἀγὼ ἀναπαύσω ὑμᾶς· ἄρατε τὸν ζυγόν μου ἐφ᾽ ὑμᾶς, . . . καὶ εὑρήσετε ἀνάπαυσιν ταῖς ψυχαῖς ὑμῶν.

ἐφ᾽ ὅσον οὐκ ἐποιήσατε . . . Καὶ ἀπελεύσονται οὗτοι εἰς κόλασιν αἰώνιον, οἱ δὲ δίκαιοι εἰς ζωὴν αἰώνιον.

Matthew alone has (1) Christ's promise of rest to those who do His will—such persons ' finding rest ' ; (2) the warning as to κόλασις αἰώνιος (only here in N. T.) for those who do not His commands, as set forth in the Judgement Scene, while the prize is ἡ (μέλλουσα) βασιλεία and ζωὴ αἰώνιος. Hence it is hard to escape the impression that our homilist is using this Gospel directly or indirectly.

d

(23) 2 Clem. iii. 2.

Matt. 10³² (Luke 12⁸).

λέγει δὲ καὶ αὐτός· Τὸν ὁμολογήσαντά με [ἐνώπιον τῶν ἀνθρώπων, om. Syr.], ὁμολογήσω αὐτὸν ἐνώπιον τοῦ πατρός μου.

πᾶς οὖν ὅστις ὁμολογήσει ἐν ἐμοὶ ἔμπροσθεν τῶν ἀνθρώπων, ὁμολογήσω κἀγὼ ἐν αὐτῷ ἔμπροσθεν τοῦ πατρός μου τοῦ ἐν οὐρανοῖς.

Clement's quotation is nearer Matthew than Luke (who has ὁ υἱὸς τοῦ ἀνθρώπου . . . ἔμπροσθεν τῶν ἀγγέλων τοῦ Θεοῦ). But even retaining ἐνώπιον κτλ. (Matthew and Luke have ἔμπροσθεν κτλ.), Clement's wording is sufficiently different to suggest the direct use of another source altogether, whether oral or written. See the next note.

(24) 2 Clem. iv. 2.

Matt. 7²¹.

λέγει γάρ· Οὐ πᾶς ὁ λέγων μοι, Κύριε, Κύριε, σωθήσεται, ἀλλ᾽ ὁ ποιῶν τὴν δικαιοσύνην.

οὐ πᾶς ὁ λέγων μοι, Κύριε, Κύριε, εἰσελεύσεται εἰς τὴν βασιλείαν τῶν οὐρανῶν, ἀλλ᾽ ὁ ποιῶν τὸ θέλημα τοῦ πατρός μου τοῦ ἐν οὐρανοῖς.

Σωθήσεται may simply echo οὐ γὰρ τοῦτο σώσει ἡμᾶς, just
before (cf. iii. 3, also i. 1, 4, ii. 2, 4, 7), especially as Matthew's
phrase is rather Jewish ; and δικαιοσύνην may be a paraphrase
to suit the context, which has *Christ's* will directly in view
(cf. xi. 7, xix. 3 for Clement's use of the phrase). Or the
quotation may have stood in this form in the same source from
which iv. 5, v. 2–4 seem to come, the subject being akin.
Or, again, it may come from oral tradition.

(25)   2 Clem. vi. 9.   Matt. 22¹¹ f.

ἡμεῖς, ἐὰν μὴ τηρήσωμεν τὸ βάπτι-   ... ὁ βασιλεὺς ... λέγει αὐτῷ,
σμα ἁγνὸν καὶ ἀμίαντον, ποίᾳ πεποι-   Ἑταῖρε, πῶς εἰσῆλθες ὧδε μὴ ἔχων
θήσει εἰσελευσόμεθα εἰς τὸ βασίλειον   ἔνδυμα γάμου,
τοῦ Θεοῦ ; ... ἐὰν μὴ εὑρεθῶμεν ἔργα
ἔχοντες ὅσια καὶ δίκαια ;

Here resemblance turns on the meaning of τὸ βασίλειον. It
is true that it can mean 'kingdom,' but rather in the abstract
sense of 'sovereignty,' as in xvii. 5 ἰδόντες τὸ βασίλειον τοῦ
κόσμου ἐν τῷ Ἰησοῦ—a sense which ill suits the contrast here,
where it is a matter of 'entering into' τὸ βασίλειον 'with
assurance.' Elsewhere βασιλεία is used of the Kingdom men
hope to enter, see xi. 7 εἰσήξομεν εἰς τὴν βασιλείαν αὐτοῦ. Hence
βασίλειον may well have the usual sense of 'royal palace,'
and so allude to the situation in Matthew's parable of the
Wedding Garment, here represented by the baptismal garment kept pure by a holy life (ἔργα ἔχοντες ὅσια καὶ δίκαια),
cf. *Acta Barnabae*, 12 τὸ ἔνδυμα ἐκεῖνο, ὅπερ ἐστιν ἄφθαρτον εἰς
τὸν αἰῶνα.

UNCLASSED

(26)   2 Clem. xvii. 1.   Matt. 28¹⁹ f.

εἰ γὰρ ἐντολὰς ἔχομεν [ἵνα, Syr.]   πορευθέντες οὖν μαθητεύσατε πάντα
καὶ τοῦτο πράσσομεν (-ωμεν, Syr.),   τὰ ἔθνη, βαπτίζοντες αὐτοὺς εἰς τὸ
ἀπὸ τῶν εἰδώλων ἀποσπᾶν καὶ κατη-   ὄνομα τοῦ πατρὸς κτλ. ... , διδά-
χεῖν, κτλ.   σκοντες αὐτοὺς τηρεῖν πάντα ὅσα
                                          ἐνετειλάμην ὑμῖν.

Just a possible allusion, in view of the reference to missionary
ἐντολάς : yet ἀπὸ τῶν εἰδώλων ἀποσπᾶν καὶ κατηχεῖν rather recalls
the gist of the *Kerygma Petri*.

K 2

D

Luke   **d**

(27)   2 Clem. ii. 5, 7.   Luke 19¹⁰.

τοῦτο λέγει, ὅτι δεῖ τοὺς ἀπολ-   ἦλθε γὰρ ὁ υἱὸς τοῦ ἀνθρώπου
λυμένους σώζειν . . . οὕτως καὶ ὁ   ζητῆσαι καὶ σῶσαι τὸ ἀπολωλός.
Χριστὸς ἠθέλησεν σῶσαι τὰ ἀπολ-
λύμενα, καὶ ἔσωσεν πολλούς, ἐλθὼν
καὶ καλέσας ἡμᾶς ἤδη ἀπολλυμένους.

Here, in spite of certain echoes (e. g. ἐλθὼν καὶ καλέσας) of
ii. 4, discussed below (30), there might be good reason to suspect
allusion to the passage in Luke, but for the fact that Clement
certainly uses at least one non-canonical Gospel.

(28) 2 Clem. xiii. 4.   Luke 6³², ³⁵.   Didache i. 3.

ὅταν γὰρ ἀκούσωσιν   καὶ εἰ ἀγαπᾶτε τοὺς   ποία γὰρ χάρις, ἐὰν
παρ᾽ ἡμῶν ὅτι λέγει ὁ   ἀγαπῶντας ὑμᾶς, ποία   ἀγαπᾶτε τοὺς ἀγαπῶν-
Θεός, Οὐ χάρις ὑμῖν εἰ   ὑμῖν χάρις ἐστί ; . . . τας ὑμᾶς ; . . . ὑμεῖς δὲ
ἀγαπᾶτε τοὺς ἀγαπῶντας πλὴν ἀγαπᾶτε τοὺς ἐχ- ἀγαπᾶτε τοὺς μισοῦντας
ὑμᾶς, ἀλλὰ χάρις ὑμῖν   θροὺς ὑμῶν... καὶ ἔσται ὑμᾶς, καὶ οὐχ ἕξετε
εἰ ἀγαπᾶτε τοὺς ἐχθροὺς   ὁ μισθὸς ὑμῶν πολύς.   ἐχθρόν.
καὶ τοὺς μισοῦντας ὑμᾶς.

No sure argument for the use of Luke can be based on this
passage.   It departs considerably from Luke's wording ; while
it is simply as one of ' God's oracles ' (τὰ λόγια τοῦ Θεοῦ) found
on Christian lips that it is cited.   The addition of καὶ τοὺς
μισοῦντας ὑμᾶς finds parallels in *Did.* i. 3 and Justin, *Apol.* i. 15
ἀγαπᾶτε τοὺς μισοῦντας ὑμᾶς.   Such a variant for τοὺς ἐχθρούς
would arise naturally in common use as a more exact antithesis to ἀγαπᾶτε.   Possibly, however, 2 Clement quotes the
whole saying as known to him in an apocryphal Gospel.

UNCLASSED

(29)   2 Clem. viii. 5.   Luke 16¹⁰ f.

λέγει γὰρ ὁ Κύριος ἐν τῷ εὐαγγελίῳ·   ὁ πιστὸς ἐν ἐλαχίστῳ καὶ ἐν πολλῷ
Εἰ τὸ μικρὸν οὐκ ἐτηρήσατε, τὸ μέγα πιστός ἐστι . . . εἰ οὖν ἐν τῷ ἀδίκῳ
τίς ὑμῖν δώσει ; λέγω γὰρ ὑμῖν ὅτι   μαμωνᾷ πιστοὶ οὐκ ἐγένεσθε, τὸ
ὁ πιστὸς ἐν ἐλαχίστῳ καὶ ἐν πολλῷ   ἀληθινὸν τίς ὑμῖν πιστεύσει ;
πιστός ἐστιν.

Iren. *Adv. Haer.* ii. 34, 3 'Et ideo Dominus dicebat ingratis
exsistentibus in eum : *Si in modico fideles non fuistis, quod magnum
est quis dabit vobis?* significans quoniam qui in modica temporali
vita ingrati exstiterunt ei qui eam praestitit, iuste non percipient
ab eo in saeculum saeculi longitudinem dierum.

Cf. Hippol. *Refut.* x. 33 ὑπάκουε τῷ πεποιηκότι καὶ μὴ ἀντίβαινε νῦν, ἵνα
ἐπὶ τῷ μικρῷ πιστὸς εὑρεθεὶς καὶ τὸ μέγα πιστευθῆναι δυνηθῇς.

While the latter part of Clement's citation of Christ's words 'in the Gospel' agrees exactly with the beginning of the passage in Luke, its former part differs so widely that it is best to regard the whole as quoted from another source altogether. For Irenaeus, followed by Hippolytus, discountenances the idea that the deviation of form is accidental (or represents a glossing of Matt. 25²¹, ²³). That Irenaeus is not quoting Luke 16¹¹ seems clear from the way in which he introduces the words, viz. 'Dominus dicebat ingratis exsistentibus in eum,' which (a) does not suit Luke's context [rather that of Matt. 25¹⁴⁻³⁰], while (b) dicebat is not his usual phrase in citing a definite passage in our Gospels, but points rather to some *logion* handed down as characteristic of his attitude to a class of hearers. Thus, whatever the exact relation of the saying in our two witnesses, they point to its currency outside our Gospels; and if we may argue from the divergence in form—οὐκ ἐτηρήσατε (which must stand, in view of what follows) and *fideles non fuistis*—it was not confined to one circle before Irenaeus's day. Cf. (31), which relates to the same context in Luke (16¹³), also (34).

(II) The Synoptic Tradition.

(30)   2 Clem. ii. 4.

καὶ ἑτέρα δὲ γραφὴ λέγει ὅτι Οὐκ ἦλθον καλέσαι δικαίους, ἀλλὰ ἁμαρτωλούς.

Matt. 9¹³; Mark 2¹⁷ (Luke 5³²).

οὐ (γάρ, Matt.) ἦλθον καλέσαι δικαίους, ἀλλὰ ἁμαρτωλούς.

Cf. Barn. v. 9 ἵνα δείξῃ ὅτι οὐκ ἦλθεν καλέσαι δικαίους, ἀλλὰ ἁμαρτωλούς.

The parallelism with our two first Synoptics (Luke has οὐκ ἐλήλυθα . . . εἰς μετάνοιαν) is exact; and Clement, unlike Barnabas, cites it as 'a scripture.' But what the Gospel writing referred to may be, is a question complicated by Clement's known use of some source distinct from our Gospels; see Introduction ad fin.

(31)   2 Clem. vi. 1 f.

λέγει δὲ ὁ Κύριος· Οὐδεὶς οἰκέτης δύναται δυσὶ κυρίοις δουλεύειν· ἐὰν ἡμεῖς θέλωμεν καὶ Θεῷ δουλεύειν καὶ

Luke 16¹³; Matt. 16²⁶.

Verbally as Luke 16¹³; Matt. 6²⁴ lacks οἰκέτης.

μαμωνᾷ, ἀσύμφορον ἡμῖν ἐστίν. Τί
γὰρ τὸ ὄφελος, ἐάν τις τὸν κόσμον
ὅλον κερδήσῃ, τὴν δὲ ψυχὴν ζημιωθῇ;

Nearer Matt. 16²⁶ (cf. Mark
8¹⁶) than Luke 9²⁵; neither
has τί τὸ ὄφελος;

It looks as if Clement knew both Matthew and Luke, or a
document based on them (cf. Introd. ad fin.).

(32)   2 Clem. ix. 11.

καὶ γὰρ εἶπεν ὁ Κύριος· Ἀδελφοί
μου οὗτοί εἰσιν, οἱ ποιοῦντες τὸ θέλημα
τοῦ πατρός μου.

Luke 8²¹.

μήτηρ μου καὶ ἀδελφοί μου οὗτοί
εἰσιν οἱ τὸν λόγον τοῦ Θεοῦ ἀκούοντες
καὶ ποιοῦντες.

Matt. 12⁴⁹ f· (Mark 3³⁵).

ἰδού, ἡ μήτηρ μου καὶ οἱ ἀδελφοί
μου· ὅστις γὰρ ἂν ποιήσῃ τὸ θέλημα
τοῦ πατρός μου τοῦ ἐν οὐρανοῖς, αὐτός
μου ἀδελφός, κτλ.

Epiphanius, *Haer.* xxx. 14 οὗτοί εἰσιν οἱ ἀδελφοί μου καὶ ἡ μήτηρ, οἱ
ποιοῦντες τὰ θελήματα τοῦ πατρός μου.

Clem. Alex. *Ecl. Proph.* 20 ἄγει οὖν εἰς ἐλευθερίαν τὴν τοῦ πατρὸς
συγκληρονόμους υἱοὺς καὶ φίλους· Ἀδελφοί μου γάρ, φησὶν ὁ Κύριος, καὶ
συγκληρονόμοι οἱ ποιοῦντες τὸ θέλημα τοῦ πατρός μου.

Here we seem to have a fusion of the structure of Luke
with the phrasing of Matthew. Yet the resemblance between
2 Clement and the *Ecl. Proph.* suggests that these both
knew the saying in the same form, whether written or in
traditional use. Epiphanius seems to be citing the Ebionite
Gospel, or our Gospels loosely in his own words. See also (35).

(33)   2 Clem. iii. 4 (cf. 5).

ἐξ ὅλης καρδίας καὶ ἐξ ὅλης τῆς
διανοίας.

Mark 12³⁰, cf. Matt. 22³⁷; Luke
10²⁷.

'A reference ultimately to Deut. 6⁵; but as both words
διανοίας and καρδίας do not seem to occur in that passage in
any one text of the LXX, we must suppose that the writer
had in mind the saying rather as it is quoted in the Gospels,
especially Mark xii. 30 ἐξ ὅλης τῆς καρδίας σου . . . καὶ ἐξ ὅλης
τῆς διανοίας σου . . . (comp. Matt. 22³⁷; Luke 10²⁷).' So
Lightfoot ad loc. Yet Mark may follow a current LXX text.
The same may be said of Clement's deviation from Cod. B of
the LXX in the quotation from Isa. 29¹³ which immediately
follows. This appears in a form found also in 1 Clem. xv. 2
and closely related to אAQ of the LXX. See p. 62.

(III) Apocryphal Gospels.

(34) 2 Clem. iv. 5.

διὰ τοῦτο . . . εἶπεν ὁ Κύριος ['Ιησοῦς, Syr., cf. v. 4]· 'Εὰν ἦτε μετ' ἐμοῦ συνηγμένοι ἐν τῷ κόλπῳ μου, καὶ μὴ ποιῆτε τὰς ἐντολάς μου, ἀποβαλῶ ὑμᾶς καὶ ἐρῶ ὑμῖν, ὑπάγετε ἀπ' ἐμοῦ, οὐκ οἶδα ὑμᾶς πόθεν ἐστέ, ἐργάται ἀνομίας.

Luke 13²⁷.

καὶ ἐρεῖ, Λέγω ὑμῖν, οὐκ οἶδα πόθεν ἐστέ· ἀπόστητε ἀπ' ἐμοῦ πάντες ἐργάται ἀδικίας.

Matt. 7²³.

καὶ τότε ὁμολογήσω αὐτοῖς ὅτι Οὐδέποτε ἔγνων ὑμᾶς· ἀποχωρεῖτε ἀπ' ἐμοῦ οἱ ἐργαζόμενοι τὴν ἀνομίαν.

Ps. 6⁹ ἀπόστητε ἀπ' ἐμοῦ πάντες οἱ ἐργαζόμενοι τὴν ἀνομίαν. Justin, *Apol.* i. 16 καὶ τότε ἐρῶ αὐτοῖς· ἀποχωρεῖτε ἀπ' ἐμοῦ, ἐργάται τῆς ἀνομίας, cf. *Dial.* 76 καὶ ἐρῶ αὐτοῖς· ἀναχωρεῖτε ἀπ' ἐμοῦ.

The points in common with Luke, ὑμῖν, οὐκ οἶδα . . . πόθεν ἐστέ, ἐργάται, point to knowledge of the saying in his form rather than Matthew's. Nor need the setting be different from Luke's, as would be the case if its imagery were that of sheep and their shepherd, as in Isa. 40¹¹. This, indeed, would suit the thought of the whole section iii. 2 (or iv. 2)—v. 4. But another interpretation of συνηγμένοι is possible, which would make it continue the imagery of Luke 13²⁷ ἐφάγομεν ἐνώπιόν σου, κτλ. Yet compare (29), (35).

(35) 2 Clem. v. 2–4.

λέγει γὰρ ὁ Κύριος, "Εσεσθε ὡς ἀρνία ἐν μέσῳ λύκων· ἀποκριθεὶς δὲ ὁ Πέτρος αὐτῷ λέγει· 'Εὰν οὖν διασπαράξωσιν οἱ λύκοι τὰ ἀρνία; εἶπεν ὁ Ἰησοῦς τῷ Πέτρῳ· Μὴ φοβείσθωσαν τὰ ἀρνία τοὺς λύκους μετὰ τὸ ἀποθανεῖν αὐτά· καὶ ὑμεῖς μὴ φοβεῖσθε τοὺς ἀποκτέννοντας ὑμᾶς καὶ μηδὲν ὑμῖν δυναμένους ποιεῖν, ἀλλὰ φοβεῖσθε τὸν μετὰ τὸ ἀποθανεῖν ὑμᾶς ἔχοντα ἐξουσίαν ψυχῆς καὶ σώματος, τοῦ βαλεῖν εἰς γέενναν πυρός.

Luke 10³ ; Matt. 10¹⁶.

ἰδού, ἐγὼ ἀποστέλλω ὑμᾶς ὡς ἄρνας (πρόβατα, Matt.) ἐν μέσῳ λύκων.

Luke 12⁴ f.

μὴ φοβηθῆτε ἀπὸ τῶν ἀποκτεινόντων τὸ σῶμα καὶ μετὰ ταῦτα μὴ ἐχόντων περισσότερόν τι ποιῆσαι . . . φοβήθητε τὸν μετὰ τὸ ἀποκτεῖναι ἐξουσίαν ἔχοντα ἐμβαλεῖν εἰς τὴν γέενναν.

Matt. 10²⁸.

καὶ μὴ φοβηθῆτε (ἀπὸ) . . . τὴν δὲ ψυχὴν μὴ δυναμένων ἀποκτεῖναι· φοβήθητε δὲ μᾶλλον τὸν δυνάμενον καὶ ψυχὴν καὶ σῶμα ἀπολέσαι ἐν γεέννῃ.

Justin, *Apol.* i. 19 μὴ φοβεῖσθε τοὺς ἀναιροῦντας ὑμᾶς καὶ μετὰ ταῦτα μὴ δυναμένους τι ποιῆσαι, εἶπε, φοβήθητε δὲ τὸν μετὰ τὸ ἀποθανεῖν δυνάμενον καὶ ψυχὴν καὶ σῶμα εἰς γέενναν ἐμβαλεῖν.

Here the phenomena of 2 Clem. (34), (29) recur, viz. closer verbal resemblance (in the parts common) to Luke than to

Matthew, though the reference to ψυχὴ καὶ σῶμα is found only in Matthew—where moreover both passages occur in the same discourse. The like is true of Justin's citation, which also shows the change of construction from φοβηθῆτε ἀπό to φοβεῖσθε with accusative. All this points to the use by Clement of a source fusing the forms found in Luke and Matthew (as Justin does), and adding fresh matter, in the form of question and answer, tending to connect two *logia* not thus connected even in Matthew, where they are in the same address. In this same source (*ut vid.*) the idea of Christ's lambs is perhaps also introduced to give a context to another *logion* (see above). [Whether this source be identical with that used in xii. 2. which was probably the *Gospel according to the Egyptians*, may be considered an open question. Its character corresponds more nearly to what we know of the Oxyrhynchus *Sayings of Jesus*, than to that Gospel as usually conceived. But it is quite likely that the Egyptian Gospel embodied much matter from earlier Gospels, including the Oxyrhynchus 'Sayings' or Gospel (? cited by Clem. Alex. *Strom.* ii. 9. 45 as the local Gospel κατ᾽ Ἐβραίους); in which case the *Gospel according to the Egyptians* may be the one source cited by 2 Clem. throughout.—J. V. B.]

(36)   2 Clem. xii. 2.

ἐπερωτηθεὶς γὰρ αὐτὸς ὁ Κύριος ὑπό τινος, πότε ἥξει αὐτοῦ ἡ βασιλεία, εἶπεν· Ὅταν ἔσται τὰ δύο ἕν, καὶ τὸ ἔξω ὡς τὸ ἔσω, καὶ τὸ ἄρσεν μετὰ τῆς θηλείας οὔτε ἄρσεν οὔτε θῆλυ.

Clem. Alex. *Strom.* iii. 13, 92.

διὰ τοῦτό τοι, ὁ Κασσιανός φησι, πυνθανομένης τῆς Σαλώμης πότε γνωσθήσεται τὰ περὶ ὧν ἥρετο, ἔφη ὁ Κύριος· Ὅταν τὸ τῆς αἰσχύνης ἔνδυμα πατήσητε καὶ ὅταν γένηται τὰ δύο ἕν, καὶ τὸ ἄρρεν μετὰ τῆς θηλείας οὔτε ἄρρεν οὔτε θῆλυ.

Clem. Alex. vouches that what Cassian cites occurs in the Gospel κατ᾽ Αἰγυπτίους, and it looks as if 2 Clement quotes from the same passage. Only 2 Clement omits its opening clause, as not to his purpose (perhaps as liable to Encratite exegesis); while Cassian omits the third clause, καὶ τὸ ἔξω ὡς τὸ ἔσω, as not to his purpose.

TABLES OF RESULTS

TABLE I

	Barnabas.	Didache. 'Two Ways.'	Didache. Rest.	1 Clement	Ignatius.	Polycarp.	Hermas.	2 Clement.	Author affording first marked trace.
Synoptic Tradition	+	?	+	+	+	+	+	+	{ Barnabas { Didache
Matthew	D	...	C ? [D]	...	B	...	C	C*	Didache
Mark	...	...	...	...	D ?	...	C	...	Hermas
Luke	?	...	D [D]	...	D	...	D	D*	Didache
John	?	...	?	...	B	C	D	...	Ignatius
Acts	...	D ?	...	C	D	C	D	...	1 Clement
Romans	B	D ?	...	A	C	B	D	?	{ Barnabas { 1 Clement
1 Corinthians	D	...	D	A	A	A	B	D	1 Clement
2 Corinthians	D	...	...	D	C ?	B	...	...	Polycarp
Galatians	...	...	...	D	C	B	...	...	Ignatius
Ephesians	C	...	...	D	B	B	B	D	{ Barnabas { Ignatius
Philippians	...	...	...	D	C	B	...	...	Ignatius
Colossians	D	...	...	D	D	D	...	...	? Barnabas
1 Thessalonians	...	...	...	...	D ?	...	D	...	? Hermas
2 Thessalonians	...	...	...	...	D ?	B	...	...	Polycarp
1 Timothy	D	...	...	D	C	B	...	?	Ignatius
2 Timothy	D	...	...	...	C	B	...	...	Ignatius
Titus	D	...	...	C	C	...	...	...	1 Clement
Philemon	...	...	...	...	D ?	...	...	...	
Hebrews	C	?	...	A	D	C	C	C	{ Barnabas { 1 Clement
James	...	...	...	...	...	...	C	D	Hermas
1 Peter	D	...	[D]	D	D	A	D	D	Polycarp
2 Peter	...	...	...	...	...	...	...	?	
1 John	...	...	...	D	...	C	...	...	Polycarp
2 John	...	...	...	...	...	...	...	...	
3 John	...	...	...	...	...	...	...	...	
Jude	...	?	...	...	...	...	...	?	
Apocalypse	?	...	...	D	...	...	...	...	? 1 Clement

? = 'Unclassed,' or to qualify the value of the letter which it follows.
[ ] = Did. i. 3–ii. 1, not witnessed to by other early documents.
* To be taken in connexion with the suggestion on p. 123, note, that the apocryphal source known to 2 Clement itself used Matt. and Luke.

TABLE II

The following classification is not in all cases to be taken strictly, but in the light of the qualifications indicated in the body of the work itself. References to 'Synoptic Tradition' have been omitted altogether, as not seeming to admit of any such classification.

Barnabas.   B   Rom.
           C   Eph. Heb.
           D   Matt. 1 Cor 2 Cor. Col. 1 Tim. 2 Tim. Titus, 1 Pet.
           Unclassed: Luke, John, Apoc.

Didache.   (i) 'Two Ways': D ?   Acts, Rom.
                     Unclassed: Heb. Jude.
           (ii) Rest: B   Synop. Trad.
                   C? Matthew.
                   D   Luke, 1 Cor. 1 Pet.
                   Unclassed: John.

1 *Clement.*   A   Rom. 1 Cor. Heb.
           C   Acts, Titus.
           D   2 Cor. Gal. Phil. Col. 1 Tim. 1 Pet. 1 John, Apoc.

Ignatius.   A   1 Cor.
           B   Matt. John, Eph.
           C   Rom. 2 Cor. (?), Gal. Phil. 1 Tim. 2 Tim. Titus.
           D   Mark (?), Luke, Acts, Col. 1 Thess. (?), 2 Thess. (?),
               Philem. (?), Heb. 1 Pet.

Polycarp.   A   1 Cor. 1 Pet.
           B   Rom. 2 Cor. Gal. Eph. Phil. 2 Thess. 1 Tim. 2 Tim.
           C   John, Acts, Heb. 1 John.
           D   Col.

Hermas.   B   1 Cor. Eph.
           C   Matt. Mark, Heb Jas.
           D   Luke, John, Acts, Rom. 1 Thess. 1 Pet.

2 *Clement.*   C   Matt. Heb.
           D   Luke, 1 Cor. Eph. Jas. 1 Pet.
           Unclassed: Rom. 1 Tim. 2 Pet. Jude.

I

INDEX OF NEW TESTAMENT PASSAGES EXAMINED

II

INDEX TO PASSAGES OF THE APOSTOLIC FATHERS EXAMINED

ERRATA

N T in Apostolic Fathers

www.ingramcontent.com/pod-product-compliance
Lightning Source LLC
Chambersburg PA
CBHW060312100426
42812CB00003B/756